CU00923634

LORDS OF THE EAST

LORDS OF THE EAST

THE EAST INDIA COMPANY AND ITS SHIPS
(1600 – 1874)

JEAN SUTTON

CONWAY
MARITIME PRESS

Copyright © 2000 Jean Sutton

This new edition first published in Great Britain in 2000 by Conway Maritime Press,
a division of Chrysalis Books Ltd, a member of the Chrysalis Group plc,
9 Blenheim Court, Brewery Road, London N7 9NT
www.conwaymaritime.com

First published in Great Britain in 1981.

A member of the Chrysalis Group plc

British Library Cataloguing in Publication Data
A record for this title is available upon request from the British Library

Jean Sutton has asserted her moral right under the Copyright,
Design and Patents Act 1988, to be identified as the Author of this work.

ISBN 0 85177 786 4

All rights reserved. No part of this publication may be reproduced,
Stored in a retrieval system or transmitted in any form or by any
means electronic, electrostatic magnetic tape, mechanical,
photocopying, recording or otherwise, without prior permission
in writing from the publishers.

Every effort has been made to locate and credit the copyright holders of
material reproduced in this book, and the Publishers regret any errors or omissions.

Designed by Stephen Dent.
Maps by Grainey Graphics.

Printed and bound in Spain by Book Print, S.L., Barcelona.

CONTENTS

Acknowledgements

I wish to thank the following people for their help: my old friend Trevor Hearl for his many contributions on St Helena and for supplying several pictures; all the people who have written to me since the publication of the first edition giving details of their forebears' service with the company; all the staffs of the various museums for their constant help, particularly Dr Andrew Cook at the Oriental and India Collection at the British Library for his unstinting help and advice on navigation and the selection of the charts; Eleanor Heron at the National Maritime Museum, Bob Aspinall at the Museum in Docklands and Jeremy Wise at the Guildhall Library for their help with finding appropriate illustrations. I am abidingly grateful to all the people in India who went out of their way to help me in my search for surviving remains of the Company and to my friends Rachel Allenby and Jean Bailey who uncomplainingly suffered frequent discomfort in locating them. Last but by no means least I wish to thank my husband Bryan for his unswerving support over many years.

Frontispiece: The drawing on the cover of the journal belonging to Captain Pike of the *Stringer*, 1713, depicts merchants bearing the luxuries of the East before the wealth and might of the East India Company. The figure descending on a dragon probably represents the various interlopers – men who defied the Company's monopoly – or European pirates operating in the Arabian Sea. Both threatened the viability of the recently reorganised company for many years. *(BL OIOC)*

$\mathcal{I}$NTRODUCTION

On 31 December 1600 Queen Elizabeth I granted to a group of London merchants the exclusive privilege of trade, with relief from customs, between England and the lands 'beyond the Cape of Bona Esperanza to the Straits of Magellan' for fifteen years, provided the trade proved profitable to the Crown.[1] Management of the Company of Merchants of London trading to the East Indies was vested in a governor and deputy governor assisted by a Court of 'Committees' with twenty-four members; these were elected by the General Court comprising all the freemen of the company.

There were initially twelve separate stock voyages, all expenses including the purchase of ships being paid from members' subscriptions. This approach was abandoned in 1613 as voyages overlapped and factors competed with one another in the purchase of return cargoes, 'each striving for his own voyage' and forcing up the cost of the goods. These were replaced with series of voyages, generally termed the 'joint stock voyages'.

From the start, the Verenigde Oostindische Compagnie (the Dutch East India Company formed in 1602), pursued a policy of financing its European imports from the profits of the inter-Asian trade, whilst the English faced a continuous barrage of criticism for exporting bullion, believed to constitute the country's wealth, to pay for its inward investment. The ships carried chests of *reals* – called pieces of eight in the seventeenth century and Spanish dollars in the eighteenth. The *reales de a ocho* were exported from Mexico and Peru by the Spaniards, and were accepted as the standard currency in the east through distribution by the Chinese. The *real* was worth about twenty-five pence.

During the first English voyage, Lancaster made trade agreements with the ruler of Achin and left factors and seamen at Bantam, one of the chief centres of the age-old Asian trading network. The third fleet brought back a rich cargo of pepper from Bantam and cloves, mace and nutmegs from the Moluccas, the legendary Spice Islands, realising an enormous profit.[2] Therefore it was spices which the subscribers wanted above all, but the Dutch had no intention of relinquishing the initiative their earlier arrival in the area had given them. After a short honeymoon between the two Protestant countries, English fleets arriving in the Moluccas were opposed by the superior force of the Dutch East India Company.

Forced to find alternative goods the English company turned to the west coast of India, where they had acquired a foothold at Surat in the Gulf of Cambay in their search for the cotton cloths which the inhabitants of the Moluccas tradi-

Part of the list of one hundred and one names of merchants and citizens of London who met at the Founders' Hall on 22 September 1599 and subscribed over £30,000 to a fund to finance a voyage to the East Indies.

(BL OIOC)

To the Honourable the Court of DIRECTORS of the UNITED-COMPANY of Merchants of ENGLAND trading to the EAST-INDIES this View of Cape of Good Hope done after the Painting in the Court Room of the Companys house in Leaden Hall Street is most humbly Dedicated — by their HONOURS most obliged and most devoted Servant John Bowles.

Printed for T. Bowles in St Pauls Church Yard, & J. Bowles at the black Horse in Cornhill. E. Kirkall f.

One of the United Company's 'great ships' and other shipping off the Cape of Good Hope, in a picture symbolising the Company's great achievement.
(National Maritime Museum)

tionally demanded in barter for their spices. Surat, forty miles up the River Tapti, was the Moghul emperor's chief emporium with links to the Red Sea and the Persian Gulf to the west and Calicut and Bantam to the south, and the port of departure of the pilgrims for Mecca.

Here Portuguese opposition was the problem. A Surat factor wished 'there might a sufficient man be sent to the emperor's court at Agra . . . such a one whose person may breed regard, for they here look much after great men'.[3] The arrival of 'such a one', Sir Thomas Roe, as accredited ambassador from the Court of St James, coincided with the trouncing of the whole Portuguese fleet on the west coast of India by four English ships. This demonstration of superior naval force by

the English, which could be used to protect rich pilgrim fleets bound to the port of Jedda on the Red Sea, was probably the factor which persuaded the Moghul emperor to grant a *farman*, or permit to trade, to the Company. In 1629 Surat became the headquarters of the English Company and its chief presidency in the east. The cottons of Gujerat gradually filled the vacuum created by the Company's exclusion from the spice trade. From factories opened at Patna, Agra and Lahore, saltpetre and indigo travelled down the ancient caravan routes to Surat. Persian silk purchased under generous terms in return for help in expelling the Portuguese from Hormuz was added to the ships' cargoes. Supplies of other types of fine cottons produced on the Coromandel coast were secured with the

Sir Thomas Smythe, a leading Elizabethan entrepreneur and promoter of trading expeditions to all parts of the world, was Governor of the East India Company during its first twenty years. *(BL OIOC)*

Sir Thomas Roe, whom James I sent as his ambassador to the Mogul Emperor's court at Agra in 1615 to obtain a firm trading agreement for the Company. *(BL OIOC)*

acquisition of a strip of land on which the Company built Fort St George, around which grew the affluent settlement of Madras, created a presidency in 1641. From there Company agents successfully established trading links with Balasore and Hooghly to secure the finer cottons and silks of Bengal.

The solid foundations of a profitable trade, laid with much ingenuity and not a little suffering and loss of life, were jeopardised by two decades of civil unrest at home. Fortunately, Oliver Cromwell realised that a healthy Company formed an integral part of his policy of achieving superiority over the Dutch at sea, and provided a charter which changed it from a medieval into a modern joint stock company. This charter provided the Company with permanent capital, regular auditing and provision for the retirement of old and the admission of new shareholders. Seventeen settlements were selected in

the east and sufficient agents and bullion sent out to put them on a good trading footing. Charles II was equally positive in his support. The Company's position was strengthened by his gift of Bombay, which had come to him as part of Catherine of Braganza's dowry but had proved a financial embarrassment. The Company grudgingly accepted it in 1668, muttering about the 'great burden and expense' while secretly delighted to have a place of its own which it could fortify. As the Hindu Marathas advanced northwards to regain their lost territory and rampaged throughout the Moghul dominions, disrupting the trade at Surat, Bombay succeeded it as a presidency in 1687. Another useful acquisition from the Crown in 1673 was St Helena which became a port of call for homebound shipping, and in 1685, to compensate for the loss of Bantam – from which they were driven by the Dutch in 1683

– the Company developed pepper plantations along a three hundred mile stretch of the west coast of Sumatra, controlled from Fort Marlborough at Benkulen. By the end of the century the Ccompany had successfully established a trade at Canton to secure supplies of increasingly popular tea, which was to replace Indian cottons as the chief import by the end of the following century.

The thirty years to the expulsion of James II were years of unparalleled success for the revived Company, chiefly the result of an explosion in the import of Indian textiles in response to increasing demand both at home and abroad. The 'India craze' swept the country. Ladies in high society were soon wearing nothing but muslin, at first considered fit only for servant girls, and decorating their homes with *chintz*, the painted cloths of Coromandel. Dividends rocketed; covetous eyes were turned on the holders of Company stock and frustrated voices raised angrily when it was discovered that most of it had been appropriated by a small clique round the king. Complaints came also from the Spittalfields silk weavers and

HET HUIS VAN DEN
OOST INDISCHE COMPAGNIE IN
LON DEN

THE OLD EAST INDIA HOUSE IN LEADENHALL STREET 1648 TO 1726
FROM A PAINTING IN THE POSSESSION OF Mr PULHAM OF THE INDIA HOUSE 12 INCHES BY 8

The home of Lord Craven, Lord Mayor of London, in Leadenhall Street, the third headquarters (1648-1726) of the Governors and Company of Merchants of London trading to the East Indies. *(BL OIOC)*

the nascent dyeing industry. These had already been partly appeased by the imposition of duties on chintzes and wrought silks from the East, but as demand soared in spite of them, an act was passed prohibiting the wearing and use of them and a duty was put on white calicoes.

Sir Josiah Child dominated the small, unaccountable group around the King who were accused of setting up 'an uncontrolable Power in themselves'. In 1685 he persuaded them to agree to his policy to secure by aggression territory in Bengal, where the Company could carry on its trade free from harassment by Moghul officials and soldiers. Ill-planned and badly executed, the subsequent war waged against the Moghul emperor by the Company brought ignominy on the name of the English in India. However, dependent as he was on the Company's ships to safeguard his pilgrim fleets the emperor was prepared to readmit the Company's agents to trade.

With the restoration of peace, the former chief factor at Hooghly, Job Charnock, retired to a bend in the River Hooghly where he had moored his ships after escaping from the Moghul Viceroy's troops in 1686. He had recognised in this fever-ridden spot the essentials for a new Company settlement: the deep-water anchorage was ideal for the Company's ships, whose big guns could protect the factory, since the Moghul emperor permitted no fortifications in his dominions. Charnock and his staff worked through the rains, many dying, many mutinous, to develop this settlement, even fortifying it in 1696 on the pretext of a local revolt. Around Fort William developed the city of Calcutta, which by 1700 was sufficiently established to become a presidency.

The discredited cabal was swept away with the accession to the throne of William III when all those elements formerly excluded from a share in the profitable eastern trade successfully petitioned for the formation of a new Company. For several years the two Companies, the new and the old, competed in a spirit of bitter rivalry. Both realised that neither would benefit in such conditions. The inevitable union came in 1708 with the formation of the United Company of Merchants of England trading to the East Indies, with much the same organisation as the old company. Only the titles used changed: the governor became a Chairman, the 'Committees' became Directors, and the subscribers met in a General Court of Proprietors. The Company was awarded the monopoly of trade with the east subject to parliamentary sanction, renewable every twenty years, in return for a loan to the government of £3.2 million which constituted its whole equity stock. Its parliamentary foundation lent the Company legitimacy while its role as a major creditor to the government established it as a pillar of the nation along with the Bank of England.

In India the company's envoy, John Surman, 'with a little patience and good bribery', succeeded where other European countries' companies failed by securing a new *farman*. This

James Town, St Helena, port of call for all Company ships on the homeward passage.

(National Maritime Museum)

permitted the Company to trade free of customs on payment of a nominal annual sum. No doubt he was helped by the timely intervention of the Governor of Bombay who hinted that the Company might withdraw completely from Surat, and by implication, no longer protect the pilgrim fleets. The Company embarked on a long period of improved trade in India, reflected in half a century of stability and increasing value of stock at home despite renewed efforts to share in the trade by those excluded from the Company's coveted position. The chief thorn in the Company's side was the Ostend Company, chartered in Vienna in 1722 following the acquisition of the south Netherlands by the Emperor of Austria. There was a great deal of spare capital looking for profitable investment and many Jacobites and Irish successfully persuaded the Emperor that a lucrative trade was to be had smuggling China tea into England, France and the United Provinces. It was operated principally by unemployed Scottish company captains and financed by silver provided mainly by Jacobite exiles in Spain. The English East India Company and VOC pressure brought it to an end within ten years, but both men and capital found a new home in the Swedish company

The courtyard at Crosby Hall, the Company's headquarters for a few years. The Directors continued to rent the magnificent great hall which they used as a warehouse until 1787 when they acquired the whole building.

(Photo Bryan Sutton)

established in 1731.

It was the dynamic reconstituted French Compagnie des Indes of 1722 which ultimately presented the greatest challenge to the United Company, bound up as it was in the two nations' struggle for empire. The French and British naval operations reached the Bay of Bengal in the mid-eighteenth century, while the genius of two men, both officials turned general, Robert Clive at Madras and Joseph Dupleix at Pondicherry, were pitted against each other on land. Clive with royal military and naval support emerged victorious while Dupleix was recalled. But it was in Bengal that British supremacy in India really began. When the Moghul Viceroy took Calcutta in an attempt to curb the English Company's aggressive trading activities, Clive – supported by royal troops and naval ships – brought about his overthrow. Within ten years events left the Company as the undisputed ruler of the richest region of India.

This change in situation threw the Company in London into confusion. It lost control of its servants in India who were amassing huge personal fortunes while disturbing rumours of the company's imminent bankruptcy, despite its huge revenues, threatened financial stability at home. Government intervention to safeguard this substantial insti-

tution was essential: its collapse would have had widespread repercussions. The government loaned the Company £1.4 million to tide it over the crisis while the situation was reviewed and reforms put in place. The Regulating Act of 1773 provided for a Governor-General and Council in Bengal to rule over all the Company's territories to stabilise the situation and to halt expansion. Warren Hastings failed to do either, necessitating increased government intervention.

During the years 1782-84 debate on the Company's future dominated domestic politics. By the India Act of 1784, introduced by William Pitt the Younger, the government assumed control of diplomatic and political policy in India through a Board of Control. This was appointed by the Crown in London, and a Governor-General sat in Bengal with enhanced powers over his own council and those of the other presidencies. The Company's agreement to relinquish a major part of its power was gained by leaving the appointment of

The ship *Septer*, one of the paintings by Edward Barlow in his *Journal* depicting the ships in which he served. As Captain of the *Septer*, Barlow foiled an attack by Captain WIlliam Kidd. *(National Maritime Museum)*

Henry Dundas (1742-1811) managed Indian affairs virtually single-handed from his appointment to the Board of Control in 1784 until 1801 when he resigned. Created First Viscount Melville in 1802.

personnel and the right to recall all servants – including the Governor-General – in Company hands. This arrangement continued in substance until 1857, and with minor changes until 1947. A further incentive was the virtual removal of the duty on tea. Henceforth the Company dominated the China trade, carried on under poor conditions, which a protracted and expensive embassy led by Lord Macartney in 1793 failed to improve.

A period of trusteeship of the Indian people and their impressive civilisation ended with the French revolutionary war. Lord Wellesley, the Governor-General, exploited the French threat to India to pursue an aggressive imperialist policy which greatly increased British territory in the subcontinent and the Indian Ocean. In the eastern seas the Royal Navy's primary role was trade protection which benefited not only the Company but also the country trade. This inter-Asian trade, by this time dominated by Indian-based British merchant houses employing ships officered by British seamen, increasingly contributed to financing Wellesley's wars and subsequent British expansion.

Pressure from these groups in India and from northern manufacturers at home desperate for markets for their products, partially forced the Company to open up trade to India

at the renewal of the charter in 1793. In 1813 it entirely relinquished its monopoly of trade with the east – except for the China trade which was considered best left in the company's safe hands until 1833.

In the final settlement of the Treaty of London in 1824 following the Napoleonic wars, all Dutch possessions in India, Ceylon and Malacca, were confirmed as belonging to Britain, while Benkulen was handed over to the Dutch, setting the pattern for future development. Sir Stamford Raffles convinced the Company that a station was needed in the Straits of Malacca to pre-empt any future Dutch attempt to reimpose a monopoly. Penang, renamed Prince of Wales Island, acquired in 1795, had proved disappointing. Raffles bought the sparsely populated island of Singapore from the Sultan of Johore, and by 1826, when the island replaced Penang as the chief presidency in the Straits Settlements, it had developed into a thriving port with a population of ten thousand.

At the renewal of the Company's charter in 1833 its stewardship was continued for another twenty years. However, as it was considered unseemly for a commercial concern to govern an empire with an enormous standing army and an annual revenue many times greater than that of Britain, the Company was required to withdraw completely from trade and to sell all

Fort St George, Madras, the Company's first fortified trading post, seen here in a painting dating from 1731 by George Lambert and Samuel Scott. *(BL OIOC)*

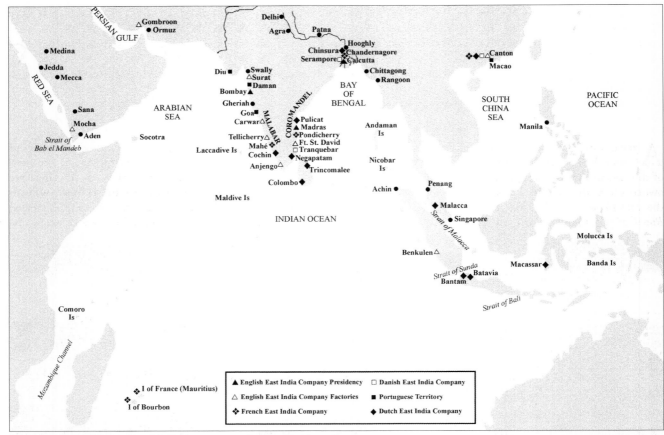

The main centres of European activity in the eastern seas in the mid-eighteenth century.

its property and possessions.

Up to 1818, when the last remnants of the great Maratha confederacy of central India were finally defeated, the Company's expansion had taken place within the borders of India. By 1833 the Bengal Presidency had become so large that it was divided into the Presidency of Bengal and the North West Provinces, Calcutta becoming the new capital of India. Over the remaining forty years of 'company *raj*', Russophobia replaced the Francophobia of fifty years earlier to justify expansion to the north and northwest. Its armed forces, supported by the Bombay Marine and aided by intense surveying of the oceans, ports, harbours and major rivers by its officers, attacked Afghanistan and Nepal and annexed Scinde and the Punjab. Lengthy and costly campaigns over thirty years secured British control of the whole of the east coast of the Bay of Bengal north of Siam to safeguard the sea route from India to China. Aden was seized to provide a coaling station when steam communication was established between Bombay and Suez.

What Macaulay described as 'the strangest of all governments . . . designed for the strangest of all empires' did not survive the great upheaval of what has been absorbed into British tradition as the 'Indian Mutiny'. The Company became the scapegoat; the charade of its rule over Britain's Indian empire ended and the British '*raj*' began. Its army passed to the Crown; its marine, which had been renamed the Indian Navy, was disbanded in 1863. After the demolition of the prestigious East India House in 1861, a skeleton staff wound up the Company's affairs from small offices hired in the City. On the expiration of its charter on 1 June 1874, one of the largest, most extraordinary organisations the world has ever known passed unnoticed from the scene.

Notes:
1. Madden, FW, and Fieldhouse, DK, eds, *Select Documents on the Constitutional History of the British Empire and Commonwealth*, I, 235-6.
2. An investment of £20,000 yielded a profit of 234%. The cloves, which cost only £2048 to buy, sold in London in 1609 for £36,287. Krishna, Bal: *Commercial Relations between India and England, 1601-1757*, 54.
3. BL, OIOC Letters Received by the East India Company from their Servants in the East, Foster, Sir William, ed, (1896-1902), I, 307

CHAPTER 1

THE OWNERS

A glance at the names of the ships employed in the Company's trade with the East Indies in the last decades of the seventeenth century gives a fair idea of the men who owned them: the *Berkeley Castle*, the *Bedford*, the *Tavistock*, the *Streatham*, the *Howland*, the *Josiah*, the *Martha*, the *Russell* frigate, the *Wentworth*, the *Beaufort*, the *Massingbird*.

These names suggest a small group of men with affinities of blood, marriage and interests, deeply involved in the company's affairs during a thriving period of its trade. There are members of the aristocracy close to the throne: William Russell, Marquis of Tavistock and Duke of Bedford, created Baron Howland on the marriage of his grandson to the

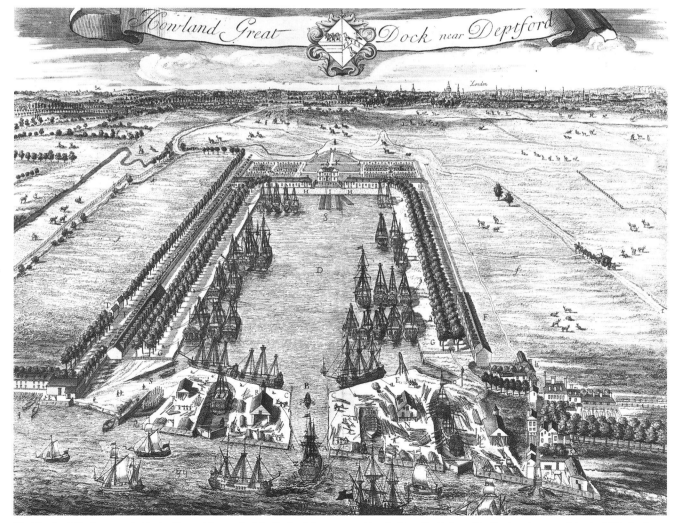

The Howland Dock was probably the first public wet dock in England. It was owned by the Russells, Dukes of Bedford, and managed by the Wells family.
(Museum of London)

daughter and heir of John Howland of Streatham;[1] the Earl of Berkeley, for nearly forty years a 'Committee' of the Company and one of the six peers selected to invite Charles to return to England in 1660, married to the daughter of John Massingbird, a treasurer of the Company (the Earl's son was also a 'Committee' in the last years of the century);[2] the Duke of Beaufort and his brother, the Marquis of Worcester, Charles II's godson, both of whom sat on the Court of 'Committees' in the 1680s.[3]

Closely connected with these men were others who had made their fortunes from large holdings in India stock and ownership of the ships employed in the Company's trade – fortunes which they used to ensure the continued support of the impecunious Charles II, who rewarded them with what they most desired, a baronetcy. With this rise in their social status, furthered by their purchase of country estates, they were able to leave behind them their plebeian background and marry into the aristocracy. Josiah Child, three times governor of the Company and 'Committee' for a quarter of a century, created a baronet in 1688, bought Wanstead Abbey with part of the £200,000 fortune he was credited with in 1683. He married one of his daughters to John Howland, another to the Marquis of Worcester.[4] The two Henry Johnsons, senior and junior, both knighted by Charles II and owners of estates at Bradenham, exercised great influence over the Company's affairs for half a century. The younger Henry Johnson married Martha Lovelace, later Baroness Wentworth; his daughter married Lord Stafford.[5]

Of the twenty part-owners of the *Beaufort*, at least twelve were 'Committees'. Their names appear time and again in lists of owners of ships in the Company's service at this time: apart from the Duke of Beaufort, there were Sir John Lawrence, John Howland, Joseph Herne, Sir Josiah Child, Sir Thomas Davall, Sir Jeremy Sambrooke, Richard Hutchinson, and Charles Duncombe. The others, like these men, were all leading City merchants, Members of Parliament, or holders of important posts in the City and the country. Amongst them were also company commanders, as was usual: Captain Nicholson, commander of the *Beaufort*, and one other.[6]

Chief amongst the owners of ships at this time were Sir Josiah and the two Henry Johnsons, who wielded enormous power in all aspects of the company's affairs. Typical of Sir Josiah's power were his instructions to Captain Knox of the little *Tonqueen Merchant*, of which Sir Josiah was the chief owner, to arrange for the ship to be cut in half and lengthened 12ft to improve her sailing qualities. Although the cost was to be met out of the profits of her first voyage no reference was made to the other owners, who dare not approach Sir Josiah to object. Later, when Captain Knox fell foul of Sir Josiah – as did everyone sooner or later – and the ship he tendered for employment in the Company's trade was refused, he realised there was no point in approaching the other members of the

Sir Josiah Child, a clever economist and a great believer in securing trading concessions in the East by force, was virtual dictator of the Company in the final decades of the seventeenth century. *(British Library)*

Court, for Sir Josiah's 'Interest & Unfluence I Knew to be so great by plasing & Displaseing whome he pleased.'[7]

This concentration of ownership of the ships employed by the Company in the hands of a small group of its governing body by no means reflected the wishes of the vast body of subscribers to the Company. On the contrary, it was to become one element in the great barrage of criticism levelled against these men in the late 1680s and 1690s for their dealings in all aspects of the Company's affairs, all of which were motivated by self-interest.

On the Company's formation, the acquisition, equipping and provisioning of the ships constituting the first fleet had been left to a few 'Committees' who purchased suitable ships, chief of which was the Earl of Cumberland's *Malice Scourge*, built as a privateer and renamed the *Red Dragon*. As succeeding voyages were organised, with good prospects of a continuation of the trade, the Company's surveyor, William Burrell, a 'Committee', pointed out that purchase in the open market was a costly way of acquiring the ships needed, and suggested that the Company build its own. The Court of 'Committees' acted on his advice and for the thirty years following 1609, the Company built ships in yards acquired at Deptford and Blackwall, a policy which bore out Burrell's predictions while trade flourished.

With the taking of several of its ships by the Dutch in 1620, the blow to the company's spice trade in the Malayan archipelago by Dutch monopolistic policy, and the halt in the Indian cotton textile trade brought about by the famine in Gujarat, the huge ships lay idle at anchor in the Thames and the yards became a financial burden. The policy of continued building became a subject of debate in the mid-1620s and lasted for a quarter of a century. On one hand, subscribers could not be persuaded to invest their money in ships which might prove to be white elephants since they were unsuitable for any other type of trade; on the other, ship owners were unwilling to let their ships out on freight, even at £30, £40 or £50 a ton, for such long and dangerous voyages in seas infested with Portuguese and Dutch ships of war.

However, events favoured those who supported the policy of freighting ships. The gradual increase in the nation's commerce resulted in more ships of the right type becoming available, while diminished hostilities in the Eastern Seas encouraged their owners to consider hiring them to the Company. In 1639 the *Caesar* was freighted for a voyage to Bantam.[8] This marked the end of the Company's thirty-year experiment in building its own ships. By the end of the 1650s, the Company had given up its yards and fully adopted the policy of freighting the ships required for its trade.

With the charter restoring the Company's exclusive trading privilege in the East Indies in the late 1650s, the speedy supply of suitable ships became an urgent and pressing problem. Not surprisingly, their provision was left to a small group of 'Committees' who knew something about shipping. Amongst them were the owners of smaller ships freighted by the Company for the re-export of spices to Italy, men who had been active for some years in support of the extension of the freighting system to the East Indies trade.

The Company's and the nation's needs coincided at this time: both required large, stout, defensible ships; both encouraged building by financial rewards. In 1662, the King offered as bounty to anyone who built such ships a remission of the customs on the goods carried — very attractive in the low bulk, high value India trade. In 1668, as tenders were still not coming in fast enough, the Company offered extra freight of twenty shillings per ton to anyone who tendered a ship of a similar type.[9]

Not unnaturally, as shipowners, this small group of men were not slow to take advantage of these conditions themselves. They were part-owners of many of the 'great' ships built during the following decades: of the ships named at the

Two views of an East Indiaman of about 1700, in the time of William III, displaying the Company flag.

(National Maritime Museum)

beginning of this chapter, only three were less than 400 tons, and five were over 700 tons, the largest ships employed at that time. There is no doubt that they provided the right ships at the right time, but not at the right price. The element of pure self-interest which motivated their organisation of the shipping employed by the Company — providing many of the ships themselves on a rota basis and influencing the Court in deciding the freight which they would receive as owners — was bound ultimately to upset those who were not allowed to enjoy similar advantages, and those whose dividends were reduced by the high freight rates.

Sir Henry Johnson, Sir Josiah Child, Sir Jeremy Sambrooke, Sir Thomas Davall and other members of this small group, which evolved into the Committee of Shipping and managed the Company's shipping affairs during the time of the 'Old Company' and throughout the life of the new United Company, saw the possibility of further advantages for themselves in the declining fortunes of the Company in the mid-1680s when ships wasted time at Surat waiting for vessels to arrive from England with treasure to buy a cargo. In these circumstances, the 'Secret Committee', the small inner-circle of 'Committees' which decided all important issues and of which Sir Josiah was the leading member, resolved in 1688 that twelve Company ships should be sent to the East and in addition 'to give permission to such free ships as shall desire to trade for their own account in India on such terms as may be most advantageous to the Company'.[10] The Court voted that members of the Company could trade on their own account up to the amount of stock they held on payment of eighteen per cent, a decision very profitable to large holders of stock. Those excluded from making huge fortunes were roused, becoming vociferous in 1695 when the Court followed up this departure by another, equally advantageous to the powerful inner group – using Company money to subsidise ships built for the Company's trade.[11] By this time, as a result of substantial losses of ships during the French wars – sixteen between 1691 and 1698, of which at least five were 'great ships' over 600 tons – the situation was reversed, and the Company was reduced to advertising publicly for ships, though owners were reluctant to let out their ships on freight to the East where recent Company policy had brought the English into disrepute.

The enlarged circle which formed the membership of the United Company of Merchants of England trading to the East Indies in 1708 was obviously intent on putting an end to what must have appeared at the time to be the chief abuses. As early as 1709 the new Court of Directors – in a spirit of reform which was evident form some years – passed two bylaws aimed at preventing future Directors being concerned in the ownership of ships employed by the Company, and preventing Company money being invested in them.

The spirit of the second bylaw was observed from that time on, though under changed circumstances the Company did become an owner of ships in the last years of the eighteenth century; but this 'shipping interest' which grew into such a powerful group during the following decades was never without its representatives in the Court of Directors. In the rationalisation of the Company's shipping system in 1796, Directors were henceforth required to swear on oath that they had no financial interest in the ships employed.

All the elements of this 'shipping interest' are present among the owners of the *Boscawen*, a ship built at Blackwall in 1747 and taken up by the Company the following year for a voyage to Bombay, the Persian Gulf and Mocha.[12] There were eighteen owners whose status and activities were very similar to those of the *Beaufort*. The Directors were still there: Sir William Baker Kt, William Braund, John Harrison and Henry Crabb were all large holders of India stock and one-time directors. Henry Crabb, later Sir Henry Crabb-Boulton, was several times Chairman of the Company during his period as Director from 1753 to 1773, and paymaster to the Company immediately before this.

These men, and others among the owners, were leading City merchants, with interests in the foremost commercial concerns of the day, and men of influence in the country's affairs. Sir William Baker, one of the Duke of Newcastle's chief advisors on economic questions, Henry Crabb and Charles Pole were all Members of Parliament. Samuel Nicholson was the Commissioner of the Lieutenancy of the Militia.

East India families had their representatives in the Court, in the factories and presidencies in the East, amongst the ships' commanders, and amongst the suppliers to the Company and its ships. The most striking feature of the lists of owners of Company ships is the repetition of names of the people comprising this small inter-related circle. The family of Samuel Braund, the *Boscawen*'s manager, was well represented: his brother William, his son-in-law John Harrison and his brother-in-law Leonard Pead all held shares. Sir William Baker's brother-in-law, Jacob Tonson, stationer to the Company, and the nephew of his business colleague Brice Fisher – himself a leading India shipping owner – were also part-owners.

Shares in the India shipping as in other types were in multiples of ¼. The ¹⁄₃₂ share was favoured in the seventeenth century. Sir Henry Johnson Jr held shares of varying denominations: ¹⁄₃₂ in the *Bengal Merchant*; ²⁄₃₂ in the *Barnardiston*; ⁴⁄₃₂ in the *Modena*, and ⁸⁄₃₂ in the *Loyal Merchant*.[13] In the eighteenth century, the ¹⁄₁₆ had replaced this, though the ¹⁄₃₂ remained for the smaller shares. An original share was a part of the total cost of building, equipping and provisioning a ship for her first voyage, subsequently changing hands freely at values varying with the fortunes of the ship and her prospects of earning a profit. The whole, or part, of the share could be sold or bequeathed. Sir Henry Johnson Sr acquired a ¼ share of the ship *Hercules* from Robert Brunninge of Wapping in 1669, then resold a ¹⁄₁₆ share to William Noord[14]. Samuel Mover bequeathed to his son a ¹⁄₃₂ share in the *Defence*, the *Royal Resolution* and the *Williamson*.

The shares could be paid outright, or in instalments, the manager charged with the running of affairs calling in the capital as required. A typical arrangement can be seen in Appendix 1 showing the shares paid by the part-owners of the *Boscawen* in 1747-51.

The cost of the shares during the Company's trading life naturally reflected the cost of building and equipping a ship at different times. Sir Henry Johnson's shares show that the 'great ships' were extremely costly. For a ¹⁄₃₂ share in the 600-ton *Bengal Merchant* and the 700-ton *Defence* he paid £500 and £550 respectively but only £140 for a similar share in the little 260-ton *Smyrna Merchant*.[15] In the mid-eighteenth century, William Braund paid £680 for a ¹⁄₁₆ share of the *Boscawen* of 650 tons, but by the 1770s the cost of a ¹⁄₁₆ share had passed the £1000 mark. The shares in his later ships, which were over 700 tons, exceeded £1000: £1023 for a ¹⁄₁₆ shares in the *Norfolk* in 1771; £1073 for a ¹⁄₁₆ share in the *Granby*.[16] By the early decades of the nineteenth century, the cost of a ⅟₁₆ share had passed the £2000 mark, when the cost of building and fitting out a 1200-ton ship had risen to over £33,000.

Of course, even though each of the partowners contributed only a fraction of the cost, several hundred pounds were at stake. The owner protected himself by spreading his risks and by insurance. Most owners of Company shipping had shares in several ships. Sir Henry Johnson held ninety ⅟₃₂ shares in his thirty-nine ships, of which thirty-three were employed in the East Indies trade.[17] William Braund held shares in twelve ships between 1746 and 1773 and Richard Benwon, an East India Company Director and ex-Governor of Madras, held shares in fourteen India ships in the early 1770s.[18]

The stone building that was erected in 1726 on the site of the old East India House after its demolition. *(BL OIOC)*

Insurance was available from the earliest times, and it was customary for the part-owners to insure their own shares. Sir Henry Johnson's papers contain many policies for insuring his shares in India ships. It appears to have been the custom then, as later, to insure only a part of the amount of the share. Sir Henry's policies show that he followed a general habit of insuring £300 of his £500 shares; six people each underwrote £50 of his share in the *Bengal Merchant* in 1676, at a cost of £3 each, two underwriting £100 and £200 of his share in the *Williamson*.[19] Richard Benyon, a hundred years later, usually insured £400 or £500 of the total cost of his shares of about £1000 each.[20]

Although insurance was available and was much facilitated by the opening of Lloyd's Coffee House in the late seventeenth century, it was not always reliable and the rates shot up at the slightest hint of war. During the growing animosity between England and Spain in the 1730s, a broker for Thomas Hall, a great owner of India shipping, wrote with delight in 1735 to tell Hall he had got him 'several topping gentlemen out of the way, that does not write but now and then' to insure his ships for fourteen per cent.[21] Fluctuations were extreme even within a short space of time: in 1770 Richard Benyon paid twelve guineas per cent to insure his shares in six ships. Ten months later he insured shares in six more ships with the reputable London Assurance House for seven guineas per cent, and thirteen months later, in 1773, six more for eight guineas per cent – again with the London Assurance.[22]

It would be misleading to make any general statement concerning dividends. The very fact that owners spread their risks so widely indicates their uncertainty and variation. William Braund earned a net profit of £900 on his £640 shares in the *Edgecote* between 1746 and 1763, £800 on his share in the *Boscawen* between 1748 and 1757, but only £100 on his £750 share in the unfortunate *Grantham* (which had general bad luck and was finally lost on her fourth voyage) between 1747 and 1759.[23] Richard Benyon earned the following on his share in the *Greenwich*: first voyage, £210 per ⅟₁₆; second voyage, nil; and third voyage, £200 per ⅟₁₆ – not very much, but even this was better luck than he had with the *Stafford*.

'At the time I received from the India House the Accounts of what was due to the Owners of the *Stafford*', wrote the 'husband' Thomas Liell on 8 June 1770 to Richard Benyon, 'for freight outward and for Passage of the Military to India. I had great hopes of returning you a Balance of between fifteen and twenty pounds on account of what you had paid for your sixteenth; but I am sorry to acquaint you that the Charges at Brest in consequence of the Ships' Misfortune will make a sixteenth Share (by the Calcul[latio]n I am at present able to make) amount to upwards of £1225 . . .'[24]

With the loss of control over the Company's shipping affairs of the clique of seventeenth century 'Committees' and their friends, the management of the ships passed into the hands of men who were always referred to in the world of India shipping as 'ship's husbands', and by the Company officially as 'managing owners'. The husbands were the princes of the India shipping world, holding amongst the owners a position of eminence recognised by the Company in their address of 'esquire'. The commanders of the Company's ships, holding though they did a position of great respect in society, and one which offered every opportunity of making a fortune, nevertheless had one more ambition – to become husbands on their retirement from the sea.

The *Neptune* East Indiaman, 809 tons, leaving St Helena in 1788 homeward bound from China.
From an aquatint by Robert Dodd (1748-1816).

(Photo Trevor Hearl)

Individually, through the patronage of the ship which was by custom considered their privilege, the husbands reaped immense benefit for themselves and their families. As a group, through their control of the shipping interest, they exercised a powerful influence on Company affairs in the eighteenth century, an aspect of their activities that will be fully dealt with in Chapter 2.

For the moment it is necessary to look at the type of man who became a husband, his work as manager of a ship, and the rewards – financial and other – of this position. Most husbands had previous experience of some kind in ships trading in the East Indies: Raymond, Crabb, Cotton, and Larkins, some of the powerful India husbands, had all been commanders of company ships. Another leading husband, John Durand, made his fortune as commander of country ships, trading from port to port in the Eastern Seas under licence from the Company.

Thomas Hall, perhaps the most powerful of all, started his career at sea in the Company's service early in the eighteenth century, but was one of many who, disgusted by the Company's restrictions on their private trade, went over to what was, in effect, an English-run interloping company – the Ostend Company – whose ships flew the flag of the Emperor of Austria and imported tea for smuggling into England. Having made his fortune from his *paccotille* – his private trade venture – he negotiated for his return to England, and in 1727, the Court of Directors were pleased to accept his sincere apologies and 'two thousand one hundred pounds in full compensation . . . for Captain Hall's trading to the East Indies contrary to the laws'.[25]

Robert Wigram, at one time surgeon on Company ships, had turned a disability – near blindness – to advantage by opening a drug business, with the proceeds of which he entered a ship-owning career with the purchase of a share in the *General Goddard* East Indiaman in 1778. By the second decade of the nineteenth century, he had become one of the leading husbands, combining this with the ownership of the Blackwall yard and an interest in Reid's Brewery and Huddart's Ropewalk, both suppliers to India shipping. Pitt created him a baronet in 1805 in return for his support in overthrowing the Addington administration. Many were also MPs, joining with other representatives of the company's interests – the army, civil servants, and commanders – to form a powerful vested interest of which the government had to take notice in the days before the development of political parties.

In East India shipping families, like the Larkins and the Wordsworths, husbanding was the natural progression from a few years as commander of a ship in the Company's service, as can be seen from the chart in Appendix 2.

Apart from a special knowledge of the requirements of a ship in the India trade, the husbands' activities were very similar to those of the other owners. They were usually merchants – Dr Burney's definition of a husband in 1815 was: 'among merchants, the person who take the direction and management of a ship's concerns upon himself' – their faces as familiar on 'Change' and at Lloyd's as in the Jerusalem Coffee House, which became the hub of the East India shipping business during the eighteenth century. What the husbands possessed in addition to their experience of the eastern seas was a 'bottom' – not simply a ship, but all future ships to replace that ship.

This enviable position enjoyed by the owners of India shipping rested on two pillars which had developed through custom like the British constitution, and, like any part of that constitution, an Act of Parliament was eventually required to regulate them. One of these pillars was the customary right of employment for life of any ship taken up by the Company; the other, the right to replace any ship worn out or lost in the company's service.

As Captain Eastwick, who served in all types of ships, including those of the Royal Navy, at the turn of the eighteenth century, put it:

> There was never any written engagement on the part of either the owners or the Company as to the continuance of these charters, but the custom of contract was so well-established that both parties mutually relied upon it, and considered themselves bound by ties of honour to observe their implied customary engagements. When, therefore, a ship's turn arrived to be

The *Bengal*, built for the East India trade by Steel and Carswell for Liverpool owners, and the first ship built at Greenock for that service. As painted by Robert Salomon, she is heaved to in order to pick up a pilot.
(Science Museum)

employed, the owner, as a matter of form, submitted a tender in writing to be engaged, and proposed a particular person as captain, and this tender and proposal were always accepted. [26]

The system originated in the difficulty of obtaining the right sort of ships for the East Indies trade in those early years of revival following Cromwell's charter. Encouragements such as King's bounties, relief from part of the customs, and extra freight for building large defensible ships would have had little effect if the owners had not been assured that their ships would be employed for more than one voyage. As early as 1668, when the offer of twenty shillings extra freight for ships over 450 tons was made by the Company, it was stated that it would be for the first two voyages, indicating there would be more to follow, a custom naturally encouraged by the small group of 'committees' charged with arranging the supply of ships.

The other basic feature of the Company's shipping system was the replacement of ships worn out or lost in the Company's service. One of the chief reasons for this development was the need for the Company to retain its experienced commanders in those early days when few had experience of the Eastern Seas and the Company's trade. The Company encouraged the owners of ships worn out or lost to build another ship for the commander. This custom of building in the room of worn out ships must have been fairly generally accepted by the 1680s, especially amongst that 'inner circle' of

powerful owners, for the Earl of Berkeley and the other owners of the *Berkeley Castle*, which had been declared by the court in the previous year as no longer fit for the Company's service, 'being fifteen years old and having brought home the Company's goods very much damaged', tendered a new ship of the same name, of 650 tons, for employment by the Company.[27] As the only possible use for such a ship was service in the East India trade, its acceptance must have been pre-arranged. Certainly this had become customary by 1723 when Captain Micklefield asked the court 'for leave to build a Ship in the room of the *Marlborough* and that she may be taken up in turn', a request the court complied with without stipulations.[28] Such a system naturally resulted in the concentration of ownership in a few hands. In the 'old company' as we have seen, control was exercised by a small group of influential 'committees'. With the formation of the new United Company, power shifted to the chief owners, the husbands, to whom permission was given to replace a ship that had been lost at sea or was worn out – to build on her 'bottom' – a system which came to be known as 'the doctrine of the hereditary bottom'.

A feeble attempt was made in the early years of the United Company to introduce competition and keep down the excessive freights. A public advertisement gave notice of the Company's shipping requirements: tenders were received, ships selected, and as a result of this healthy breath of competition and the close of the war with France, freight rates dropped a little. In 1715 they stood at £21 and £24 a ton for China, but

A view of the improved and enlarged East India House in 1815.

(BL OIOC)

there they stuck. The following year the owners demanded the same freight, leading the court to believe 'there was a confederacy among the owners to improve the freight they demanded on the Company.' The court therefore decided that 'the two ships whose owners shall first declare their acceptance of the Company's freight of £20 and £23 a ton and are of burthens fit for China voyages shall have those voyages provided they answer the Company's survey . . . these two resolutions to be put on the boards of the Exchange and at this House'. Only one ship was tendered, and this was withdrawn when most of the other owners submitted a paper to the court demanding the freight for the previous year.[29]

The Directors' stand, no doubt weakened by the presence in their midst of the close relatives and friends of those holding shares in the ships, did not survive for long in the face of the closed ranks of the owners. In 1717 the court decided to give the same rate as the previous year and so avoid conflict, and from that time on, in deciding what freight should be charged, the Company was increasingly in the hands of the owners, led by a small group of leading husbands who held the 'bottom' rights of the 30 ships which constituted the Company's fleet in the early decades of the eighteenth century. With the Court's decision of 12 August 1724, that ships that had already performed one voyage to India and back should be taken up again without ballot, and that 'ships which are or have been in this Company's service shall for the future be employed in order as they return home', the system was formally recognised.[30]

There was no question of the owners selecting the husband to manage their ships, since without him there was no ship to manage. It was he who, when a ship of which he had been husband wore out, approached the Court of Directors for permission to build a new one to replace her, and invited a group of people, usually the part-owners of the previous ship, to join him in ownership. His position was usually formalised by the signing of legal documents by both parties: one formally

appointing him signed by the owners, and a bond signed by the husband in which he promised to manage the ship according to agreed rules, paying dividends at arranged times. Examples of these documents can be seen in Appendix 3.

Such formalities were not always effected, with the result that towards the end of the century, when new men were attempting to break into the oligarchical structure which the system encouraged, the Court ruled that such a procedure was necessary. William Moffat sent to the Court of Directors a letter of 1 March 1785, signed by the owners of the *Duke of Grafton*, authorising him to build a ship on her 'bottom', but the Court granted leave to her previous husband, John Durand, as was usual. As the dispute raged, the Committee of Shipping decided that no ship should be built to replace the *Grafton* '. . . till it shall be determined between the parties in whom the right of building on that bottom is legally vested'. Following on this dispute and others:

> The Committee taking into consideration the many inconveniences which have arisen from disputed claims to build on the bottoms of ships lost or worn out in the company's service recommend to the Court that in future it should be a standing order that previous to any Managing Owner having permission to build on the bottom of any ship, worn out or lost, he be required to produce to the Court an Instrument in writing from the majority of owners signifying their consent to his making such application.[31]

Once appointed, by a gentleman's agreement or a legal instrument, the husband acted alone, exercising complete freedom in all aspects of the ship's business. He alone signed the contract with the builder. His name and that of one other owner – a hang-over from that period in the seventeenth century when the power was in the hands of one of the leading Directors, and the work later done by the husband was done by the commander – appeared on the charter party, the contract between the Company and the owners stating the terms on which the ship was to be hired. He settled all accounts, calling in the share capital to pay the instalments to the builder and meet the demands of the suppliers of all the equipment, stores and provisions. He arranged for the insurance while the ship was in dock and at anchor in the Thames. He was responsible for paying the crew their advance money before sailing from Gravesend; the rest he deposited with the Company's paymaster, who paid absence money to relatives during the voyage, and the balance to the crew on the ship's return. It was his job to settle the accounts with the Company for freight and demorage (nowadays called demurrage – a fine payable by either party for delays) and transporting troops. Finally, he called the owners to a meeting – usually at the Jerusalem Coffee House – to show them the accounts and declare the dividends, the first shortly after the ship's arrival in

The launch of HEICS *Edinburgh* at Blackwall in 1825 depicted by William John Huggins, a seaman in the Company's service who later became marine painter to the king.
(National Maritime Museum)

the River, the second when the accounts with the Company had been finalised. The summary of the accounts for the *Boscawen*'s first voyage in Appendix 4 show the financial aspect of the husband's work.

There is little guide as to what the husbands received for their services. In Samuel Braund's ledger of the accounts of the *Boscawen* appears 'husbanding – £50'. This covered the period from mid-1747 to mid-1752. Obviously there was more to it than that. It is difficult to find other exact sums quoted: 'he shall be paid the usual and accustomary agency or commission by the . . . owners' stated an indenture of February 1793 by which John Fiott was appointed by the owners of a new ship, but documents are reticent as to what this 'accustomary agency or commission' was in terms of hard cash.[32] It appears to have taken the form of a lump sum in the earlier period and been commuted into a percentage on all monies passing through his hands later.

Certainly by the end of the century the husband had become more financier than manager, a trend already apparent from Samuel Braund's handling of the capital for the *Boscawen*'s first voyage, shown in the chart in Appendix 1. He

bound himself 'to render an Acc[oun]t to ye Majority of ye said Owners . . . which Acc[oun]ts are to be laid before ye Owners in two Months after ye Acc[oun]ts of Freight & demorage is Settled with ye East India Company'. The final payments by the Company were made in July 1751. Only one month before, on 6 June, the £1120 covering Braund's ⅙ and ¹⁄₃₂ share was entered in the ledger to enable him to draw his dividend of £315. No doubt his share capital had been earning a healthy interest elsewhere for the previous four years, the voyage being financed by the other owners. As he managed seven ships, this was a neat way of earning large sums of money through husbanding.

Whatever financial benefits were to be gained they were the tip of the iceberg: the real attraction of husbanding lay in the accretion of his influence, and the consequent advantages to himself and his family, through the patronage of the ships he managed.

That the husband had pretty well undisputed right to the patronage of the ship is evident from the case of Mr Douglas of the *Plassey*.[33] She returned in the Spring of 1768 from a voyage to St Helena and Canton, during which she had touched at Benkulen, where the Captain had died and the chief mate, John Waddell, had assumed command of the ship, the second and third mates, Rogers and Douglas, moving up accordingly. On her return to the River, the husband, John Durand, since he had no objection to Waddell or the others, confirmed these new positions, as was customary. Preparations went ahead for her next voyage to the Coast and China in the autumn of 1768, Rogers and Douglas working on the ship, Douglas refusing offers of positions of second mate on other ships. Two days before the swearing in at the India House of the commander and the first four officers prior to sailing, Durand approached Captain Waddell and asked him to agree to his putting another man in as second officer. Waddell considered this a gross injustice, but Durand told him he was pressed by 'a quarter of so much weight, such importance to his own interest' that he would have to do it if it meant turning out his own son. At the swearing in, Captain Waddell refused to accept Durand's protégé, Chisholme, to the consternation of the directors who were torn between their abhorrence of this obviously glaring injustice and their friendship with Durand. The swearing in was adjourned to give time for a settlement to be reached, during which time Durand's friends brought pressure to bear on both Waddell and Douglas to influence each other, but Waddell was immovable. At the swearing in he refused to accept Mr Chisholme, who was, nevertheless, forced on him by the court.

Samuel Braund was furious when circumstances deprived him of the chance of replacing the second mate of the ship *Warren*, of which he was husband.[34] Her commander, Captain Glover, wrote to Braund by his Purser from Gravesend in March 1754:

I am sorry to inform ye yt Mr Halkeston 2nd Mate did yesterday early in ye morning make away with him Self . . . As Soon as I was informed there of (as I knew ye was not in town) I thought it proper, not only for Reason of Prudence, but as it was my duty, to make Mr Chauncy the Compliment of Serving one of his friends, he has accordingly provided one of which he has wrote me this day.

From Lee Roads a few days later, on 29 March, Captain Glover wrote again, obviously worried about his actions: 'I have not heard from ye since [I] left Town, which should be glad to know if ye approve of my acting in regard to an officer.' Braund's replies have not survived but Glover's reaction to them leaves no doubt as to the temper of the letters.

Downs 4/4/54
At my arrival here I have read your four letters . . . which will answer in there turns vizt y[ou]r not being first acquainted with Mr Halkerst[ons] death, was no fault of mine, I heard it

coming out of Town and did expect to find ye at Gravesend & I thought it would be agreeable to ye that Mr Chauncy should be served soon than anybody else & there was no time to be lost. I stopt at Blackheath at Mr Wells and consulted with him who you are sensible is an owner, he thought I did right to give him ye offer.

and, after a lengthy defence of many other actions on which Braund attacked him, repeats: 'I think I did right and for the Interest of ye & all ye Gentlemen concerned'.

The accumulated power of the husbands and their control of all those connected with the company's shipping – the 'shipping interest' – was a crucial factor in the Company's affairs throughout the eighteenth century. Before we look at this aspect, it is necessary to consider the terms on which the ships they managed were taken into the Company's service.

Notes:
1. *Dictionary of National Biography*.
2. Gibbs, Vicary (ed): *The Complete Peerage* (1910).
3. *Ibid*.
4. *DNB*.
5. *Ibid*.
6. BL: Papers of Henry Johnson. Additional MSS 22, 184, f77.
7. Knox, Robert: *An Historical Relation of Ceylon* (Glasgow, 1911), 371.
8. BL, OIOC, Sainsbury, E B: *Calender Court Minutes of the East India Company, 1635-1679*, Vol 1, xxix, xxxii, 317, 329.
9. BL, OIOC, *Brief Historical Sketch*, L/MAR/C1, 12.
10. *Ibid*, 14.
11. Knox, Robert: *An Historical Relation of Ceylon*, 374.
12. Essex Record Office, Papers of Samuel Braund, D/Dru B26, f90.
13. BL: Add MSS 22, 184, f151.
14. *Ibid*, f25.
15. *Ibid*, f151.
16. Sutherland, L S: *A London Merchant* (1933, reprinted 1962) 120, 121.
17. BL: Add MSS 22, 184, f151.
18. Berkshire Record Office, Reading. Papers of richard Benyon. D/E by B6.
19. BL: Add MSS 22, 184, f151.
20. Berks R O. D/E BY B6.
21. Gill, Conrad: *Merchants and Mariners in the Eighteenth Century* (1961), 65.
22. Berks R O. D/E BY B6.
23. Sutherland: *op cit* 120-121.
24. Berks R O. D/E BY B6.
25. Gill: *op cit* 44.
26. Eastwick, R.W. (edited by H. Compton): *A Master Mariner* (1891), 41-42.
27. BL, OIOC, Court Book 34, f154, 4 November 1685.
28. BL, OIOC, *Brief Historical Sketch*, L/MAR/C1, f31.
29. *Ibid*, f26.
30. BL, OIOC, Danvers, F.C., *Introduction to the Marine Records*, xii.
31. BL OIOC L/MAR/C530, 304.
32. *Ibid*, 531, 742ff.
33. Hickey, William (edited by Alfred Spencer): *Memoir* (1913), Vol 1, 146ff.
34. Essex R.O. D/Dru B20 f34ff.

CHAPTER 2

HIRING THE SHIPS

The preamble of a typical mid-eighteenth century charter party stated unequivocally that the East India Company 'have hired and taken to Freight all the said Ship for a Voyage with her to be made, (by God's blessing) . . . in Trade as also in Warfare.'[1] This contract between the Company and the husband covered all the terms on which the ship was to be hired: freight, impress and demorage; the tonnage to be allocated to the Company's cargo and treasure, and that allowed for the commander and officers' private trade; provision for accommodating the Company's personnel; the schedule, manning and armament and the conditions on which the ships could be detained for extraordinary duties in the East.

An important section of the charter party was naturally concerned with freight rates, which rose steadily throughout the period, at the same time fluctuating wildly in wartime, often doubling the peacetime rate. The rates quoted for China were always lower than those for the Indian settlements. Rates were lower for 'gruff' or 'gross' goods such as sugar, saltpetre, cowries, pepper, lacquer and chinaware; and a higher rate for fine goods such as chintzes and calicoes, silks, spices and tea.

Passengers always formed an important part of the Company's effects on outward-bound ships, existing as a trick-

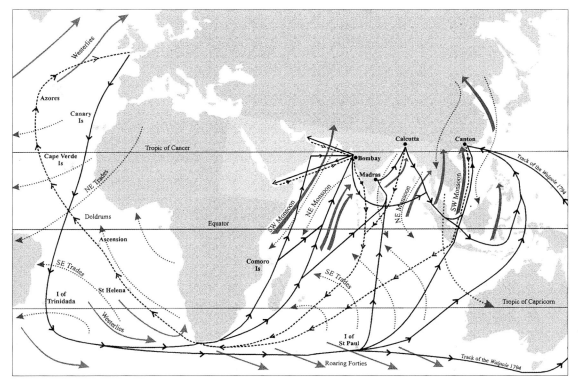

The wind systems of the oceans and the routes followed by the company's ships.

le during the greater part of the Company's life, and becoming a flood in the last few decades. From the earliest years, the great cabin was considered the Company's preserve on each vessel. This provided accommodation for the two or three factors going out to take up posts in the Company's settlements or supercargoes who went out and came home with the ship, conducting the trade at ports where there were no resident factors. These were charter party passengers, who were accommodated and received the ship's ordinary diet at the captain's table at no extra charge.

Soldiers formed the greater part of the rest of the Company's personnel – a rather sorry collection of down-and-outs for the defence of the Company's factories, swelled on the outbreak of hostilities with the French in the mid-eighteenth century by royal troops. Slaves from Madagascar for the Company's plantations at St Helena and Benkulen also had to be transported. The *Suffolk* in 1749 carried soldiers for the garrison at St Helena and some administrative workers; her charter party stated that her owners were to receive 'for all Soldiers and Passengers carried to ye S(ai)d Island £5 a head' and one ton was to be deducted for each person from the 333 tons reserved for the Company's cargo. Having unloaded her soldiers and clerks, the *Suffolk* was to take on board:

> so many blacks, Males and Females, at the Said Island as the Governor's Council shall tender to the Said Master, & ye Said Ship can conveniently take in, and transport them to Benkulen or elsewhere On the West coast of Sumatra . . . for which ye said part-owners and Master are to be paid after ye rate of £4 a head.[2]

Provision for impress and demurrage completed the financial aspects of the contract. Impress was an advance paid by the Company towards the costs of the voyage. Demurrage (or demorage), a fine payable by either party for delays, rose from about £12 a day at the beginning of the eighteenth century to around £20 in the last few decades of the Company's existence. The bane of both the owners and the Company was the commanders' habit of touching at ports en route for the purpose of their own private trade. Owners' instructions to their commanders leave one in no doubt that this was their chief concern. Samuel Braund's instructions to Captain Oliver of the *Grantham* began with the words 'You are to use your utmost Endeavour for a quick Passage'; after stressing the necessity for not stopping at any port the ship was not consigned to, and

On the Coromandel coast, catamarans were always at hand to pick up any passengers washed out of the boats used to bring them ashore through the surf. *(BL OIOC)*

Benkulen, the chief port of the Company's settlement on the west coast of Sumatra, with Fort Marlborough on the left. *(BL OIOC)*

insisting that the reasons for any such stops should be written down and countersigned by the officers or the ship's surgeon, Braund placed responsibility for any financial loss so caused on Captain Oliver:

> the Owners will charge you with the Demorage that they shall loose by such Detention, Or if you put into any Port after you are dispatched you shall be answerable for the time so lost and if by such detention you loose your Passage round the Cape you shall be answerable for the Demorage.[3]

The revised charter party of 1787 was specific: heavy fines were laid down for any master who took in goods at any western, Madeira or Canary Islands or any other this side of a consigned port outward, or touched at Ascension, American ports or islands, Barbados, Western Isles, Plymouth or other ports in England, Ireland or Europe homeward.[4]

The Company's agents in England and in the East made sure that the ships were 'tight' and sufficiently manned, equipped and provisioned before leaving any port. The ship's seaworthiness was checked by the Company's surveyors before she left England; if there was any doubt about her condition on arrival at an Eastern port the agent there could insist on a survey and any necessary repairs at the owners' expense. 'A Survey was ordered on us . . .' Captain Burdett wrote from Fort St David on 25 September 1750, 'on which we were found capable of proceeding home with a Cargo but ordered to put up new

Standards fore and aft.'

The ships had to be 'sufficiently mann'd' and armed according to schedules laid down for each category of ship, the owners being liable to fines if the prescribed men, guns, powder and shot fell short during the voyage. The ships taken into the Company's service were not only its trading vessels; they constituted the Company's navy in times of emergency, acting alone or in conjunction with the Navy. The charter party provided for the detention of ships for the defence of the Company's settlements in the East for a period not exceeding twelve months on full demorage. There was no question of a commander refusing orders of this nature, and Captain Douglas' experience shows that it was unwise to air opinions on the subject. His ship the *Queen* was among the Indiamen of the season at Bengal in 1790 awaiting despatch for Europe when word went round that some ships were to be taken up to convey sepoys and baggage to Madras for Lord Cornwallis's campaign in the Carnatic. Captain Douglas's loud and incautious denial of the Governor-General's power over Indiamen and his threat to ignore any orders concerning the *Queen* reached the ears of the authorities. As a result, three Indiamen were taken up to convey sepoys and baggage, while three hundred bullocks, desperately needed by Lord Cornwallis for transport, were sent on board the *Queen*. Captain Douglas was given to understand that if he refused, or in any way failed to see that the animals received proper attention during the voyage, he would be removed from his command and sent a prisoner to England.[5]

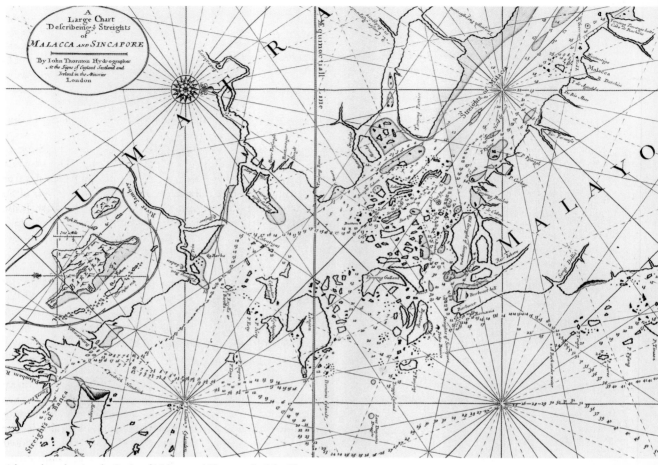

A large chart showing the Straits of Malacca and Singapore by John Thornton.

(BL OIOC)

The terms on which the ships were hired and the freight were negotiated by representatives of the owners and those directors constituting the Committee of Shipping. The existence of a powerful owners' organisation was fully revealed in 1751. For some years previously the number of ships taken up by the Company had resulted in excess tonnage, as it was not simply a case of an extra ship being taken into the service but an extra 'bottom' created, perpetuated by the custom of replacing the ship when worn out. The nucleus of most powerful husbands, finding their returns diluted by the ships having to spend a year at home between voyages, determined on consolidated action to reduce the number of 'bottoms' and so recover their former control. One of these husbands was Samuel Braund, whose ledger for 5 March 1753 contains the entry: 'Paid towards defraying ye expenses of making ye owners agreement to reduce ye numbers of Ships in ye Service: £1.1s.0d.'[6] They decided that::

if the said Company shall think necessary and have occasion to encrease the number of hired Ships in their Service, in such Case We do hereby respectively agree that we will use our utmost and best endeavours that every such Ship which may be so built for the said Service shall be built upon the bottom or bottoms, and to replace the Ship or Ships first worn out or lost in their Service . . .[7]

and went on to state that they would 'prevent even any or every application to the Company for the purpose of adding to that number or anything relating thereunto.' They agreed that as ships wore out or the commanders died, the 'bottoms' should lapse and be brought back into the service again as occasion required.

In spite of the husbands' firm resolve expressed in the agreement of 1751, their control was not absolute. Directors seeking to increase their influence occasionally managed to persuade the Court to take up a ship whose owners were out-

Letter tendering a ship for the East India trade by its managing owner, Samuel Braund.
(Essex County Record Office)

the circumstances they were 'not only enabled to obtain too high a freightage, but were likewise exempted from the necessary Control'.[8] The Secret Committee pointed out that freight and demorage paid by the Company in the ten years 1762-1772 amounted to £4,777,902, of which it felt that one third could have been saved. However, as the ships always carried a surplus at a lower rate, this was an exaggeration.

A concurrent enquiry into the causes of the scarcity of timber for the navy concluded that the general increase in shipping was the cause, 'but the Increase has particularly been in the East India Company's ships, which from 30 Sail, their Number 30 Years ago, are now 90 Sail, one of which ships of 800 Ton would take the same scantling as a Ship of War of 50 or 60 Guns: that within these 20 Years the East India Company have greatly increased the Tonnage of their Ships.'[9] The twin aims of reducing freight through reducing wasted tonnage and taking pressure off scarce resources to benefit naval building were the motives behind the Act Geo. III 12th year ch.54 providing for cessation in new building until the Company's shipping was reduced to 45,000 tons. By-law number 40 of 1773 stated that only ships taken up for four voyages at a fixed rate of freight calculated on an estimate of the cost of building a ship, fitting her out and equipping her with stores and provisions for a certain number of months were to be employed. To compensate the owners ships were to be taken up in future at builders' measurement, for many years greatly exceeding the 499 tons at which the ships were chartered, to fit in with an act of the following year providing for 'one certain rule' to replace the myriad of local rules for measuring tonnage. The method of measurement embodied in the Act of 12 Geo. III c74 of 1720 applied to ships carrying brandy and other prohibited goods was adopted for all ships: length by the keel by breadth by half-breadth divided by ninety-four.

Within a few years all controls collapsed as the American colonists' struggle for independence plunged the country into crisis. Insurance rates rocketed, the costs of manpower and stores rose, while large numbers of ships were required to take military and naval stores and men out to the eastern seas. By 1781 freight had risen to £47.4s a ton.

The 'old owners' grasped the opportunity to regain some control. In January 1780 they influenced their friends in the court to suspend the 1773 by-law limiting a ship's life to four voyages. The following week the *Queen* was taken up for a fifth voyage. As peace returned in 1782 John Robinson at the Treasury requested the Court of Directors to enlighten him on the state of the Company's shipping. The Directors, anxious to co-operate to keep at bay further government encroachment on the Company's charter rights, assured him that though the tonnage had exceeded the legal limit, and four ships had been taken up for a fifth voyage, the tonnage would be reduced to the permitted level by natural wastage by

side the oligarchic association of the most powerful husbands, and 'bottoms' again began to proliferate. In 1760, at the height of the Seven Years' War, the Company expressed itself 'distressed for tonnage' and some lapsed 'bottoms' were brought back into commission. By 1763 there were sixty-eight afloat or on the stocks, occasioning a further agreement between the husbands, this time approved by the Court of Directors; but despite this there were eighty-five ships afloat or on the stocks by 1769.

Despite several years of peace, by 1772 the freight had climbed to £34 and £37, only a little short of the peak wartime rate of 1760. This fact came to light during the enquiries of the Secret and Select Committees set up in 1772 when the government loaned the near-bankrupt Company £1.4 million. Gabriel Snodgrass, the Company's Surveyor of Shipping, summed up the situation when questioned: 'that from the great Numbers, Opulence and various interests of the Owners of Shipping, due economy was prevented' and in

1784. In 1783 the Committee of Shipping tried to reduce the freight but the old owners all offered ships at £37.4s a ton. On the basis of the rates then operating for building and equipping a ship in the River the Committee estimated that a rate of £32 would produce interest at £11 per cent per annum and that price should not be exceeded. The owners reduced their offer to £35. The Committee responded with a proposal of £33, which the old owners declined.

The Committee decided to advertise, receiving tenders for twenty-eight ships from a variety of sources including some 'new shippers' anxious for a share of the lucrative eastern carrying trade, but Mr Snodgrass found some of the ships weak, others old, the French ships too slightly built and some in need of repair. The Committee wavered. In the event, they decided that the difference in price between the ships tendered and those of the old owners was insufficient to risk taking up unknown ships in preference to those they knew to be well built and surveyed and much more serviceable in the event of war. This capitulation disgusted the 'new shippers' and those who objected to the old owners' rapacity.

The following year the tonnage required for the China trade doubled as a result of the drastic reduction of the duties on tea. The new shippers grasped the opportunity to break into the charmed circle, Anthony Brough offering to supply the Company with eighty ships at £22 and £24 for China, producing a saving of £150,000 in one year. Emboldened by this offer the Committee advertised, inviting tenders. They responded to the old owners' complaints that they deserved preference by pointing out that they would be engaged to bring back the same amount as before, 712,000 lbs each, plus a surplus, but the additional 12,800 tons required would be taken up by persons tendering suitable shipping; four ships had already been engaged totalling 3,000 tons, leaving 9,800 if offered on better terms.

Sir Robert Preston, chairman of the Managing Owners of Shipping, complained bitterly that they were being 'cruelly injured in property and credit' and 'precluded from finding owners for ships actually upon the stocks'.[10] They looked to the Company to restore confidence and prevent any doubts concerning the security of the large property now afloat. In its new found confidence the Court ignored the old owners' complaints, simply informing them that their tenders should be presented by 3 February next. Mr Brough continued pressing his case, claiming public support. 'The business has got abroad' he informed the court, and people were getting impatient, asking whether the delay was due to his own doubts or the Directors' timidity.[11]

The Committee finally refused Mr Brough's eighty ships on the grounds that he could not deliver on time and they wanted larger ships for greater economy. They settled for only three from Mr Brough, one from another new shipper, John Fiott, and one from a Captain Tanner for a 1000 ton ship, on the explicit understanding that none of them would have the right to build on their 'bottoms'. The new shippers now came up against another section of the Shipping Interest. Mr Fiott could find no builder on the Thames willing to build his ship and resorted to Itchenor. Captain Tanner came to a verbal agreement with Mr Randall of Randall and Brent of

The East India yard at Deptford (about 1670) where the Company built its own ships in the very early years.   *(National Maritime Museum)*

Above: William Hickey, seen here in old age with his Indian servant, record-ed details of many voyages to the East made in the eighteenth century, pro-viding a valuable picture of a passenger's lie on board Company ships.
(National Portrait Gallery)

Left: Sir David Scott, successively Director, Deputy-Director and Chairman of the Court of Directors, worked tirelessly to persuade the Company to reform itself to avoid bankruptcy. Mezzotint by John Young of the painting by George Romney. *(National Maritime Museum)*

Rotherhithe, one of the leading builders of East Indiamen and naval vessels. On enquiring later why no progress was being made with his ship, Mr Randall confessed that he and Mr Brent had pledged themselves 'jointly with others, not to build for those who would tender at the reduced freight.' The Court consulted their Counsel as to whether this constituted a conspiracy in restraint of trade, but he felt there was insuf-ficient evidence for a charge. It is hardly surprising that the River builders were reluctant to desert those very powerful old owners at the first whiff of speculative competition. Their relationship was long-standing, and the actual building of the ships was only a part of the work involved as will be explained in the following chapter.

The House of Commons and Henry Dundas, now President of the Board of Control, were concerned that tax-payers' money should not go straight into the pockets of some of the richest men in the kingdom. On 13 June the Court of Directors were ordered to lay before the House 'an account of the freight and demorage paid between 21 January 1784 and

1 March 1786 and from these estimated up to 1790, distin-guishing each year; also the savings on the ships taken up at low freight and the savings per annum if all the ships were taken up at the same low rates.'[12]

The old owners responded to the increased pressure by ral-lying their support. At a special meeting of the General Court called on 28 June, by an awesome three hundred and sixty-two votes to ninety-four, the proprietors recommended to the Court of Directors that they consider the following resolution passed at a General Meeting of the Managing Owners of Shipping at the London Tavern on 21 June: 'that an offer be made to the Court of Directors to accept £24 a ton for China for the coming season only, and whether under any possible regulations or conditions ships built by the present owners can be afforded at so low a rate.'[13] The Court of Directors fee-bly accepted the old owners' offer. Mr Fiott vented his disgust in an address to the Proprietors in which he railed against the Society of Old Owners 'which, like an enormous succor, has robbed the parent tree of its vital juices.'

A VIEW OF THE EAST INDIA DOCKS.

This painting by William Daniell shows the East India Docks developed on the eastern side of the Isle of Dogs at the turn of the nineteenth century. Greenwich and Deptford are just visible in the distance on the right.

(BL OIOC)

The old owners reinforced their position by the successful repeal of the by-laws 30 and 40, the one limiting the tonnage to 45,000, the other restricting the number of voyages to four. In their place were voted by-laws confirming that new ships to be built on the bottoms of those worn out or condemned should be the first in rotation; and ships taken or lost should have preference of building without waiting for their turn in rotation. Their position was further strengthened by the passing of another by-law establishing that no ship should be built less than 800 tons with eighteen months between laying the keel and the launch. This effectively cut out most of the new shippers' offers, which were for smaller ships, and precluded the Committee accepting tenders for new ships for the ensuing season.

The old owners' extravagant demands at last welded their critics in the General Court into an effective opposition organised by two proprietors, both lawyers, Thomas Henchman and Randle Jackson. A defining moment in the struggle was John Fiott's success in getting through at a special meeting of the General Court on Thursday 31 March 1791 a motion

That there be laid before this Court, copies of all proposals for receiving tenders for building ships for hire to the East India Company from 1st January, 1780, to this present time, with the answers and resolutions of Committees and Courts thereon, together with the prices agreed to be given for the hire of ships in each of the said years, according to their respective des-

tinations, & also of any agreements or resolutions of the Court, or Committee of Directors, which may have been made respecting any or all of the Old Ship Owners, on the subject of shipping, during the said period.[14]

All the papers were to be printed. The battle had been joined. It was a long, hard struggle because the shipping interest was London-based and very united.

There was always a body of 150-200 Shipowners and their dependants, completely organised, ready to come to Court, on receiving what was called . . . a Shipping Letter; whose general instructions it was, not to stir from their seats until the Independent Proprietors were fatigued and had retired; to vote implicitly with their leaders and above all to take care that no fair and genuine question, which might lead to a reduction in their prices, should ever reach a ballot. A sumptuous repast at the London Tavern was always ready prepared to recruit their spirits when the debate was over.[15]

Fourteen months later, following consideration of selected of the printed papers at a meeting of the General Court, a motion that it was 'the opinion of this Court that owing to the long practised mode of conducting the shipping concerns of the Company an higher price than necessary has been paid for many years past and now paying for the freights in its service' was only narrowly defeated, revealing a shift in support for the opposition.[16]

The old owners' friends in the Court of Directors continued to secure their position. Their underhand refusal of two ships offered by John Fiott the same year were deemed 'contrary to every principle, detrimental to the commerce of India, and injurious to the Company's interests' according to one Director who deprecated the deviousness of the Court, comparing the Directors' behaviour to that of the old English company which had been censured by Parliament for similar practices.[17]

At the renewal of the charter in 1793 the Shipping Interest successfully fought off the bid of the northern manufacturers at home and the merchants in India to end the Company's monopoly: the Company was required to make only 3000 tons a year available for the private trade. Immediately afterwards the old owners secured a very favourable freight which confirmed them in a profit of £80,000, and a revision of the supply of shipping which provided for a class of large ships, so reinforcing their position.

Henry Dundas was becoming increasingly impatient with some of the Directors' collusion with the old owners, and he now had support inside the direction. David Scott had made his fortune as a partner of the Bombay firm Scott, Tate and Adamson, one of the large Houses of Agency that invested company servants' money in goods exported to Europe. Scott soon won the ear of Henry Dundas who welcomed his experience in an unrestricted free market and was receptive to his arguments for breaking down the Company's monopoly culture which was driving the Indian trade into foreign bottoms and to foreign ports. Writing to the Governor General Lord Cornwallis on 11 August 1789, Dundas said Scott was 'now one of the Directors and intimately connected with Government. He is endeavouring to make the Court of Directors act in a very new Character, I mean to make them think now and then as Merchants, in place of viewing themselves only in the light of sovereigns and Great Generals.[18]' David Scott recognised that the old owners had some genuine grievances and worked hard to redress them. He wrote to a friend, 'the times of their ships sailing and returning are, since I came into the direction . . . drawn so accurately with the proper seasons, that they can have no more fear of unnecessary detention in India, and the ruin which so often followed it. They have no longer to wait for from two to three years for payment of their freight, but have ready money as soon as it is possible to make up their accounts,' as well as many private favours.[19] But he was determined to introduce free and open competition in the shipping, otherwise the Company would be bankrupt.

In April of that year Dundas wrote to the Court of Directors expressing his view that 'the freight respecting the shipping now in the employ of the East India Company should be settled once for all on a fair and equitable footing'.[20] He also requested the Court of Directors to set up 'some per-

manent system upon principles of fair, well-regulated and open competition which would not affect existing ships which should continue at a fixed rate and in preference', adding that 'persons whose property is embarked should not be kept in constant agitation by discussions on tenders of speculators.' This was supported in the General Court.

Events in October 1794 strengthened the growing antipathy to the old owners. The Committee of Shipping, using the estimates that it had prepared annually for the previous ten years and taking into consideration the commencement of hostilities with France, offered £31.4s a ton. Finding the old owners immovable, they finally accepted the lowest offer of £35 5s, a difference of £80,000 between the Company's offer and the one accepted. Henry Dundas at the Board of Control reacted angrily to this abysmal surrender by the Committee, asking if there was some influence at work in the Court of Directors. In the General Court Henchman and Jackson, redoubled their efforts, publicising every development and putting the old owners before the 'Bar of the Public'.

The following April Scott was elected, with government support, to the Deputy Chair and immediately proposed a plan to the court. A meeting of the independent Proprietors

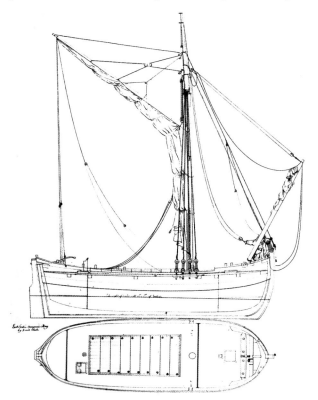

A plan of an East India Company hoy of the type used in the victualling of Indiamen. The original draught is in the Chapman Collection in Stockholm.   (*Sjöhistoriska Museum, Stockholm*)

A splendid painting by Dodd (dated 1807), showing a convoy of East Indiamen and their naval escort dropping anchor at Spithead after the long voyage from the East.

(National Maritime Museum)

was convened at the Crown and Anchor Tavern on Thursday 16 April 1795 to support the resolution of the Court of Directors for fair and open competition in the shipping affairs of the East India Company. It was also to consider what further measures were necessary for the real interest of the Company. They bemoaned the alarming increase in freight which 'has materially checked the import of the manufactures and products of our Oriental Territories into Great Britain' and believed that 'the mode of building ships for the service of the East India Company . . . by fair and open competition . . .is equitable, judicious and economical and that it ought to be carried into effect'[21] while at the same time supporting the continued employment of existing ships.

Despite substantial opposition, by-laws finally passed in the Court in March 1796 revised the shipping system: a lower freight was agreed; the Court advertised for ships to be tendered; the regular ships were continued in the service, but hereditary bottoms were abolished.

The system was not yet secure. Henry Dundas wrote to Scott, 'You know it has always been my opinion that the Shipping question could only with certainty (be) settled in Parliament . . . It must end there sometime or other and if the little faction at the India House go on to tease in the manner they have done I believe I shall favour them with a bill in Parliament to prevent their bringing matters forward by surprise.'[22]

As the 'little faction' never ceased their efforts to bring about the collapse of the new system an Act which received the royal assent on 12 December 1799 embodied the bylaws passed in 1796.[23] The Court of Directors advertised publicly for the shipping required, stating:

the burden of the . . . ships wanted, the dimensions or scantlings of timbers and planks, number of guns, manner of building, providing, furnishing and storing such ships . . . and the said advertisement shall fix a time (not less than four weeks from the publication) for receiving proposals in writing, sealed up, for building and freighting the same to the Company, such proposals to specify the lowest rates of freight . . . required for such ships for six voyages to and from India or China, or elsewhere within the limits of the Company's exclusive trade . . .'

The tenders were to be placed in a locked and sealed box and opened publicly in a Court of Directors on a certain day, the lowest tenders being accepted 'without favour or partiality' provided they were low enough. The Court was to choose by ballot between similar tenders. For the ship owners' guidance, the Master Attendant drew up estimates of the cost of building, equipping and fitting out a ship of 800 tons and one of 1200 tons for six voyages and displayed them in appropriate public places.[24] On their part, the Company recognised the huge capital investment represented in the provision of ships suitable for the Company's trade by hiring the ships 'for six voyages certain' at a given peacetime freight with an additional sum to cover 'war extraordinary' to meet the higher costs resulting from the war; and ships unavoidably taken or lost during the period of the contract were to be replaced. The by-laws already in operation were to continue: no Director was to retain shares in ships in the Company's service; tenders of ships were to contain the names of all the owners; and the

ships were to be employed in rotation according to the times of their arrival home.

Two additional voyages were permitted in 1803 through pressure on scarce resources; again in 1810 an act authorised the company to engage a ship beyond eight voyages provided she was found fit on repair, and to take up by private contract ships carrying stores or convicts to New South Wales to bring home cargoes from India and China.

In the freight service one of the chief obstacles to the solution of the shipping problem had been the difficulty of laying down a permanent and fixed rate of freight when the outbreak of war had an immediate and startling effect on costs not only of insurance but of wages, stores and provisions. Now a system had to be devised to ensure that these additional costs were fairly met: the freight for each voyage was laid down, starting at a higher rate for the first voyage and decreasing

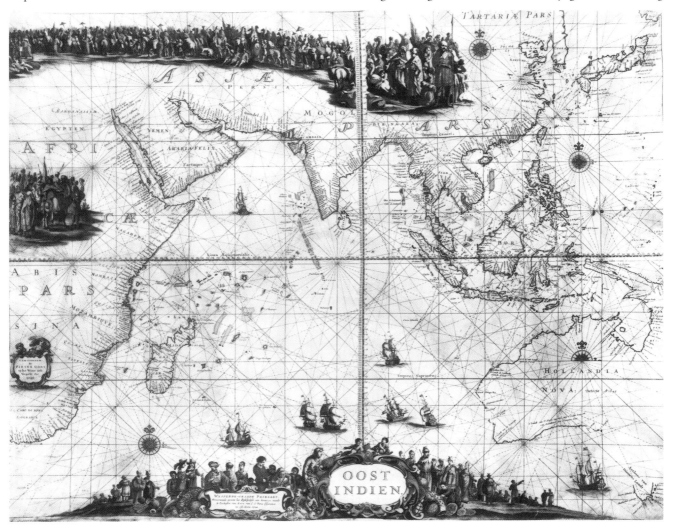

An early Dutch map and chart of the East with a rudimentary indication of dangerous rocks and shoal waters. *(National Maritime Museum)*

progressively until the sixth voyage. Owners' complaints that the rates of fitting out and repair greatly exceeded the estimates on which the freights had been based resulted in the passing of two further Acts of Parliament in 1803 and 1816. The Court was empowered to make extraordinary allowances to the owners of certain ships, the act of 1816 stating that it was 'fair and reasonable' that the *Herefordshire, Atlas, Bridgwater, General Harris, Vansittart,* and *General Kyd . . .'* should receive additional payment. In all, the owners of thirty-four ships presented their grievances to the Court in 1816, pointing out that the average freight they were receiving was £18 while contracts for building since the peace had exceeded £26 per ton, but not all were fortunate.

The new shippers merged with the old owners to resist any further encroachments on their position. Together they set their faces against the threat from Indian-built shipping. The Act of 1772, which aimed at taking pressure off scarce resources to benefit naval building, had also empowered the Company to build ships in India for its service, but the shipping interest was opposed to any intrusion into its province. The Company had not objected to line of battle ships and frigates being built in India, but their use for commerce was 'an affair of so great consequence, and requires so much consideration, that the Court think it highly necessary to request the instructions of the General Court, before the Court can offer an opinion therein.'[25] A few ships were built in Bombay from the late 1780s for the port to port trade in the eastern seas but only occasionally appeared in the European trade. The capital accumulated in India, chiefly by the Company's servants, far exceeded all the means the Company could provide for remitting it to England for their retirement, the 3000 tons provided by the Company in 1793 proving wholly inadequate. A series of bad harvests in England forced the Company's hand. Extra ships were sent to India to bring back rice, but Indian-built ships were also chartered to bring rice to England and were allowed to fill up with general cargo. Their performance demolished all the arguments the shipping interest had used against their employment: they were fast, sailed out of season and unloaded and reloaded in record time. As William Money remarked, the arrival of these ships caused a 'sensation among the Monopolists, which could never have been exceeded if a hostile fleet had appeared in the Thames.'[26] Henry Dundas encouraged their use and supported the Governor-General, Lord Mornington's, efforts to get back to England in Indian-built shipping 'that portion of trade which at present is purloined from us by foreigners, in a great measure trading upon our capital.'[27]

Vested interests were unable to stem the assault on the walls of protection. As the time for the renewal of the charter approached the struggle for the opening up of the eastern trade was launched with increased vigour on two fronts: the northern manufacturers at home and the English merchants in India. In vain the 'Petition of the managing owners and other owners of ships built for and in the service of the United East India Company' claimed that if the system on which the trade was conducted were changed they would suffer immense losses, 'such ships being wholly unfit for any other trade or employment . . . there are now in the service of the East India Company: 115 ships of 1400 down to 500 tons each, amounting in the whole to a tonnage of 115,000 tons and upwards, and in value to above £6,000,000 of money, ships better prepared to resist an enemy', ships which had men 'eminently useful to government'.[28]

Lord Liverpool's Act of 1813 ended the Company's monopoly of commerce with all areas in the east except China.

Notes:
1. Essex R.O.Papers of Samuel Braund: D/Dru, B18,19.
2. *Ibid*, B20.
3. *Ibid*, B20.
4. BL,OIOC, L/MAR/C530 f442. Appendix 826.
5. Hickey, *op cit*, Vol 4, 1 and 5.
6. Essex R.O., Papers of Samuel Braund, D/Dru, B22.
7. BL,OIOC, L/MAR/C1, *Brief Historical Sketch*, f33-35.
8. *Ibid*, f39.
9. Horne, D.B. and Ransome, M: English Historical Documents, vol 10, 597.
10. BL, OIOC, L/MAR/C530. Append. 580 and 581.
11. *Ibid*, Append. 576.
12. *Ibid*, f266 26 May 1786.
13. *Ibid*, f285, 28 June 1786.
14. *Ibid*, Introduction.
15. Philips, C.H: *The East India Company, 1784-1834* (Manchester 1940) 81n.
16. BL, OIOC, L/MAR/C531, f520 9 and 15 May 1792.
17. *Ibid*, f536 22 August 1792.
18. PRO 30/11/115 f93-95v.
19. Philips, C.H. ed: *Correspondence of David Scott 1797- 1805*, Vol.I, no. 26, Scott to William Fairlie, 30 March 1795.
20. BL,OIOC, L/MAR/C531 f568 3 April 1793.
21. *Ibid*, Append.1755.
22. Corresp. David Scott, *op cit*, Henry Dundas to David Scott, no129 6 February 1798.
23. 39 Geo III, c89.
24. MacGregor, op cit, Part IV, 179: eg Captain Joseph Bolderson compiled following list in 1809 for ships of:

	1200 tons	800 tons
First voyage	£64,580	£45,931
Second voyage	£16,737	£12,828
Third voyage	£19,508	£14,777
Fourth voyage	£29,071	£20,944
Fifth voyage	£19,663	£14,609
Sixth voyage	£20,353	£15,111

25. BL, OIOC, L/MAR/C530 f105 26 February 1782.
26. Bulley, Ann: *Free Mariner*, 166, Money W.T. quoted.
27. Ingram, Edward (ed): *Two Views of British India*, Henry Dundas to Earl of Mornington 23 July 1799.
28. Parliamentary Papers House of Commons 1801-1900 v.IV: Petitions respecting the East India Company Charter, 6 May 1812, v.xxiii f49,50,51.

CHAPTER 3

THE $\mathscr{S}$HIPS

The popular perception of an East Indiaman as a very large, superbly-built ship carrying a crowd of sail is based on portraits of the large China ships painted in the last few decades of the Company's trading life. Even the term East Indiaman was adopted quite late, documents referring to 'India ships', 'East India ships' or 'the East India Company's shipping' until the latter years of the eighteenth century.[1] Over the two hundred and thirty-four years of the Company's operations the shipping it employed varied considerably in size and quality, but it is generally true to say that the ships that took out the bullion and broadcloth and brought back the cottons and teas were the largest, most soundly constructed British merchantmen afloat. The ships changed little over the years of the company's trading life: there were refinement, but few technological advances. The seamen on the *Trades Increase* in 1610 would have handled the *Farquharson* in 1827 without great difficulty.

Although the founders at first hesitated to buy the *Malice Scourge* of 600 tons to be admiral of the first fleet, 'her burthen being so great, whereby the Tunage agreed upon shalbe so greatly exceeded'[2] they soon favoured much larger ships – partly to combat the huge rival Dutch and Portuguese ships of war encountered in the eastern seas, partly to provide increased tonnage as trade prospects improved. Prestige also counted for a great deal in the early days when the Company was trying to get a foothold at Surat inside the Emperor Jahangir's dominions and combat the influence of the Portuguese, those 'prating Jesuits . . . who prevail much with him, telling him we are a base people and dwell in a little island of no force, and that we can send no more ships hither until those that were last here return . . .'[3]

The first twenty years of the Company's life therefore witnessed the building of some exceptionally large ships: the *Trades Increase*, the *Palsgrave*, the *Charles*, the *Royal James* were 1000 tons and more; the *White Bear*, *Elizabeth* and *New Years Gift* were over 850 tons, and there were several of 600 and 700 tons. The disappointing sailing qualities of some of these larger ships and the blow to the spice trade in the 1620s discouraged the Company and by the 1640s the fleet had dwindled to a few ships averaging about 500 tons. Large numbers of small craft were used in conjunction with these huge ships in the eastern seas: prefabricated pinnaces were taken out and assembled on arrival at foreign ports; small native Indian craft or Chinese junks were bought or freighted for use in the coastal trade or among the islands of the Malay archipelago, seeking out cargoes which they transferred to the holds of the large ships remaining in port.

With the return of confidence under Cromwell and Charles II the Company 'inclined much to encourage the building of good able 3 decked ships of 450 or 500 tons which will be fittest for their employment.'[4] Government policy accorded with this aim. The *Royal Katherine* must have been one of the first ships to take advantage of the act offering remission of customs to owners of large ships: launched in November 1662 she sailed from the Downs for Coromandel the following March. She was 435 tons, 90ft long and 30ft

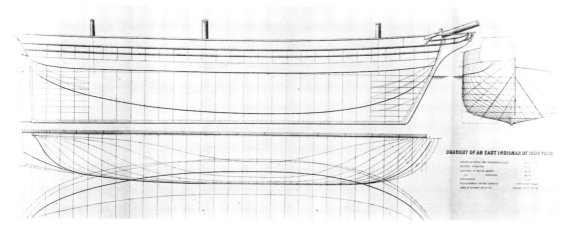

DRAUGHT OF AN EAST INDIAMAN OF 1000 TONS

Draught of a 1000-ton East Indiaman of the final generation (about 1830).
(*Science Museum*)

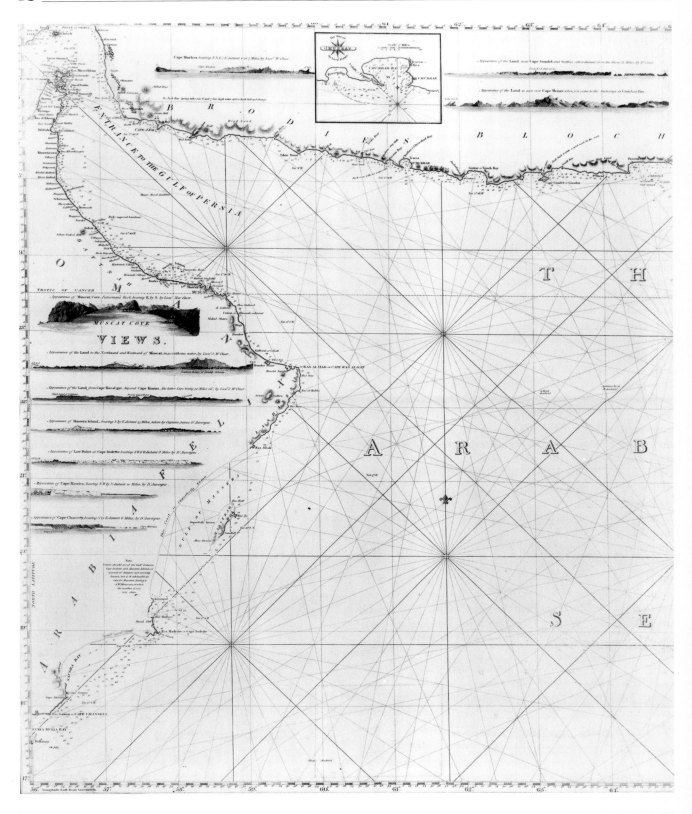

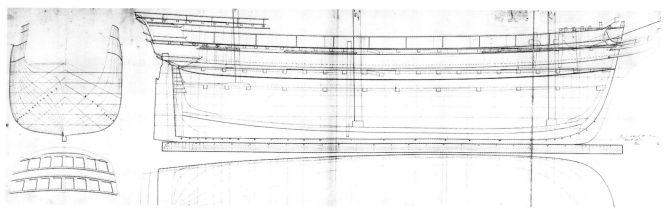

Sheer plan of the 'extra ship' *Coromandel* of 576 tons burthen, taken up for one voyage in 1819.　　　　　　(*Science Museum*)

wide, with an orlop, gun deck, upper deck, forecastle and quarterdeck. On 30 September 1664 her owners requested a share of ⅒ part of the customs on the goods she carried 'and that she hath three decks and 5 feet between each deck and is mounted with 30 peeces of ordnance and other ammunition proportionable and that this is the first voyage she hath made.'[5] Reinforced by the Company's offer in 1668 of 20s a ton extra freight for ships of this size and the growing 'India craze' the owners responded. The size of the ships reached that of the earlier years: the *Bedford, Rochester, Modena, Charles II, Defence* and *Beaufort* all exceeded 700 tons. These 'great ships' remained at the main settlements where they filled up with cargo collected by smaller ships and returned home to collect the customs. Smaller ships were also employed in seeking out the trade, chiefly to get access to the legendary luxuries of China and the Japanese silver required to finance them. There was no point in sending ships capable of carrying huge cargoes until there was some assurance that there would be a cargo to carry. These voyages were often prolonged, ships losing their passage while their commanders and supercargoes conducted lengthy negotiations with local rulers. The ships in which Edward Barlow served between 1670 and 1703 reveal the range: the *Experiment*, 260 tons; the *Delight*, 100 tons; the *Kent*, 130 tons; the *Rainbow*, 250 tons; the *Sampson*, 600 tons; the *Sceptre*, 360 tons; and the *Fleet Frigate*, 270 tons. Of the thirty-three ships in which Henry Johnson had an interest only twelve were over 500 tons and nine were 250 tons or less.

By the early eighteenth century changed conditions favoured smaller ships of a more uniform size. The King's bounty lapsed in 1704, while some daunting losses during the war with France exposed the error of building very large ships. The pioneering voyages of the small ships had borne fruit in

Left: A section of a chart of the Persian Gulf based on a survey by Lt John McCluer, Indian Navy, in the 1770s and published by Dalrymple. The latter encouraged the drawings of coastal features.

(*National Maritime Museum*)

the establishment of settlements. With the formation in 1708 of the United Company of Merchants of England trading to the East Indies, the trade was settled in established channels and for most of the century the Company's policy was similar to that agreed by the Court of Committees in 1615, that 'ships of 300 tons and so forth to 600 and 700 tons were fittest.'[6] The Company's chartered tonnage exactly mirrored the trading conditions: a steadily increasing trade was carried on in ships gradually increasing in size and numbers. By 1773 when the Company changed to the policy of taking up ships at builder's measurement, the standard size was equivalent to the 'great ships' of a hundred years earlier – 750 to 800 tons.

The 'new shippers' responded immediately to the sudden trebling of the tea imports after 1784. John Fiott's two ships, the *Hartwell*, 938 tons and *Belvedere*, 987 tons, both built at Itchenor in 1786, blazed the way for large China ships, but within a few months they were surpassed by the *Nottingham*, 1152 tons, launched later that year at Gravesend. The committee of Managing Owners roundly condemned this departure from the customary 750-800 tons. A few months later the return of the *Nottingham* confounded the Court and caused much soul-searching in the Committee of Shipping. She brought home almost twice the 712,000 lbs customarily brought home in an 800 ton ship. Those in sympathy with the old owners pointed to the captain's abuse of the rules in dismounting sixteen of her guns to stow cargo on the gundeck and encumbering her upper deck with stores and waterbutts.[7] The debate whether or not proceedings should be taken against her owners ebbed and flowed into the new year, but in the end no charges were made. The argument was won. Larger ships followed in succeeding years. The *Maidstone Journal* reported on 3 November 1789 the launch of the *Royal Charlotte*:

of the largest burthen of any ship that has ever been in the Company's service, being 1252 tons; seven or eight hundred tons being the size they have of late years employed; but we (their ships) to such a state of perfection as to make them surpass the shipping employed in almost any service whatever, the Navy of Great Britain perhaps not excepted.' Though written towards the end of the Company's life, these comments were valid throughout the period.

The turn of the sixteenth century had been an auspicious time for the Company to enter the market for ships. Historical development had resulted in the replacing of the vulnerable Royal Dockyards at Harwich and Portsmouth by Deptford and Woolwich. From London Bridge to Woolwich Reach the River was seething with new ideas expounded by men intent on replacing the old medieval rule of thumb methods by scientific principles. From the start there was no division between naval and merchant building. The men in charge of the royal dockyards – the 'master shipwrights' created by Henry VIII – had their own yards on the River where naval vessels rose on the stocks alongside merchant ships. Edward Stevens, appointed master shipwright in 1603, built in his own yard the *Malice Scourge*, bought by the company and renamed the *Red Dragon*, 'admiral' of the first fleet. Several of the ubiquitous Pett family had yards at Wapping and Limehouse which they ran in conjunction with the supervision of royal docks at Chatham, Woolwich and Deptford.

William Burrell, a Ratcliffe shipbuilder and a 'Committee' of the company, was chosen as the first Surveyor General of the Company's ships, combining this post with that of Commissioner for the Navy. In the royal dockyard at Deptford he built naval vessels while in the adjoining Company yard, acquired in 1609, he controlled the building of the Company's ships. It was here that James I, his queen and the young prince, with a great deal of pomp befitting the occasion, witnessed the launch of the *Trades Increase*, designed by Burrell and named by the King. Burrell organised the Company's yard on exactly the same lines as the royal dockyards, co-ordinating and controlling all the different operations: he designed the ships, made patterns from light battens which he personally took to the forests to find suitable timber, and arranged the transport. He designed the wet and dry docks, the wharves, warehouses, storehouses and workshops; even the housing, feeding and paying of the workers were his responsibility. On additional land acquired at Deptford a foundry was set up for making anchors, chains and nails, a spinning house for the manufacture of cordage, a whole range of storehouses for timber and canvas, a slaughterhouse and salting house and a powder mill where gunpowder was manufactured from the saltpetre brought back from Surat.

The same standards, exacted by careful survey, were demanded in the Company's ships as in naval vessels. A suggestion in 1615 that ships could be built more cheaply in Ireland was turned down because William Burrell would not be able to keep his eye on them during building, 'whereby many faults would be to their great prejudice and danger of the shipping.'

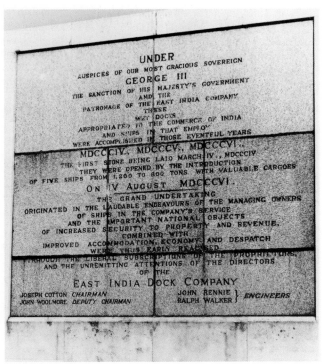

The inscription built into the main gate, East India Dock Road.
(Museum of London, Docklands Collection)

find, so long back as the year 1610, when King James the First gave the Company their Charter, they built a ship of 1200 tons, called the *Trades Increase*, which was unfortunately lost going to Bantam . . .

The old owners were not slow to jump on the bandwagon. If large ships were required, then they would make sure they were the chief beneficiaries. In 1793 their supporters revised the company's shipping requirements to meet the changed pattern of trade. Two classes of ships would in future be chartered: thirty-six ships of 1200 tons for the China trade and forty ships of 800 tons for India. Extra ships of about 500 tons would be chartered as required with no guarantee of further employment, providing flexibility from time to time to bring home 'gruff goods'.[8] This set the general pattern for the remainder of the Company's trading life, though the numbers of ships increased.

There is no shortage of contemporary accounts stressing the quality of the ships in the Company's service: 'the aristocrats of the seas', 'the finest ships that ever sailed on the high seas'. These were by no means exaggerations. In the opinion of Captain Eastwick, who saw service in all types of ships including those of the Royal Navy, 'no finer fleet sailed the seas than that which was directed from Leadenhall Street'. Another writer went even further: 'the Company brought

As production and repair work exceeded the capacity of the Deptford yard in the early years, Burrell was asked by the court to acquire more land for the building of additional docks. Company ships were already in the habit of mooring off the remote marshy area in the north-east corner of the Isle of Dogs where the River Lea flows into the Thames, and a lighter service to Custom House Quay and Wool Quay had been in existence since 1606. Travellers had long used the Stairs, linked by a causeway with Poplar Street, an open road leading to the lime kilns of Limehouse, by which they could reach the City and avoid the long trek round the Isle of Dogs. This remote area was soon transformed into a thriving shipyard, employing two hundred and thirty-two men by 1618, having an upper dry dock and a lower wet dock. The first ship to enter it was, appropriately, the *Red Dragon*. With their docks at Deptford and Blackwall the Company became the major shipbuilder on the Thames and one of the largest employers of labour in the London area.

The Blackwall Yard carried on as a thriving concern until in the dark days of the 1650s the Company took the decision to sell it. Henry Johnson bought it to build naval ships, but with the regeneration of the Company under Cromwell company ships rose on the stocks. Pepys recorded in his diary in January 1661: 'We took barge and went to Blackwall and viewed the docks . . . which is nearly made there, and a brave new merchant man which is to be launched shortly, and they say to be called the *Royal Oak*'. The yard carried on under Henry Johnson Jr and after his death under his manager Philip Perry whose son John succeeded him in 1776, taking over the whole yard in 1779. In 1790 he opened the Brunswick Basin, known as Perry's Dock, to accommodate thirty large and thirty smaller vessels. This was enlarged and converted into the East India Dock opened in 1806, financed by private and company money, to provide secure moorings for the returning India ships. After John Perry's retirement in 1810 Sir Robert Wigram bought the yard, continuing the partnership.

Many shipyards on the River, mainly at Limehouse, Rotherhithe and Deptford, expanded during the eighteenth century to build ships on contract for the Navy Board and East Indiamen. Death, bankruptcies, intermarriage and expansion caused confusing permutations amongst the owners of these yards, but there was a core of excellent shipwrights who were highly respected. The Wells family had a long tradition of shipbuilding. One member worked with Phineas Pett; others managed the great Howland wet dock, which they bought in 1763. They developed a very large yard at Rotherhithe that they sold in 1798 when they joined the Blackwall partnership which became Perry, Wells and Green. Randall and Brent took over the Wells' yards at the entrance to the Howland Dock as well as a large yard at Rotherhithe.

In 1763 William Barnard, who had worked for his father

Jamsetjee Bomanjee Wadia, Master Builder, Bombay Dockyard, 1790-1821, a member of the famous Parsee shipbuilding family.

(National Maritime Museum)

building ships for the Navy Board at Ipswich and the King's Yard at Harwich, leased a yard at Grove Street, Deptford, with his partner William Dudman. It was financed by a third partner, Henry Adams, who owned a shipyard at Beaulieu in Hampshire where he built ships on contract for the navy. Dudman and Adams had both been overseers at Deptford Royal Dockyard, adjoining the Grove Street yard, the facilities of which rivalled those of the Blackwall Yard: two dry docks, one extensive wet dock and three building slips. In 1779, on his own account, William Barnard took over a yard by Deptford Creek, on the site of the first East India Company shipyard. After his death his sons purchased the Wells yard at Rotherhithe with its excellent mastmaking facilities, becoming specialist mastmakers and suppliers to the Company's Bombay shipyard.

Late in the century Mr Pitcher joined this list of respected shipbuilders. With the introduction of the large class of Indiamen, the obvious place to build was at Gravesend, where most of the loading had always taken place and where ships were 'lightened' before continuing up-river to Blackwall. Thomas Pitcher moved to Northfleet from Deptford and started business with the launch of the *Royal Charlotte*; he followed her up with thirty-four other East Indiamen until

1825. Pitcher was joined by a group of enterprising India husbands – Messrs Larkins, Fraser, Dent and Clements – in developing moorings at Northfleet for use by company ships and naval vessels.

The major part of the work of these yards was maintenance and repair., each ship returned to the yard where it had been built at the end of each voyage. With the extension to six voyages, the fourth voyage became the repairing voyage, which was almost as costly as the original building. When eight voyages were permitted the sixth voyage also became a repairing voyage. A long relationship often developed between a husband and a builder: Robert Williams, one of the leading husbands, had ten ships built at Barnard's yard between 1764 and 1792, the Larkins family five. Papers in the Navy Board archive indicate that naval vessels also returned to these yards for cleaning, repair and refitting. The Company's records reveal that the Directors respected these men's knowledge, experience and expertise. Their opinions were frequently sought on possible improvements in design, and there is evidence of regular consultation between them and the Company's Master Attendant and Surveyor of Shipping.

Considering the fact that the Indiamen and naval vessels were built side by side in the same yards, by the same men, under similar stringent survey by the owners, the Company and the Navy Board, it is surprising that the Company's ships were superior in so many ways. Early in the French revolutionary wars an exasperated Gabriel Snodgrass listed possible improvements to the Navy in a letter to Henry Dundas who had taken over responsibility for the conduct of the war.[9] He complained that it was 'twenty-four years since I first introduced . . . the mode of fastening on the outside and inside plank with bolts, and leaving the treenail holes open for air until the ships were nearly finished and ready for caulking which . . . is now universally acknowledged to be the best method of seasoning the timbers and plank' but not practised in naval yards or included in the contracts for building ships of war in merchants yards. His considerable experience had taught him that the old type of rudder coat was very dangerous and seventeen years earlier he had introduced into company ships round-headed rudders requiring no rudder coats, 'now universally acknowledged to be much superior, in every respect, to the square-headed rudders of the ships of the Navy.' The aim was to produce a rudder head which rotated about its own centre, so minimising the size of the rudder port in the stern and dispensing with a coat. He condemned the 'thin bottoms' of the naval ships, which had 3in bottoms as opposed to the 4in bottoms of the East India Company's ships. In his opinion 'no ships of four hundred tons and upwards should have less than a bottom of 4" oak plank . . . and all ships should have the addition of wood sheathing.' The merchant yards charged with converting five 1200-ton East Indiamen to 64 gun ships in 1795 received plans of cap-

stans from the Navy Board but Snodgrass assured Dundas that 'every old capstand (sic) in the King's ships should be fitted with an iron spindle and catch-pauls' which would prevent men 'being thrown from the bars, crippling and killing the people.' Snodgrass claimed to have added iron knees under the beams to all old ships in the Company's service, and shortly afterwards all new East Indiamen were required to have iron knees. Not only did this save using large scarce angled timbers, but Snodgrass believe the separation of the sides from the beams was a major cause of foundering in several naval ships. 'I am persuaded that the loss of most of the ships of war and even merchant ships that have foundered at sea, has been occasioned by their having been insufficient in point of strength.' The East India House published on 2 November 1797 a list of twenty-six ships in the Company's service built with iron fittings – seventeen of them were over 1400 tons.[10] By 1810 all East Indiamen were required to be fitted with iron knees and standards, as well as iron hold pillars and hooks. Mr Snodgrass had served for several years in the Bengal shipyard where he had been impressed by the large ships built like oblong boxes. This experience was at the root of his campaign to reduce the ridiculous 'tumblehome' of ships, a view he failed to persuade the navy to adopt.

Some of Snodgrass's ideas were incorporated into naval ships after 1801 when Joseph Tucker was appointed as assistant to the Master Shipwright of Plymouth Dockyard. Trained as an overseer of ships building and repairing in the Company's service up to 1784, he graduated to assistant surveyor and became a surveyor of the Royal Navy in 1813. In 1805 twenty-two ships of the line, eleven frigates and a storeship were repaired by doubling their hulls and bracing their frames as recommended by Snodgrass in 1795, and the tumblehome of warships was greatly modified. Snodgrass was motivated by the need to economise on the use of large 'compass' timber required in such quantities by the navy and the need to maximise capacity while achieving great security for the valuable cargoes.

In one of the greatest technological advances in ship design of the eighteenth century the navy was far ahead of the Company. Starting with the *Alarm* frigate in 1761, the whole fleet had been coppered by 1782, while William Hickey noted in 1779 'scarcely any of our ships were copper-bottomed.' The old owners dragged their feet on coppering. As late as 1786 their friends in the Court tried to get through a motion to prohibit copper-bottomed ships being employed in future as the copper was injurious to the hull and very expensive, adding £100 on each ¹⁄₁₆ share.[11] The new shippers and the supercargoes in Canton had a more positive attitude. Anxious to get a belated lot of fine silks sent to London in 1788, they decided to send it by the *Belvedere* as she was 'a coppered Ship and we think it of consequence that this article should go by the speediest conveyance . . ..'[12] By 1790

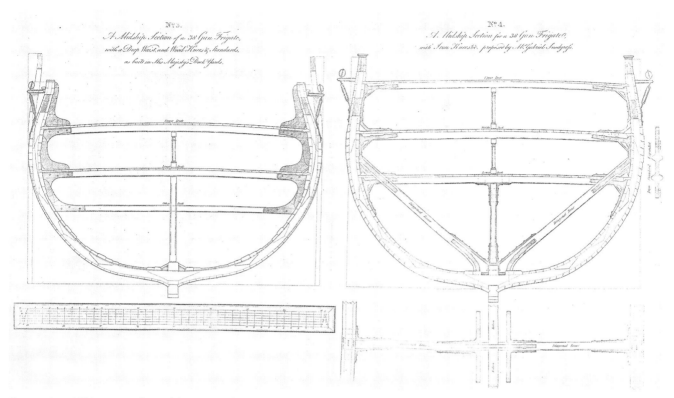

Comparative midship section of a naval frigate (as built in the 1780s – left) and as proposed by Gabriel Snodgrass, Surveyor to the East India Company. Frigates were closest in size and scantlings to the 800-ton Indiaman, and Snodgrass proposed that they adopt features (such as iron knees and brackets and a flush upper deck) that he had already adopted for the Company's ships.

twenty-two company ships had been coppered.

By the end of the eighteenth century the husbands and builders were forced to look further afield for timber. The new shippers Fiott and Moffat and Hurry built in Liverpool, chiefly extra ships of low burthen, though Humble and Hurry of Liverpool built the regular ships *Charlton*, *Asia* and *Europe*. In the south Henry Adams used the timber of Hampshire to build Indiamen on the Beaulieu River and supply his partners Barnard and Dudman of Deptford; other Indiamen were built in yards in Sussex and in the East coast ports as far as Hull and Durham.

In the last years of the eighteenth century, as the French wars put increasing pressure on the already dwindling reserves of English oak, the Company's fleet received a fresh infusion of quality with the introduction into the European trade of ships built in India of teak – the 'oak of Hindostan'. The Company's council in Bombay had brought the Parsee ship-builders down from Surat early in the century and ships of unsurpassed quality were built there for the navy, the Bombay Marine and the East India Company. According to a visitor to Bombay in 1775 (when Manackjee Lowjee was the head builder):

It boasts such a dry dock as, perhaps, is not to be seen in any part of Europe, either for size or convenient situation. It has three divisions and three pairs of strong gates, as to be capable of receiving and repairing three ships of the line at the same or at separate times . . . the outermost and the second ship can go out and the others be received in their places without hindrance to the workmen employed on the third or innermost ship.[13]

To practice their art the shipbuilders had the finest material – teak, rated 'very durable' for shipbuilding. Teak grows in profusion in many parts of India and Burma, but the finest grows on the Malabar coast. It is resistant to marine borers such as the dreaded 'teredo navalis', the scourge of oak-built ships, and requires only a brief period of seasoning. Its oily nature preserves ferrous metals so that the ships could be fastened with iron spikes. A commercial revolution occurred in Western India with the carrying of cotton to China. The Company built ships in Bombay to participate in the trade – the *Britannia* in 1779 and the *Sir Edward Hughes* in 1786 – but the vast amount was carried by large country ships owned

One of the finest ships ever built for the East India service, the *Earl Balcarras* was built of Indian teak by the famous Parsee firm of shipbuilders in the Bombay dockyard for the China trade. It is easy to understand how such vessels were mistaken for ships of the line. *(Science Museum)*

by the agency houses or private Parsee, Indian or English owners. The *Scaleby Castle*, 1215 tons, built by Bruce Fawcett was bought by the Company. From 1808-1811 the Company built one ship a year for the Bombay-China trade: the *Bombay, Charles Grant, Earl of Balcarras* and *Minerva*. The longevity of these ships was legendary: the *Bombay* frigate of the Company's Bombay Marine served continuously in tropical waters for more than sixty years. The hostility of the shipping interest successfully excluded their employment to any great extent in the European trade.

The East India ships were not without their defects. These became more pronounced in the later period. The alarming number of ships which foundered in 1809 concentrated the minds of the Directors who sought opinions from all the authorities including Captain George Millet, an ex-East India captain elected to the direction. Replying to a request from the Chairman, Charles Grant, for his advice regarding advertising for tenders for the season 1810, Captain Millet stressed the necessity of abandoning 'the scale and plan of the 800 ton ships now in use . . .'[14] It was the practice of increasing the 'encumbrances aloft' following the general adoption of the flush upperdeck ship that most exercised Millet. The first

three-decked ship built for the Company's service was the *Boscawen*, launched in 1749. A passenger aboard her on her first voyage noted the increased safety resulting from her flush upper deck:

> . . . when a Sea broke in thereabouts, I mean at Midships, the Gunwall not being more than a foot above it, it passed off immediately; whereas in a Two-decker the Waste is entirely open to it, and when full, contains so great a Body of Water, as to make them liable to fatal Consequences. I shall wonder if the Company don't order all their Ships to be built in the same Manner.[15]

Her commander, Captain Braund, was of the same opinion. After encountering a gale off Cape Agulhas, he wrote to his uncle, the husband, 'we all believed had it not been for our third deck (ye Seas running so high and breaking short) we must have foundered'.[16] Gabriel Snodgrass constantly agitated for flush-deck ships but there were still waisted ships about in the early nineteenth century. Captain Millet pointed to the *Boddam*, built in 1787 on the scantling of an 800 ton ship, 'having the forecastle raised four feet above the upper deck, the bows raised fifteen inches, the ship's hearth risen with the forecastle, the hogsties, and sheep-pens, brought on the upper deck, and the sides birthed up a midships and with dimensions of 128'1" keel and 38'9" breadth and 15'6" Depth in the hold she hasn't the breadth to compensate for the elevation of the additional weight.' Millet claimed 'The modern 800 ton ships have not only all the incumbrances aloft of the *Boddam*, but they are beginning to bring the gallies up on the upper deck altogether, until they are become . . . so extremely crank, as to be unfit for the service they have to perform.'

As for the 1400 ton ships, everyone had had sufficient experience 'to be thoroughly satisfied they will never answer'. The problem arose from the method of measuring: the depth of the hold did not figure in the calculation and so made no difference to the price. Ship owners had abused this omission for years, instructing builders to build ever deeper ships. Although additional beams had been fitted 'to strengthen the immense space unsupported' it would not do, and Millet felt it was necessary to fix some limit.

The 1200 ton China ships, though too long for their breadth, met with his approval, 'certainly by far the best class that were ever built for the China trade.' But 'It is the opinion of the best informed builders, that a ship of 900 to 950 tons burthen, will require no more scantling than what is given to the present class of 800 tons' and since the 800 ton ships were in his opinion over-masted, they would require no more men and need draw no more water. This was an important consideration as ships bound to Bengal had to draw no more than 17ft in order to navigate the River Hooghly. Captain Millet said, 'I know there is a pretty general coincidence of opinion in favour of 900 ton ships and upwards, among the owners, the maritime officers, and the builders.' He suggested a letter be written to the principal builders, '(say Messrs Wells and Co, Messrs Barnards, and, if you think proper, Mr Brent and Mr Pitcher)' asking them to furnish a plan of a ship of about 930 tons, bearing in mind all the necessary requirements. Barnard's reply has not survived but Wells responded three months later, 'We are of the opinion we cannot improve on the construction of the *Warren Hastings* of 1,000 tons,' (actually 997 on the Blackwall ship list) 'which ship is of great stability and capacity, and draws less water than the ship of 800 tons.'[17] It was the opinion of Gabriel Snodgrass and the Master Attendant, expressed earlier, that as far as ships 'that may prudently be built with the same scantlings as the present ships of 800 tons, we are of opinion, that, with the exception of the beams, provided copper bolts be used instead of treenails, that the scantlings would be sufficiently large for ships of 1200 tons.'

Naval ships and East Indiamen were built side by side by the same people in the same yards to the same high quality specifications and very nearly the same scantling. Why, then, many people asked, could the East Indiamen not be readily converted into ships of war? It was a debate that ebbed and flowed for decades. The 800 ton ships were often compared to frigates while the large China ships were frequently mistaken for ships of the line by the French. The captain of the French frigate *La Medée* surrendered without battle after a chase by the *Exeter* and *Bombay Castle* East Indiamen in 1800. Only when he saw the little guns on the quarter-deck while surrendering his sword did he suspect his error – and asked to what ship he had surrendered. On being told 'to a merchantman' he requested a repeat of the battle, a request that Captain Meriton refused. In a letter to his brother William written on the eve of his departure for China in 1805, Captain John Wordsworth described his ship, the *Earl of Abergavenny*, as 'the finest ship in the fleet; nobody can tell her from a 74-gun ship.' Certainly Admiral Linois in the 74-gun *Marengo*, accompanied by two frigates, a corvette and a brig, mistook the *Abergavenny* and a few other 1200 ton Chinamen for much more heavily armed ships. After engaging the China fleet for about forty minutes at the entrance to the Straits of Malacca, the admiral ordered the retreat, convinced his force was not equal to the Indiamen. Napoleon was not amused.

The French model was held up by the supporters of East Indiamen doubling as warships: after 1755 until its demise in 1769 the French company had built 1200 ton ships which carried at least fifty-four 12pdr cannon on the main deck. 'Armee en flute', that is with all except the upper deck guns stowed away in the hold to make room for soldiers or stores, they could take their place in the line when required, reverting to fully-armed ships when they had landed men and stores.

David Scott felt the answer would be 'to make our large ships as fit for warlike purposes as possible. If they can't be made really fit for men of war without spoiling them . . . for commerce, in such case we should endeavour to make them as fit for armed transports as possible without a necessity of cutting them to pieces and going to a great expense to make them so in any future war . . .'[18] Scott was writing just after fourteen East Indiamen had been taken into the navy, some completed ships which were converted, some near completion on the stocks. The most important change was the addition of stronger lower deck beams. William Barnard's letter to the Navy Board excusing the delay in delivering the *York*, converted from the *Royal Admiral*, bears out David Scott's view: 'The great difference in materials necessary for a ship of war from those previously provided for the ship as an East Indiaman . . . together with a variety of alterations that have to be made to frames and other parts of her construction . . .' Perry of Blackwall put down his lateness in delivering the *Agincourt* to 'the difficulties we met with in procuring gundeck beams, . . . being an entire addition, and requiring such capital timbers . . .' The only sailing report is of the *York* by

Captain Ferrier who claimed she was a slow sailer and poor steerer. The East Indiamen were lighter in draught and performed well in the shallower waters of the West Indies and Dutch waters, and their greater stowage capacity created by the bluffer bows and stern were welcomed by the naval officers.

There was always the problem of the Indiaman's lower deck ports being too near the waterline, with the problem of water getting in and damaging the cargo, but it was on the impossibility of manning a large battery with only one hundred and thirty men that the argument for Indiamen doubling as warships eventually withered and died. Nathaniel Smith, Chairman of the Company in the mid-1780s, argued that a ship was capable of defence only 'if properly manned, her guns all mounted, and the middle deck sufficiently cleared either from goods or stores' and with a minimum of one hundred and sixty to one hundred and seventy men. The state in which the *Nottingham* returned to the River in August 1788 revealed the weakness of the argument: ships could not stow large cargoes while keeping all their guns in action, and there were never enough men to man all the guns. The capture of the 1200-ton *Warren Hastings* by the French frigate *Piemontaise* on 21 June 1806 after a four hour action reveals the underlying weaknesses. The Indiaman had sailed from Canton with only one hundred and thirty-eight men while the Frenchman, only ten days out from the Isle de France, had a crew of three hundred and eighty-five. Captain Larkins reported 'in her tops were fifty men with swivels and rifles' still leaving plenty to man the big guns and manoeuvre the ship, while Captain Larkins was forced to take in 'all the steering sails, stay sails, and hanked the mainsail up, that I might have nothing to draw the attention of my crew from their quarters, save the principal sails for manoeuvring . . .'[19] He had had to find space for stores on the main deck, caulking up four gun ports and consigning the guns to the hold along with four others, probably because he lacked men to man them.

Arming the ships was never a simple business. In the early period it was a question of casting about and taking what was available, aggravated by the sheer shortage of suitable armament and the need for large ships to be well-armed to deal with Portuguese and Dutch hostility or that of local rulers. They mounted a great mixture of cast iron culverins and sakers, large calibre muzzle loaders and wrought iron breech loaders.[20] The problem of weight led to consideration of lighter brass and forged iron guns. The Company borrowed from the Tower, bought from other adventurers and other companies, from gunfounders such as Thomas Brown and the company's favoured gunfounder, Mr Turvill. The Company made its own gunpowder at Deptford from saltpetre it imported from India until 1625 when it set up its own mills at Chilworth, Sussex, which served the Company for ten years

before being taken over. On the ships' return the guns were all offloaded at Deptford for checking after which they were reshipped, consigned to be used as ballast, sold off for shot or rebored.

On the adoption of the policy of freighting ships, the Company handed over the task of arming their ships to the owners. With the peace in the 1660s the armament was standardised at thirty-six guns for a three-decker and thirty for a two-decker. The downward trend continued, the guns being reduced to twenty-four on 500 ton ships and fewer proportionately on smaller ships. By the mid-eighteenth century 9pdrs replaced 12pdrs on the gundeck. The owners constantly pressed for fewer, smaller guns and permission to have them proved other than at Woolwich which was very expensive. This problem persisted. In 1787 the owner of the *Admiral Barrington* pleaded with the Committee of Shipping that the guns 'be permitted to remain' though not Woolwich proved, protesting that it was 'a great expense and trouble' to have the guns taken out and sent to Woolwich. All had been proved at Bow Common some years earlier and the ship was only 'an occasional ship'.[21] Guns were an expensive item, always in great demand, giving rise to the persistent problem of the commanders selling them abroad. Who could gainsay a captain and his officers who noted in the ship's journal, as did Captain Glover of the *Warren*, 'off the northwest coast of India she rode out in ye open sea a violent hard Gale w[h]ich obliged me to heave 19 Guns overboard all 9 pounders to pre[ve]nt foundering.'[22] Charter parties throughout the period stressed the seriousness of this practice: the latest version of the charter party stated the owners would be charged £100 for each gun sold and the commander would be sacked.[23]

The ships of the mid-eighteenth century carried twenty-six guns. The *Boscawen* was armed with twenty-two 9pdrs and four 4pdrs in 1747, while the 800 ton *Princess Amelia* had twenty-six 9pdrs and six 4pdrs in 1786. With the increase in the size of ships for the China trade from the 1780s and the war with France the armament became part of the debate on whether East Indiamen should be built as both cargo ships and warships. In 1794 the Committee of Shipping required the large China ships to carry extra men and guns, the Company offering to pay the men's wages and contribute to the victuals.

The capture of seven East Indiamen with heavy losses to the Company between 1793 and 1801 focused the Committee of Shipping's attention. Various men of experience were consulted, amongst them Joseph Cotton, an ex-East India commander who became a Director in 1795. On his advice, each gun would in future be fitted with a proper

Right: A plan and painting of the *Falmouth*, representative of the regular East Indiamen taken up by the Company at 499 tons in the middle decades of the eighteenth century. *(National Maritime Museum)*

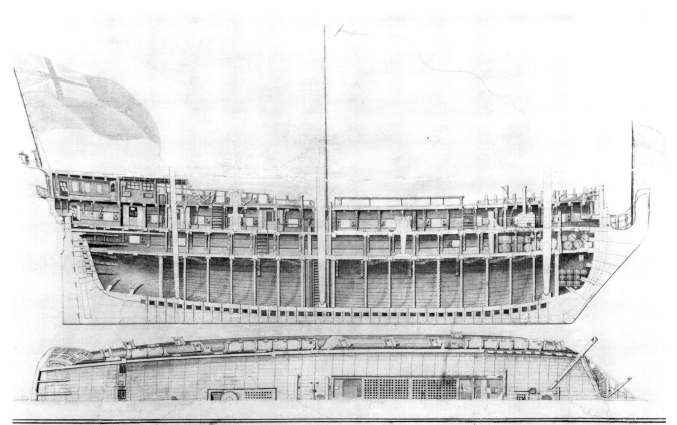

A SECTION and PLAN of the FALMOUTH *Built at* BLACKWALL *Anno* 1752

The FALMOUTH *Capt.* THO.S FIELD *Launcht at* BLACKWALL *the 14.th of August* 1752 *Length P.r Keel* 108:9, *Breadth* 34, *Burthen* 668 9⁄94

lock and chamber, and would rest on a Gover's patent gun carriage which enabled a smaller crew to operate the gun. The carriages would be paid for by the Company. After wide consultation the Court decided on the armament of each class of ship. Carronades were not popular – Robert Wigram claimed they 'almost invariably upset on being fired' – and were banned from the main deck along with light guns. A certain proportion of the guns were to be on the upper deck to ensure that there were men stationed there to repel boarders, there being a propensity amongst the heterogeneous European wartime crews of doubtful loyalty, with their large proportion of foreigners and Lascars and Chinese, to slink below at the first sign of trouble. In future all guns were to be of one calibre, and the proper charge of powder marked on each gun; two, to be mounted in the aftermost ports and to be used as stern chasers when necessary, were to be longer. 1200 ton ships were to have twenty-four 18pdrs, twenty-two on the gun deck plus two stern chasers and twelve 18pdr carronades on the upper deck; 800 ton ships were to have twenty 18pdrs plus two stern chasers on the gun deck and ten 18pdr carronades on the upper deck. The 18pdr cannonades were about 28 ½ cwt, hybrids between the long gun and the carronade, and not to be compared with the naval 18pdr. The company insisted on a minimum of 32½ cwt for the stern chasers. Advertisements for 500 and 600 ton extra ships stipulated sixteen 12pdr carronades and eighteen 12pdr carronades respectively. The large China ships of the post-Napoleonic war period appear to have mounted a similar armament. Thomas Whitcombe's painting of a ship believed to be the *Farquharson*, 1326 tons, built in 1820, shows thirty-eight guns, twelve on the upper deck and twenty-six on the middle deck, while David Steel's draught shows ten on the upper deck with two stern chasers, though she was pierced for fifty-six guns.[24]

Theory and practice were not the same thing, however. The owners found it impossible to obtain so many guns of one calibre, and the Company was forced to compromise. The minutes of the Committee of Shipping contain many reports of surveys of ships' armament by Captain Corner, the Company's Master Attendant, and his assistants and the Committee's subsequent orders to the owners. Most common were orders to replace unproved guns, to make sure of suitable guns for stern chasers, and suggestions for appropriate substitutes if the owners had difficulty in obtaining the regulation guns. On two points, however, the Court was adamant: guns of different calibre should not be mixed on the same deck to avoid mixing up the charge; the stern chasers should be longer guns.

Although the increased armament carried by the large ships in the China trade during the Napoleonic wars was impressive, such victories as were gained over French warships usually resulted from ingenuity rather than strength. William

Hickey, returning to England in 1808 on the *Castle Eden*, recorded in his memoirs: 'Our great guns were now regularly exercised twice a week, though I fear had it been our fate to depend upon the hostile use of them for safety, we should have cut but a wretched figure.'

The Company's policy regarding the security of its fleets remained the same throughout its life: commanders were discouraged from joining battle with enemy ships; a ships' guns were principally intended to keep an enemy at bay while escaping, hence the emphasis on proper stern chasers; keeping company was the chief defence of all Indiamen. A passenger on the *Abergavenny* recounted, after she was wrecked, that Captain Wordsworth was anxious to arrive first in Bengal in 1805 to sell his private trade goods at a good profit. 'His wish was to proceed as a single ship, but the orders regarding separation from the Fleet were too strict to be disobeyed.'

Samuel Braund's papers include a contract for the building of a hull by Perry & Co of Blackwall, essential features of which can be seen in the drawing of the *Falmouth*, similar in construction and lay-out to the ship in question.[25] The contract drawn up between Samuel Braund and John Perry & Co in December 1747 provided for the building of a hull for £8.10s a ton, the first instalment of £1000 being paid on signing the contract.[26] The ship was to measure 105ft on the keel and 33ft 4ins in breadth, only slightly exceeding the accepted safety principle of three times length by breadth. The greatest breadth was probably forward of amidships following the fashion in naval architecture at the time. Though this had been hotly debated for more than a century most expert shipwrights clung to the Tudor belief that if God had made fish and ducks fuller forward than aft that was the best shape for ships, and custom placed the broadest section of the ship – ambiguously the midship section – about ⅖ the length of the main deck from the bow. Maximum capacity dictated the shape of the hull which approximated to an oblong box: one of Captain Millett's many complaints was that 'the extreme breadth of their floors . . . is carried so far aft, that they have rudders given them like a west country barge, and when the sea strikes the rudder in a gale of wind, the helm is not only held with difficulty, but the seamen are frequently thrown round the wheel.'[27] For the same reason the floor was very flat but this did not endanger the ship or diminish her sailing ability provided the upper parts were light, keeping the centre of gravity low, a principle which was later abused as Captain Millet never tired of pointing out. This contract stipulated that the top timbers should 'tumble home' at least 3ft.

Headroom varied considerably: there was a generous 5ft 10ins on the lower deck, in the forecastle and under the gangways along the ship's sides, but the men had to look out in the steerage under the quarterdeck where it was reduced to 5ft. The officers and passengers had more comfort, the deck above the roundhouse rising from 5ft 10ins at the fore part to 6ft

2ins at the stern.

Practically the whole of the hull – at least ninety-five per cent – consisted of English oak. The Company's ships were invariably framed and to a large extent planked in English oak. There was even an insistence on oak grown in the south of England, as the clay soils of Sussex (and to some extent of Surrey, Kent and Hampshire) produced a superior type of oak. In this contract, John Perry & Son 'do further oblige themselves to work no North country wood, plank or timber . . . under penalty of Fifty pounds.' For a ship of this size, about 620 tons, an equivalent number of average sized oak trees of eighty to one hundred years' growth would be needed. Such a tree yielded about 50 cu ft if timber weighing 1¼ tons, producing about 1 ton of shipping in a naval vessel or company ship. Quality was demanded in every aspect of the ship's materials and construction. The iron used was 'all to be good Spanish iron', and 'a good suit of masts of the Growth of Gottenburg.' Regular inspections by the owners' and company surveyors ensured that the quality of the materials and workmanship were maintained.

The ship's construction began with laying the keel, made of elm as this preserved well under water. Stem and stern posts were fixed then the floor timbers laid at right angles across the keel. The frames were formed by joining futtocks – curved pieces of timber – to the arms of the floor timbers to form a curve to give fullness at the waterline, narrowing to form the 'tumble home'. The ship had substantial frames with little space between them. By March 1748 the framing was complete and the husband paid the builder the second instalment of £1000. The remainder of the outer planking was then secured to the frames. Dry rot was one of the chief problems of the wooden sailing ship, the area 'between wind and water',

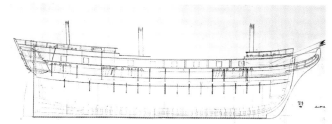

Sheer plan of the *Lord William Bentinck* (564 tons, 1827) showing the positions of iron standards and knees. *(Science Museum)*

alternately washed by the sea and dried by the sun, being the most vulnerable. The use of young supple oaks was generally considered insurance against this dry rot: the contract provided for English oak plank above the wale, the rest of the bottom to be covered with English plank, probably beech, except underwater where the traditional 'East country plank' – Baltic oak or elm – was to be used. All those parts of the ship where there was little ventilation and the air was stagnant – the breadroom, the magazine, the space between the frame timbers, the extreme bow and stern – were vulnerable to dry rot. As the use of certain foreign woods was considered to contribute to dry rot, the contract stipulated English oak only 'within board'. Special attention was to be paid to the hold where the plank was to be 'neither slappy nor sappy and well-fayed' – meaning well seasoned and close fitting. The realisation that seasoning helped to prevent dry rot was fairly recent at this time; in previous decades many methods, such as charring, pickling and steaming had been used unsuccessfully as preservatives.

On 5 May 1748 the gun deck beams being all in and fastened, the third instalment of £1000 was paid, and the fourth

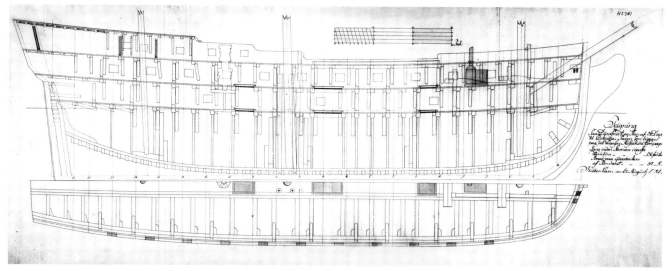

Construction plans such as this internal profile of a Danish East Indiaman of 1781 are almost unknown for English ships. Although rather larger, this ship (the *Dannemark*) has the same general layout and most of the construction features of an English East Indiaman of the period. *(Riksarkivet, Copenhagen)*

payment of £800 on 13 July, when the upper deck beams were in. The beams were to be 'well-pillar'd' and joined to the frames by knees. Some of the lower deck beams were to be strengthened by two knees at each end, one hanging, securing the beam vertically to the ship's side, the other lodging, securing the beam horizontally. These large angled timbers which could be cut only from 'grown' timber, formed where branches grew at right angles to the trunk, were very difficult to find. Even more scarce were the huge timbers used as supports where the hull was under the greatest strain: the V-shaped breasthooks which united the bows between decks, the crutches at the stern and the knee of the wing transom which was bolted across the inside of the stern-post to form the foundation of the counter. The navy was beginning to feel the pinch of Company competition at this time in the search for these large timbers.

Before the decks were planked with deals the chief fixtures were put in: the steps to take the masts; the huge timbers to secure the cable; the hand and chain pumps – the latter considerably improved in design a few years earlier by a Captain Bentinck RN; the main capstan with two drumheads to provide a drum on the maindeck and quarterdeck, used mainly to haul the anchor cable but also used to hoist the mainyard and to ship cargo and cannon; and the gear capstan on the maindeck forward.

The hull was then finished off: the frame for the quarter galleries and stern galleries was erected at the stern and the head at the bow; the catheads, huge timbers to take the anchors, were fixed on either side of the bow. On the main deck a wooden barrier called the manger was built to dam up any water that entered by the hawseholes through which the anchor cables passed. Gunports, as many as the husband decided on, were cut in the ship's sides. The rudder was fixed to the sternpost, 'the rudder head to go up into the great cabin with a hole for the Tiller' which could be used in the event of the breaking of the main tiller operated on the lower deck. A decorated box covered the rudder head in the great cabin.

Great care and attention were paid to the part of the ship's hull that would be under water. The contract provided for the usual treatment at that time: Perry & Co were to 'sheathe the Bottom with good three quarter inch board to . . . Tarr the parselling and to nail it on . . . to pay the Bottom with white Stuff and to find spunyarn and Nails.' This involved first caulking the planks, forcing spunyarn or oakum obtained from shredding 'old junk' or cables into the spaces between the planks, topped by a protective layer of hair. After this, the 'parselling', well tarred, was nailed on. The parselling was either canvas or brown paper; in this case it was probably brown paper as that is what was used on the ship which was being built alongside. Finally, the sheathing board was attached and well washed with lime, which was then considered to be a good deterrent to the teredo worm (a wood-

borer). Indeed, the biggest threat to any ship in tropical waters came not from pirates or privateers, hurricanes or typhoons, but from the teredo: the time and ingenuity brought to bear on this problem equalled that spent trying to combat dry rot. One method, sheathing with lead, was used in classical times and again in the seventeenth century, but Perry & Co undertook only to 'mark the ship fore and aft with lead'.

When the ship was finally launched at Blackwall and the last instalment paid to the builder in the autumn of 1748, the basic framework was complete and she was painted inside and out. At the stern, extending the full width of the quarterdeck and 18ft long, was the roundhouse. A door from the roundhouse led on to an open stern balcony extending the full width of the ship: two doors gave access to the quarter-galleries projecting on either side of the ship at the stern. The excellent quality demanded in the hull was continued in the appointments: 'all the sashes belonging to the roundhouse . . . to be good Crown Glass' with dark shutters fitted; the quarter-galleries were to be 'Compleatly finished with Copper Funnels to each Gallery' to provide lavatories for officers and passengers, more comfortable than those of the crew which simply consisted of holes in the ship's head, a position which would hardly attract the idler with a high sea running. Extending forward from the roundhouse, on the quarterdeck, was 'an handsome awning of whole Deal Rabbeted to come as far forward as the Mizzen Mast'. Underneath this substantial structure were the steering wheel and a quarterdeck table containing two glazed binnacles. A 'handsome Bell Ladder' at the fore part of the awning led from the quarterdeck to the poop on which, presumably, was the belfry.

An iron staircase with 'handsome turned Bannister' led from the quarterdeck down into the steerage at the rear of the main deck. Here was the great cabin immediately under the roundhouse, with similar quarter-galleries but without the stern balcony. Substantial shutters were required for fixing to the row of rear windows in bad weather. According to William Hickey, a seasoned traveller on the Company's ships, heading the list of the many inconveniences of travelling in the great cabin was 'that of being debarred from all daylight in tempestuous weather by what is very expressively termed 'the dead lights being then fixed to all the windows to prevent the sea breaking in, which nevertheless it does not effectually do . . .'

Extending forward on either side of the main cabin were 'Eighteen standing Cabbins with Lockers and shelves four Cabbins to be lined and scuttles cutt in them.' Scuttles were small apertures for ventilation. Cabins at this time often simply meant fixed beds, privacy being obtained by means of canvas partitions fixed to the deck above and below; only the 'lined' cabins had bulkheads. Apart from the pantry, which was in the steerage, all the stores and provisions were kept in rooms on the lower deck: two bread rooms, a powder room, a light room, a sail room, a lazaretto, and right in the stern a gun room – traditionally the living quarters of the Master Gunner and his mates.

After the launch, which was probably a grand affair, with a lunch at the dockyard and supper at a tavern followed by a ball for the benefit of the ladies, the ship spent about a month in dry dock, another month in the wet dock, and about four months on the mooring chains at Blackwall. During this time an army of tradesmen moved in to finish off the hull and fit out the ship. The tradesmen's bills for finishing off the *Boscawen*, another of Samuel Braund's ships which was built on the stocks alongside the ship in question, give full details of the finishing and fitting customary at the time.[28] First came the filler, while she was in dry dock, to drive seven tons of large-headed nails into the keel to keep out the teredo worm. He was followed by boys who cleaned out the ship and picked up all the nails underneath. The hearth for the galley was fitted on the main deck, complete with a furnace and air pipes. To reduce the risk of fire, always one of the chief hazards on the wooden sailing ship, the tinman fitted more than a gross of sheets of tin round the galley. He was also responsible for fixing the three huge lanterns to the poop – not as large as the lantern on the *Sovereign of the Seas* into which Samuel Pepys delighted in squeezing ten sightseers, but large nevertheless. He also fitted a glazed light in the powder room as no one was allowed to carry a naked light when the powder was being measured out. To reduce the fire risk further the bricklayer plastered the bulkheads of the powder room.

All the decks and the 'ceiling' – the inner lining of the ship – had to be caulked, the caulker driving the stranded oakum into the crevices with his caulking iron and sealing them with melted pitch. He then 'payed' all the upper parts of the ship with rosin and tallow and the upper decks with turpentine.

The carver was busy at the stern creating an effect of 'foliage and grotesque' on the stern and quarter-galleries and simulating capitals on the bulkhead of the roundhouse. There is no indication of the excesses of the Stuart period such as that noted by Francis Rogers in 1702, Captain Bowes' ship having 'the finest Quarter Deck I had seen, all the bulkhead of the roundhouse being gilt birdcages and sash glass.'[29]

The joiner planed the roundhouse floor and constructed a partition across it, probably to separate off the dining area, or cuddy, which usually opened on to the quarterdeck. He made sash doors for the roundhouse bulkhead, a pair of folding doors leading from the roundhouse on to the stern balcony, hanging shutters for the quarterdeck awning, and a coalhole bulkhead. On the poop he built a pair of coops 12ft long with gratings above and below to house the poultry, three turkey coops, four running coops, and at the breastwork – the balustrade at the fore part of the poop – two pairs of 'fatting coops' each with ninety-two holes. The painter could then

The masthouse erected at the Brunswick Dock in 1791. In this engraving by George Scharf it is seen in action hoisting a fifteen ton mainmast into position.

(Museum of London, Docklands Collection)

move in to gild or paint all the work done by the carver and joiner. A 'floor cloth' for the roundhouse was made by the sailmaker from 'Russia duck' and painted a plain colour each side. There is no mention of the extravagant decor which had been a feature of the earlier Stuart ships. When the *Sampson* drove through the wreckage of the convoy in which she was returning from Barbados, Edward Barlow saw a great deal of 'broken cabins and ceiling, painted white and brown, and some with red and branches of flowers and other paintings, which I judged came from the ship *Modena*, she having very good paintings on board of her in her great cabin and roundhouse.'[30]

The breadroom, being particularly vulnerable to dry rot, had to be dried out, and an engine brought on board 'for extracting the foul Air by Fire': the gases accumulating in the bilge were not only insupportable but positively dangerous, and the only means of ventilation at that time was by wind-

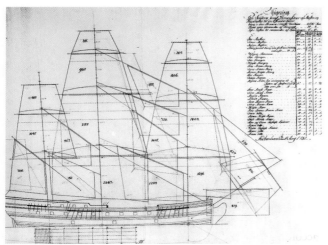

No sailplan for an English East Indiaman of this period has been found but the Danish *Dannemark* of 1781 demonstrates the usual suit of sails.

(Riksarkivet, Copenhagen)

sails, long canvas funnels let into the hatchways to allow a stream of air to reach the lower parts of the ship.

The boatmaker supplied the 30ft longboat, the pinnace, yawl and skiff; the sailmaker fitted tarpaulins to the main hatchways and those on the quarterdeck and forecastle.

Masting and rigging were carried out by a specialist rigger who probably used a sheer hulk – an old ship cut down to the level of the main deck, with a single mast amidships fitted with tackle for hoisting on board the lower masts. When the mainmast and foremast had been stepped they were secured by shrouds fixed on either side to the channels, wide platforms projecting from the ship's sides, and by stays fore and aft. The foremast was held firmly in position by the bowsprit to which was fixed the jib-boom and the flying jib-boom. After erecting the lower masts, the rigger fitted the topmasts, topgallant masts and yards. It was not until 1791 that Perry's yard acquired a mast house at the west end of the Brunswick Basin, locally known as Perry's dock. Towering 120ft into the air it signalled home for many a returning sailor until it was taken down in 1862. The first ship to be masted there, the *Lord Macartney*, had the whole suit of masts and bowsprit erected in three hours and forty minutes.

The sails were probably similar to those carried by the *Boscawen*: topgallant sails on all the masts; foretopgallants and maintopgallants had been carried for many decades. There is no mention of royals, later carried above the topgallant sails, but she was supplied with lower and topsail studding sails, forestaysail, middle, maintop and maintopgallant staysails and a mizzentop staysail. Her suit of sails included a spritsail and a spritsail topsail – a small square sail mounted under the jib boom ahead of the jib – as well as two jibs. The introduction in the early eighteenth century of the jib, a fore and aft sail spread from the jib boom which was an extension of the

bowsprit, was a great improvement over the quaint square spritsail topsail which is such a distinctive feature of the seventeenth century ships. At this time both spritsails and jibs were used but later the jib entirely replaced the spritsail. On the mizzen mast she carried a lugg mizzen and a half mizzen; these were beginning to replace the old triangular lateen sail with its excessive and unbalanced sail area.

Notes:
1. Morse, H.B: *Chronicles of the East India Company trading to China 1635 -1834* (Oxford 1926), Vol. II, 1793: 'Indiaman' and 'East Indiamen' used for first time in the records.
2. BL, OIOC, Danvers *op cit*, Introduction to the Marine Records, v.
3. BL, OIOC, Foster, *Letters received*, v.1, 307, 9 November 1613 *op cit*.
4. BL, OIOC, *Brief Historical Sketch*, f10,12.
5. BL, Papers of Henry Johnson, Add MSS 22, 184.
6. BL, OIOC, Court Book 3, 351, 30 January 1615.
7. BL,OIOC, L/MAR/C530 f394-402 *passim*, 27 August 1788 to 14 January 1799.
8. BL,OIOC, L/MAR/C531, f610, 10 October 1793, Court of Directors' opinion.
9. MacGregor, *op cit* quoted: Pt. IV, 182-183.
10.*Ibid*, 183.
11.BL, OIOC, L/MAR/C531, 15 March 1786, f257.
12.Morse, *op cit*, Vol II, ,145 13 March 1786.
13.Low, C.R: *History of the Indian Navy*, Vol 1, 175.
14.MacGregor, *op cit*, 188.
15.BL,OIOC, Tract 133, Barlow.
16.Essex R.O: Papers of Samuel Braund, D/Dru, B20.
17. MacGregor, *op cit*, 194.
18.Scott, *op cit*, Scott to Snodgrass, no. 68, 26 January 1796.
19.*Naval Chronicle*, vol.16 (1806). Accounts of battle.
20.*International Journal of Nautical Archaeology*, vol 19, no.1, 1990, 17: Ruth Rhynas Brown: Guns carried on East Indiamen.
21.BL,OIOC, L/MAR/C530, Append. 831, f456.
22.Essex R.O, Papers of Samuel Braund, D/Dru, B20.
23.Hardy, H.C: *A Register of Ships employed in the Service of the East India Company* (1820), 46, Extracts from the Charter Party.
24.MacGregor, *op cit*, cited: Court of Directors, Wednesday 3 August 1808.
25. Essex R.O: Papers of Samuel Braund, D/Dru, B20.
26.NMM, GRN/1 ff102-104:

Year	Ship's name	Husband	Price per ton	Tons	'Amount'	'Extra'
1774	*Hillsborough*	Chas Foulis	£12	723	£8628	£100
1780	*Earl of Hertford*	Chas Foulis	£14	799	£11,195	£374
1782	*Macartney*	Robert Preston	£14.14s	755	£11,111	£329
1792	*Brunswick*	Thos Newte	£12.10s	1219	£15,247	£607
1796	*Warley*	Henry Boulton	£17.19s	1449	£25,364	£363
1801	*Alnwick Castle*	John Locke	£19.10s	1257	£24,517	£708
1808	*Warren Hastings*	J P Larkins	£27	997	£26,937	£304
1811	*Prince Regent*	Henry Bonham	£27	950	£25,651	£432
1816	*Waterloo*	East India Company	£22.10s	1315	£29,588	£466
1817	*Dunira*	G Palmer	£23.10s	1315	£30,903	£262

27.Parkinson, C. Northcote: *Trade in the Eastern Seas*, 137-138, quoted.
28.Essex R.O, Papers of Samuel Braund, D/Dru, B11.
29.Ingram, Bruce: *Three Sea Journals of Stuart Times*, (1936), 187.
30.Lubbock, Basil: *Barlow's Journal* (1934), Vol.2, 448.

THE COMMANDERS

Captain Richard Pierce, Esq, exemplified the covered position enjoyed by eighteenth century commanders in the company's service.

Captain Pierce's earliest recorded post was as third mate of the *Horsenden*, one of John Durand's ships, on a voyage to China in 1762. After serving as second mate in the Pacific he acquired the command of another of John Durand's ships, the *Earl of Ashburnham*, in 1769, probably due to the influence of his father-in-law, Thomas Burston, collector of customs for Surrey. There is no record of what sum Captain Pierce paid the previous commander, but it was probably in the region of £5000.[1] An India command was by this time a piece of property which its owner could sell or pass on to a friend or relative on his retirement, and which formed part of his estate if he died in service. A commander's choice of successor was usually accepted by the husband and owners, who paid him, but on his appointment, the commander became a Company servant and as such was protected from arbitrary dismissal by the owners. Provided he carried out the owners' and the Company's instructions, he had the customary right to retain the command of his ship, and succeed to the command of any ship or ships built to replace it, until he chose to retire. When the *Ashburnham* was worn out, Thomas Burston acquired the 'bottom' and built the *Halsewell* in her room; he became the husband, Captain Pierce succeeding to the command. The *Halsewell* made two voyages before her last tragic voyage in

The type of bungalow at Calcutta where commanders of Indiamen might stay as guests while their ships were being loaded.   *(BL OIOC)*

which her commander and many others lost their lives when she was wrecked outward bound off the Dorset coast in January 1786. Captain Pierce's paternal loyalty in not forsaking his daughters who were travelling with him became a legend retold by Dickens many decades later.

Captain Pierce succeeded in making 'a competent fortune' according to a surviving mate of the *Halsewell*. Evidence for this exists in his move in 1781 from the house he owned with a rateable value of £10 per annum to the tenancy of one of the ten largest houses in Kingston on Thames rented in previous years to persons of standing – even members of the aristocracy – at a rateable value of £80 per annum.

His obviously high social standing was no doubt enhanced by the uniform the company introduced the same year: a blue coat with blue lapels and light gold embroidery, white waistcoat and breeches, the yellow metal buttons carrying the company crest. He did not live to see the change to buff waistcoat and breeches in 1787, forced on the Company by the jealousy of the Navy who felt the blue and white resembled naval uniform a little too closely.[2]

His standing was even higher when he arrived at the Company's presidencies in India. On entering harbour, his ship received a salute of guns; he himself 'was saluted with nine guns from the fort according to custom in those days' as he came ashore, and the guard turned out whenever he entered or left the fort, the same treatment as was given to a member of council.[3] On his voyage to the Coast and Bay he no doubt had, like all commanders, his 'dubash', a general steward who immediately rented a fine house for him and provided 'every household article as well as of merchandise and engages all inferior servants' while his ship was in harbour – about two months at Madras, up to four months in Bengal.[4] He could then spend his days disposing of his private trade investment and purchasing a return venture with the proceeds. In the evenings he could participate to the full in the hectic social round kept up by high society, his name included in the list of guests at receptions at Government House.[5]

At Canton, where the European traders were limited to the factories of their respective countries, he could stay at the English factory with its public apartments 'in front looking to the river: the others go inland to the depth of two or three hundred feet, in broad courts, having the sets of rooms on each side, every set having a distinct and separate entrance

with a small garden, and every sort of convenience'.[6] The council of supercargoes and any guests – commanders or passengers – dined at 2 pm daily; the rest of the day could be spent at his private factory, hired from a Chinese merchant, where he stored his private trade goods ready for the ship's departure.[7]

The coveted position enjoyed by Captain Pierce and his contemporaries was won by the incredible fortitude of the early commanders who were the cornerstone of the whole Company structure in its formative years. Right up until the formation of the United Company in 1708, the commanders were required to assume responsibilities far in excess of those of the sea-captain of the following century. The whole subsequent development of the Company hinged on the quality of the men charged with exploring the possibilities of trade in the little known Eastern Seas and establishing settlements for the conduct of a regular trade.

This is particularly true of the leading commanders of the first two decades whom the Company selected as 'generals' to take command of the fleets of the separate and joint stock voyages – men like James Lancaster of the first voyage in 1601, Henry Middleton of the second voyage in 1604 and the sixth voyage in 1610, Nicholas Downton of the first joint stock voyage in 1614. Under the general's orders were the commanders of the separate ships comprising the fleet, the sailing masters concerned with navigation, the cape merchants whose job it was to conduct the trade at places decided on by the general, and the crews of all the ships.

Armed with only a minimum of information about the vast seas he had to traverse gleaned from the few accounts available from earlier Dutch and English travellers or stolen from the Portuguese, and equipped with primitive navigational instruments, he was responsible for finding the most profitable investment for the subscribers' money and laying the foundations of a lasting trade.

Most of the generals had to face the problem of sickness and death from scurvy and the diseases of the East. Both Lancaster and Middleton, in the first and second voyages, had to put in at Table Bay outward-bound to seek fresh provisions to stem the ravages of scurvy. Lancaster stopped once more on the east coast of Madagascar as scurvy broke out again almost immediately, while Middleton, whose orders strictly enjoined him not to stop at all, pressed on – in spite of many deaths – to Bantam. Here his crews were even more decimated by the other scourge of voyages to the East – dysentery, or the 'bloody flux'. He despatched two of his ships ahead with full cargoes from Bantam, but on his return he found them at Penguin Island, Table Bay, the *Hector* having only ten Englishmen and

Two prints depicting the *Warren Hastings* East Indiaman and the *Piémontaise* just before and just after an engagement when the English ship was captured.   *(BL OIOC)*

four Chinese left.

There was also the problem of finding fresh water and fresh provisions in areas hitherto unvisited; in 1610 Sir Henry Middleton, instructed to open up a trade in the Red Sea area, left information at various places likely to be touched by succeeding generals to help them:

> If any of you chance to come into the Red Sea you shall understand that WSW from Mocha upon the Habesh coast there is an excellent harbour in the Bay of Morgain, where grow many date trees and there you shall have wood and water in abundance and some refreshing of victuals.[8]

There were also regional weather hazards to contend with in areas for which no information was available. 'If we had not found this road,' Sir Henry wrote of the Habesh shore where he had found water and provisions, 'it would have gone hard with our ships, for there is no getting out of this sea from the middle of October till the end of May, the winds continuing SE and SSE'.[9]

On arrival at a foreign port where the prospects of trade were promising, there was every likelihood of obstruction from Portuguese and, later, Dutch ships of war. Downton, Henry Middleton's lieutenant on the sixth voyage, records how, when they arrived in the Gulf of Cambay, hoping to obtain the cottons of Gujarat so necessary in the barter for spices at Bantam, they were met by:

> armies of Portugal frigates . . . who gave diligent attendance round about us to destroy and cut off as many of our people as they could spy advantage . . . or at least not to suffer any of our people to come near us with refreshing, no not so much as for the recovery of our weak sick men . . . until we were forced to check their insufferable saucy insolency, by taking one of their bragging frigates . . .[10]

As general in 1615, when the whole naval might of the Portuguese Estada da India concentrated off Swally Hole near Surat to blockade his fleet, Downton was able to square the account. He put his smallest ship at the entrance and succeeded in tempting some of the Portuguese ships into the shallows where the English managed to inflict much damage. Even the Portuguese fire ships failed to cower the English. At last the great Portuguese armada withdrew, ending all attempts to block the English trade and establishing the English as the superior European maritime force on the west coast of India, and therefore the one best suited to protect the pilgrim fleet to the Red Sea.

The 'general' and his subordinate commanders were empowered to conclude trading agreements with rulers, presenting gifts and letters from the English monarch. Lancaster signed a treaty with the ninety-five year old Sultan of Achin and Pedir

ENGLANDS GLORY.

A Fight for three Days between two English East-India-Ships, & four Portugueze-Gallions & 24 Frigats in the Mouth of the River leading to Surat, in which the Portuguezes were beaten. Pag. 432. done, &c. to Act of Parliam.
Printed for Will.ᵐ Rayner & Sold at C.Dahuus in y Old Baily.

The battle of Swally Hole between East Indiamen and the Portuguese fleet in 1613 won a foothold for the Company on Indian soil at Surat.   *(BL OIOC)*

on the first voyage. William Hawkins, arriving in the *Hector* at Surat in 1608, and finding the Portuguese, as usual, blockading the entrance of the River Tapti and refusing him permission to land, at last managed to get ashore and obtained a permit to go to the Emperor's court at Agra. There his knowledge of 'turki' enabled him to converse directly with Emperor Jahangir, though apart from the Emperor's admiration for his prodigious drinking, he achieved little in the face of the powerful hold of the Portuguese.

Obviously, the men who carried this enormous responsibility had to be more than navigators. In those days before the science of navigation had developed to any degree, the Company chose its commanders from among merchants with wide experience of commerce especially in the Middle East and of the stature to deal with Emperors and princes. The Court, considering the choice of commanders in 1614,

decided it was '. . . better to have a merchant no navigator than a navigator no merchant'.[11] Most of the commanders in the separate voyages were merchants of standing. Both Captain Keeling, who had 'an Arab tongue', and Captain Hawkins had probably been factors in Syria for the Levant company. James Lancaster, who was a founder member of the East India Company, had been a merchant in Lisbon, and, like several of the commanders, he was also a soldier.

The exalted position enjoyed by these overall directors of operations was not accepted by all, including Joseph Salbank the company's 'ancientest servant . . . in all this country and elsewhere' who raised his voice against:

this constant and inviolable custom . . . to send hither Generals as the supreme disposers and governors not only of your sea affairs but also of your land business even amongst your factors and servants planted in the country; who, because their authority is very large and in a manner unlimited, are emboldened to abuse it and exceed their bounds very immeasurable.[12]

Salbank was wrong. Above all, the general had to have a cool head in a crisis and be able to handle any situation that might arise. Such men are always at a premium. England's good name in the East was built up on the forbearance of these early commanders, in contrast with the methods employed by the hated Dutch and Portuguese who hounded and bullied the natives into accepting them as traders. The temptation to resort to force in face of the rapacity and brutality often displayed by petty rulers was frequently almost overwhelming, but it was the English commanders' capacity to stay their hand that was the foundation of Britain's lasting trade in the East. In 1610, Middleton, by then Sir Henry, demonstrated this when he arrived at Mocha in the *Trades Increase*, 'a ship of wonderful importance', accompanied by the *Darling*. On going ashore they were received 'with fair flattering speeches' but were later 'traitorously surpris'd, myself wounded, many of my people slain, the rest put in irons, neck, hands and legs, and all our goods confiscated.' When Downton, captain of the *Peppercorn*, which Sir Henry had sent to Aden where the company had suffered similar treatment, arrived at Mocha, he managed to communicate to Sir Henry his intention of blockading the port.

Middleton bade Downton kindly but firmly to stay his hand: 'We have as much leisure and better means and experience to consider the depth of things touching that point, better than you or any other that have neither been actors nor spectators of what is past and present' and to Downton's anxieties about the lack of provisions and wood and water for his ships, battered by storms usual at that time of year, urged him to try the Bab Islands off the coast of Abyssinia.'[13]

At the same time one of the merchants urged him to escape, but Sir Henry knew they could not at any rate leave until the westerlies in May, and feared reprisals against the other prisoners. When he thought the time right, after the prisoners had been returned to Mocha, he did escape – in a barrel. Shortly afterwards, the pilgrim fleet began to arrive. Immediately he acted. 'I have made seizure of all the people of the ship of Diu, together with the ship and goods, whom I purpose, with the help of God, to detain as pledges for you', he wrote to one of the merchants, Lawrence Femmel, still a prisoner'.[14]

Threatened with the deprivation of dues the governor was at last prevailed upon to disgorge, and prisoners and goods were restored.

In contrast was Captain Heath's ill-considered action in 1690 which 'almost forever ruin'd the Private and Public Trade' at Canton after decades of patient effort. When his ship, the *Defence*, was ready to sail there was a dispute between two Chinese officials over the release of the ship's mainmast. Heath took an armed party ashore and seized it, ordering his men to fire when the Chinese began throwing stones:

> In this confusion, ye poore Doctor, 3rd & 5th Mate, and 7 Englishmen on shoar, were not thought on, or neglected, the pinnace and Longboat having cutt loose ye Mast, making away from ye shoar, who had they stayed but a few minutes longer, might have reached our poor Doctor, who with some others making towards ye boat, was miserably cut downe in their sight . . . The next day a Dutchman reported that the doctor was . . . mortally wounded and drag'd by ye cruell Tartars into their . . . watch House, where lyes on ye ground chain'd in his gore most miserably, ye stinking dead corpse (after it had been carrier around ye town ye more to irritate ye Chinese) lay'd by him, and none suffered to come near or dress his wounds; and all ye rest of his people (save ye two Mates which believe have sheltered themselves amongst ye Portuguese) bound miserably in ye same house . . .[15]

Sheer endurance and management of men were the chief qualities required in a commander for the prolonged exploratory voyages to gain access to the luxuries of China. Edward Barlow described an early attempt: the *Experiment*, 260 tons, the *Return*, 340 tons and the little 180-ton *Zant Frigate*, sailed in October 1671 'bound to a place where no English ship had been in forty years before which was to the island of Formosa upon the coast of China, and also to Japan to settle a factory at both places if we could.'[16]

On arrival at Bantan, the *Zant* went on alone to Tonking where she settled a factory; the crews of the *Return* and *Experiment* loaded goods for Formosa and Japan, 'frying in the sun', and set sail in June 1672. They arrived at Formosa in July but after discharging the cargo it was too late in the year to go on to Japan. To avoid the expense incurred by two ships wintering until the coming of the south west monsoon the following April, the *Experiment* put her cargo in the *Return* and sailed for England, the *Return* continuing her voyage several months later to Nagasaki. She found the inhabitants here were intransigent on the question of trading with Europeans who might prove similar to the Portuguese. She weighed anchor, her cargo intact in August 1673, arriving in September at Macao where she remained for a year without success. In September 1674 she pressed on farther along the coast, sold some of her pepper, and in November, already more than three years out from England and her crew mutinous, she sailed for Bangkok.

Thirty years later, as captain of the *Septer*, Edward Barlow was at Mocha to protect the pilgrim ships returning to Surat from attack by European pirates based in Madagascar. After passing the Bab Islands Barlow sighted a strange ship in the

LORDS OF THE EAST

convoy. It was her unusual rig that caught his eye: she had a topgallant sail on her mizzen mast and a spritsail topgallant sail at the end of her bowsprit. She was a galley, with a tier of ports for oars on her lower deck. As there was little wind, Barlow ordered two boats out to tow the *Septer* towards the ship which had already begun firing on one of the larger ships in the convoy. The strange ship hauled off as the *Septer* came up firing and after waiting for a while out of range, she made all sail and went off. Later, Barlow found out she was William Kidd's *Adventure Galley*.

Although increasing emphasis was placed on good seamanship, throughout the seventeenth century the Company continued to look to its leading commanders to undertake positions involving wider responsibilities. For some this resulted in a complete change of function: Captain Goldsborough of the *Bengal Merchant* was knighted and appointed to replace Sir John Child on the latter's death in 1690, the 'Governors and Company reposing especiall trust and Confidence in the fidelity Prudence Justice and Circumspection' of Sir John Goldsborough appointed him Supervisor, Commissary-General and chief governor of all the Company's forts, factories and factors, officers and soldiers, in all the settlements, with headquarters at Surat.[17] Another commander, Captain Gayer, was also knighted in 1693 before sailing to take up his post as Governor of Bombay and Director-in-Chief '. . . next and under Our General Sir JOHN GOLDSBOROUGH' succeeding to the supreme command on the latter's death that year.[18]

Others were required to combine their role as sea captain with that of a sort of ambassador extraordinary. Although the Company's settlements were well established by the latter part of the seventeenth century, crises requiring the diplomatic proficiency and careful handling displayed by Sir Henry Middleton at Mocha erupted at intervals, and it was still to its leading commanders that the Company turned to find the men capable of dealing with these disturbances. Captain Grantham had displayed such diplomatic skill in resolving a revolt in Virginia and such courage in an encounter with Barbary corsairs that the King himself 'was pleas'd as a mark of his Royal Favour . . . to recommend him in a most particular manner to the Governor and Company of Merchants trading to the EAST INDIES, that he and the ship he intended to build might be entertain'd by them'[19]. The King knighted Captain Grantham on board his ship at Deptford at the launch on 8 February 1683 when he named her the *Charles the Second*.

Sir Thomas Grantham was sent on a roving commission, first to Bantam to exact reparations for demurrage to the Company's property, then on to Persia to obtain an improvement in the sums received by the Company in recent years from the revenue of the customs of Gombroon. Half of these had been granted in perpetuity in 1623 by a grateful Shah Abbas 'in Consideration of the English Blood and Treasure' expended in helping the Persians to take Ormuz from the Portuguese.

From there he was sent to Bombay with 'liberty at large' to deal with a mutiny led by Kegwin, the commander of the garrison. In spite of narrowly escaping death when a pistol was put in his back and 'but for the Providence of God Almighty . . . I had been basely and cowardly murdered,'[20] he negotiated a settlement with Kegwin and returned some days later to meet the soldiers and agree a peaceful solution.

From the first the Company recognised the value of such commanders and took steps to ensure that they remained Company servants when the freighting system was adopted. In the early days of freighting preference was given to the ships of those commanders who had already served the Company well. This soon hardened into a rule that no stranger should be employed in command of a Company ship while an old captain of good character remained unemployed. The commander's loyalty to the Company was cemented by the Company's 'indulgence' to share in its exclusive trading privilege in the East, though he took the oath declaring that he would not trade in those goods which formed the chief staples of the Company's trade. Effectively, not only would he abstain from trading in those goods while serving the Company, but also would refrain from turning interloper. Each party to this contract evidently considered it binding. Sir Joseph Child berated Captain Knox severely for breaking his oath by offering his services to the abortive Scottish company in 1694. Knox, on the other hand, felt absolved from the limitations imposed by the oath by the Company's refusal to take up a ship he had offered, while employing three strange ships and three commanders who had never served before. He also claimed that younger men with less experience had been appointed to the commands of large ships in preference to himself. In Knox's view 'my oath never bound me to serve only them & no other, no, not when they would not imploy mee to my Contentation & prefer Juniors in Command over my head before me'.[21]

A commander's continued employment depended on his having a ship to command. The Company therefore encouraged owners to build a new ship in the room of one that was worn out in order to retain the commander's services. On 2 July 1674 the Court declared that the owners of two worn out ships – the *President* and the *Antelope* – 'Shall have the preference in building the two first Ships that shall be entertained to serve the Company so as C Hide and C Goldsborough have the command of them . . .'[22]

This was the origin of two customs peculiar to the Company: the commander's name always appeared on the tender of a ship built for the Company's service even before the ship was named; a command was held in perpetuity.

The enviable position enjoyed by both commanders and husbands in the eighteenth century therefore was derived from the Company's need to retain the services of its experienced commanders during the years in which it was laying the foundations of its trade.

Not surprisingly, wealth and influence soon played a part in securing commands which assured the holder of employment for life while the Company's 'indulgence' of private trade – however reluctantly bestowed during these early years – provided him with the opportunity of making a fortune. Naturally, in the latter years of the seventeenth century, the best jobs – the commands of the 'great ships' – went to the small clique around Sir Josiah Child and Sir Henry Johnson, many of whom were inter-related. Captain Thomas Raynes was a kinsman of Sir Henry's and Captain Samuel Hide, commander of the *Berkeley Castle*, was Captain Thomas Goldsborough's brother-in-law.

Money had begun to change hands before the close of the century. Edward Barlow offered the owners of the *Maderass* £100 for the command. She was tendered, naming Barlow as commander, and accepted by the Court of Committees for a voyage to Benkulen. Influence, however, backed by money, proved more effective. In a typical piece of double-dealing, Sir Josiah, professing ignorance of the extent of the owners' commitment to Barlow, gave the command to a man of war's lieutenant, who was prepared to double Barlow's offer, at the request of the wife of the Speaker of the House of Commons. Captain Knox knew that 'thare hath bin sumes of money given to come into greate ships'[23] but was unconvinced by Sir Josiah's claim that there were those who would give him £500 to have the command of a small ship he had designed himself.

Attempts to prohibit the sale of commands in the early years of the following century failed, and with the full acceptance of the 'doctrine of the hereditary bottom' the commander's position was strengthened. After two or three voyages, sufficient to make his fortune, he could sell his command, his successor then acquiring the right to succeed to the ship built on her bottom after the customary four voyages.

With the relaxation of the Company's strict limitations on private trade (which will be discussed in the following chapter) the price of a command rocketed. By the end of the eighteenth century, according to Captain Eastwick, 'there was no service equal to it, or more difficult to get into, requiring great interest' and huge sums of money, which he put as high as £8,000 to £10,000.[24] At all times, those fortunate enough to have 'interest' in the right quarter could obtain a command very quickly. When Edward Barlow signed on in 1701 as chief mate of the *Fleet Frigate* bound for Canton, the captain, an ex-milliner who owed his command to the influence of his rich wife, offered Barlow extra pay to act as pilot and take charge of the ship from Batavia to Canton, as he had never been in the China Sea, his whole experience amounting to only three voyages.

Although company regulations from 1765 laid down that only those over twenty-five years of age who had performed one voyage as chief or second mate should be appointed to a command, and that no one who had not served the Company before should be accepted, they were frequently disregarded.[25]

William Hickey's friend Bob Pott was 'not quite fourteen' when he sailed to China in 1769 as a midshipman on the *Cruttenden*, of which his uncle, a Director of the Company, was an influential owner. In 1772 he returned to China as fifth mate, and his father confided to Hickey that he hoped to get Bob a command 'after one voyage more', by which time he would have been twenty years old, the same age as John Durand's son when he obtained the command of the *Northington* in 1776. To his father's great chagrin, Bob refused to entertain the idea of a command as he considered India captains 'a set of low blackguards' and refused to be associated with them.

Henry Meriton entered the Company's service in 1785 at the age of twenty as third mate of the *Pigot* after becoming a master in the West Indies trade. In 1786 he sailed as second mate with Captain Pierce on the *Halsewell's* ill-fated last voyage, transferring to the *Bridgewater* as first mate later that year. Lacking the necessary influence and money he remained in that station for thirteen years until the sale of commands was ended. Captain Pierce's son Thomas, born in 1776, followed in his father's footsteps. He skipped the position of fourth mate and served as third mate on a voyage to Bombay and China in 1795. In 1798 he sailed as second mate, again bound to Bombay and China. In 1800 he was sworn in as a commander only a few months after Henry Meriton was appointed to the command of the *Exeter* in which he had served as first mate since 1792.

Those who obtained commands through the 'interest' of their wealthy relatives and friends were not bad captains, but often their aim was to remain at sea for only two or three voyages, during which time they hoped to make enough money to live comfortably for the rest of their lives. They were unlikely, therefore, to pay much attention to the development of all the qualities necessary in a good commander: the ability to make the right decision in a crisis, to lead men and command their respect.

There were, on the other hand, a large number of able and dedicated men, who, though their priority was to make a fortune and advance their families' interests, nevertheless made the service their career and became excellent commanders. The East India shipping families like the Larkins and Wordsworths produced some of the best. Destined for a command from birth, they entered the service at an early age as midshipmen, and served as mates until fitted for a command. That 'worthy man and admirable seaman' John Pascal Larkins, whose career is set out in Appendix 2, displayed all the qualities of an excellent commander when only second mate of the *Nassau* on her voyage to England in 1779.[26]

The Battle of Pula Auro.
(BL OIOC)

Before leaving Madras, the *Nassau*'s commander, Captain Gore, was ordered to take on board eleven French officers and seventy French soldiers who were on parole and were to be treated as passengers. Gore's fears that they would take over the ship increased when, having waited in vain at Trincomalee for convoy, he was told that he must sail in company with the *Southampton* which also carried prisoners. Scurvy appeared on board only days out from Trincomalee, debilitating the crew to such an extent that Gore became frantic with fear and, against all advice, insulted the French officers, who were behaving impeccably, by demanding their swords. During the following fortnight, thirty-three seamen died, reducing Captain Gore to such a state that he shut himself up in his cabin, appearing only at meals, refusing to receive the sick list or to have the bell tolled at the funeral ceremonies. The first mate, William Greer, was perpetually drunk, he and Gore indulging in brawls on the few occasions they met. Only Larkins and the fifth mate were capable of performing their duties. When the crew were down to sixteen men, the French prisoners performing all the duties and the food and water supplies running dangerously low, Mr Larkins, who had approached Captain Gore privately without success, addressed the commander and company after dinner one evening and explained the desperate state the ship was in. Captain Gore asked him what he advised. Mr Larkins replied, 'Make for the Cape as soon as possible', advice which Captain Gore acted upon.

There was one method of obtaining a command apart from wealth, influence or membership of an India shipping family. One of the unwritten rules of the East India shipping world in its later years was that the new *status quo* following the death of a commander or officer at sea should be accepted by the owners on the ship's return to the River, provided there was no serious objection to the people concerned. Occasionally, therefore, chief mates who lacked the necessary 'interest' to make the final step to the top of the ladder were able to obtain a command. These were frequently men with years of experience of running a ship – in 1795 there were one hundred and fifty-six chief and second officers who had served in those posts for ten years or more – and so usually made excellent commanders. They were referred to in the service as 'God Almighty's captains'. The command still had to be purchased from the widow or whoever had inherited it, but the lucky successor was more than happy to borrow the sum required on the strength of his expected profits from private trade. Captain Waddell of the *Plassey*, on which William Hickey first sailed to the East as a young writer, had succeeded to the command on the death of her former captain at Benkulen in 1767. He was not only a remarkably good sailor, but showed that he possessed other qualities necessary in a good commander. William Hickey noted that in his treatment of Charles Chisholme, whom husband John Durand had forced on him as second mate against his will, 'Captain Waddell, conscious that no personal blame attached to Chisholme in the transaction, never betrayed the slightest resentment towards him, treating him at all times with the utmost respect and kindness'.[27]

The shadows were already closing in on Captain Richard Pierce and his fellow commanders when the *Halsewell* met her fate on the cliffs off the Dorset coast in 1786. They were affected along with every other section of the East India Company by the brush with bankruptcy in 1771 and the consequent cessation of new building to reduce waste in the Company's shipping. The commanders combined to get a motion passed in the General Court to compensate impecunious commanders for the loss of voyages. The Company

agreed to a payment of £200 per annum to a commander to commence eighteen months after leaving India and to cease as soon as his ship was taken up. At about this time changing circumstances threatened their private trade, and it was possibly this multiplicity of problems which stimulated discussions resulting in the formation of a Society of East India Commanders.[28] Thirty members agreed to subscribe £50 to a fund to relieve any member in financial difficulties. Captain Pierce was one of five captains appointed as trustees. The subscribers' addresses suggest an exclusive group of commanders of substance: the Inner and Middle Temple, the Strand, Bloomsbury Square, Queens Square, Adelphi, St James and Duke Street, Westminster. No doubt excellent meals were washed down with the best wines at their monthly meetings, which they held first at the Queens Arms Tavern in St Paul's Churchyard and the Antwerp Tavern before settling down at

the Jerusalem Coffee House until the society's demise in 1834. Not all their funds were allocated to cases of hardship. They agreed to present a piece of inscribed plate to any member's wife on the birth of her tenth living child, from which Mrs Money, Mrs Cotton and Mrs Timmins benefited in succeeding years.

Although the threats to their private trade, always central to the commanders' thoughts, most exercised the members of the Society, it was the campaign carried out with increasing fervour throughout the late 1780s and early 1790s to reform the shipping system which threatened their very existence. The ending of the doctrine of the hereditary bottom necessarily brought in its train an end to the custom of perpetuity of command. On 29 November 1794 the Society sent a memorial to the Chairman, Deputy and Directors concerning the building and hiring of ships under consideration of the

This painting, inspired by the tragic loss of the *Halsewell*, shows the captain and company in the stern galley preparing to enjoy the voyage.

(National Maritime Museum)

Court. Choosing their words carefully they pointed out that 'The long practice and usage of the service, having given rise to a transaction between a commander and his successor, in which they are deeply interested make it necessary . . . to throw themselves on the wisdom, and equity of your Honourable Court.'[29]

In the bitter propaganda war the shipping interest employed every trick in the book to secure the commanders' loyalty. Writing to William Fairlie in March 1795 David Scott reported how 'The Old Shipping had the art to persuade the too credulous captains and officers that I was only working to ruin them.' They turned 'the Jerusalem Coffee House into a canvassing shop,' alienating the commanders and officers 'who had received more favours from me than from all the other Directors together.'[30] What Scott worked for was to end the commanders being at the mercy of their ships' husbands in regard to their 'good wills'. There were frequent cases of commanders wishing to resign and finding a successor willing to pay the cost of his command, but being prevented by the husband who wanted to give the command to someone else. The commanders were entirely unprotected, having no legal redress since their purchase of the command had no legal basis. John Fiott stressed this point:

The captain's good-will, in regard to his resale, however, depends greatly on the honesty of the husband, who has leave from the Company to put in whom he pleases, though not to

turn out. Several instances have appeared where the husband has negotiated the purchase for a captain and refused him liberty to sell at the same price. A captain, for instance, has got his command at £8000, the ship's husband being the agent. Afterwards the captain, on wishing to resign the ship, has been refused leave, unless he gave up the good-will at half its cost, and in some instances for nothing . . . as the whole negociation is contrary to the By-Laws, no redress can be obtained by the captain.[31]

Injustice often resulted from political manoeuvres in a society moulded by patronage. Captain Walsby had the support of Captain Rice, husband of the *Dutton*, in his desire to succeed to the ship's command on the retirement of her captain. Sir Robert Preston wanted the command for one of his own friends and probably overcame Captain Rice's scruples by supporting his candidacy for the position of Elder Brother at Trinity House.

Scott was single-minded in his intention to do away with the old system. He cogently assessed the commanders' status in a letter to Sir Stephen Lushington, the Chairman, with whom he was hammering out the new shipping system. He felt there were certain principles which should guide them in their solutions. Cutting through all the mystique and charisma which had inflated the commanders' persona over the life of the Company, he wrote:

1. They should not be acknowledged as our captains, but as persons in our immediate employ and of course entitled to our protection. This is considering them as masters of the ships when freighted. The owners are their real employers and only let them out on freight to us as in other services.

2. . . . they could have no claim for compensation as we have deprived them of no rights. The right to perpetuity in command being an erroneous idea founded on the erroneous perpetuity of bottoms. But that we give them a consideration *merely* because if they had been mistaken the practice of the Court had led them into the mistake.

3. That the perpetuity of bottoms was a theory in direct opposition to the established regulations of the Company.

4. That the sale of commands was equally against their regulations.

5. That we were introducing no new system but in fact only renewing the old one. This last should be made as clear as the day that the enemy might not raise a hue and cry against us for breaking through established systems . . .'[32]

By-laws prohibiting the sale of commands were reintroduced and became part of the law of the land in 1799 along with the introduction of free and open competition in the hiring of ships. Swift action was taken whenever the practice reappeared.[33] All commanders and officers were to be selected from a register containing the names of all existing commanders and officers, though new officers could be admitted to the lower stations. No office on board ship was to be sold, nor any fee accepted for any such offices. The traditional importance of the commanders continued to be central to the Company's freighting policy: if a ship contracted for six voyages was lost or captured before the completion of the fifth voyage, the owners were to be permitted to replace the ship, provided the commander or the chief officer was still living, to be employed by the Company for six or more voyages.

There remained the question of compensating those who lost their commands when their ships wore out, precluding their recouping the cost from their private trade. A special committee of the Court of Directors decided on £5000 as the maximum sum: those commanders who had not completed a voyage received the full amount, others reduced sums in proportion. The fund from which the payments were made was financed by contributions of £500 each voyage from existing commanders. Payments began in 1796 and ended in 1804, a total of £355,910 being paid to eighty-seven commanders. Entries in the *List of all Pensions granted by the East India Company to the Company's Commercial Marine Service* bear witness to individual hardship. On 2 December Sir Charles Mitchell, Commander, was granted £250 annually for life from the Poplar Fund on the grounds of 'pecuniary embarrassment brought on by the alteration in the shipping system in 1796, of doing away with the perpetuity of bottoms, by

which he was thrown out of the command of his ship.'

Both husbands and Company benefited from the opportunity the change of law offered to get rid of a few commanders who had constantly abused their privileged position: conducting round-about voyages for the benefit of their own private trade; missing a voyage and resuming the command when it pleased them. The Directors had consistently refused to allow the husbands the right to sack their captains without the Court's sanction to protect the commanders from unscrupulous husbands, but were aware that many had had cause for complaint. The Company's maritime service now received a healthy injection of sound experience and ability as many chief mates whose financial and social circumstances had prevented them mounting that final rung of the ladder at last got their hands on the helm.

The Jerusalem Coffee House, viewed here from Birchin Lane, was the unofficial centre of activity for all those connected with the East India Company, particularly its shipping. This was probably the new building of 1879 which replaced the old Jerusalem. *(Guildhall Library)*

The Society of East India Commanders' memorial to the Court of Directors in November 1797 indicates the effects of the changes. They reviewed their careers, pointing to the great sacrifices their long training had entailed, and talked of the Company being their 'ultimate employers'. They had assumed their careers were permanent, but now they were under a new system, under new regulations which brought distress to many who were now deprived of employment or the prospect of it. They expressed the hope that they would continue to be employed as commanders in the Company's service, only forfeiting their commands by misconduct as in early by-laws. Though grateful for the indemnity lately granted in lieu of their right to transfer the command of their ships they felt it couldn't be considered as compensation for 'more sacred' rights.

The commanders felt no better placed fifteen years later. Thirty-nine signed a memorial to the Court pointing out that during the intervening years the new system had brought great benefits to the Company from reduced freight but the predictions of the special committee had failed to assess correctly the future state of the commanders. In only six or seven cases out of forty had the emoluments equalled those predicted and in those cases it had been achieved only by investing great amounts of capital and credit. While the pay and allowances and privileges had remained unchanged for twenty years their emoluments had been eroded by many circumstances. They pointed out that in effect commands were still bought and sold, in that it was necessary to build an Indiaman to get a command and these had doubled in price since 1796. It was now necessary to advance between £10,000 and £20,000. John Woolmore made the same point in evidence to a committee of the House of Commons in 1812, though more moderately: an officer in search of a command needed to find a shipowner in order to establish himself, so instead of giving a young man £5,000 or £6,000 a relative invested in a ship and offered it to the Company cheap simply for the patronage.[34] David Scott underlined this point when in November 1804 he replied to someone seeking the command of a regular ship for a friend in straightened circumstances. He explained it was necessary to purchase a large ship costing about £45,000 or a small one for £35,000 'and without a ship's being tendered on purpose, or having the interest of the majority of owners, no person can get a command . . . I can assure you that I might as well propose to make him archbishop of Canterbury as captain of a ship.'[35]

With the exposure to market forces and increased profes-sionalism as opposed to wealth and influence as factors in their selection, the East India commanders lost some of the awe in which they had hitherto been held. Already in 1808 William Hickey could talk of the days when the commanders 'were treated with more attention and respect than of late.' Certainly for two hundred years they were an independent, even arrogant, breed, fully aware of their unchallengeable position. The financial rewards for the services of these men who were indispensable to the Company's trade reflected their status.

Notes:

1. BL OIOC L/MAR/C530 f325 14 February 1787; Committee of Managing Owners in conference with committee of the whole Court of Directors: owners commenting on offers of ships made by new shippers at £20 per ton listed among their objections the fact that the latter could sell the commands of the ships for £6,000 which was equivalent to £2 per ton, so their own offer of £22 per ton was a fair price.
2. The uniform was modified in 1818: BL OIOC Court Book 106, p204, 27 May 1818.
3. Hickey, *op cit*, Vol 1, 167.
4. *Ibid*, 165.
5. *Ibid*, 170.
6. *Ibid*, 202.
7. *Ibid*, 202.
8. BL OIOC Foster *op cit*, Vol 1, 130.
9. *Ibid*, 131.
10. *Ibid*, 157.
11. BL OIOC Court Book 3, p71, 19 March 1614.
12. BL OIOC (Foster): op cit, Vol 4, 228.
13. *Ibid*, 65.
14. *Ibid*, 110.
15. Morse, *op cit*, Vol I, 82-83.
16. Lubbock, *op cit*: *Barlow's Journal* (1934) Vol 1, 204.
17. Hedges, William: *Diary* (1887) Vol 2, 56, clvi.
18. *Ibid*, cxxxvii.
19. *Ibid*, clxii.
20. Keay, John: *The Honourable Company* (1991) 139.
21. Knox: *op cit*, 373.
22. Hedges: *op cit*, Vol 3, 155-156.
23. Knox: *op cit*, 360.
24. Eastwick: *op cit*, 43.
25. BL OIOC L/MAR/C644.
26. Hickey: *op cit*, Vol 2, 204.
27. Ibid, Vol 1, 148.
28. Guildhall Library: Memorandum Book Ms 31376.
29. *Ibid*: item 18, 29 November 1794.
30. Scott, *op cit*, Vol I, no.26: Scott to William Fairlie, 30 March 1795.
31. Parkinson, *op cit*, 181: quoted.
32. Scott *op cit* Vol I, no 67, 24 January 1796.
33. BL OIOC L/MAR/C21.
34. BL OIOC Select Committee Report 4 (1812), 440.
35. Scott, *op cit*, Vol II, no. 475: Scott to Joseph Stratton, 12 November 1804.

CHAPTER 5

PAY AND PERQUISITES

The ambition of every lad whose parents managed to obtain a midshipman's berth for their son on an Indiaman was to gain a command and make a fortune from the 'privilege and indulgence' granted by the Company to share in its monopoly of trade with the east. As the members of the Society of East India Commanders stated in a resolution of 1812 opposing the opening up of the India trade, 'the commanders have acted as merchants'. Young men trained as navigators in order to progress to the status of merchant. This was the reason why an officer paid what would amount to at least £500,000 today for a command. Nevertheless, the other perquisites of the job amounted to a not inconsiderable income.

Least attractive at first sight is his pay of £10 a month, a standard sum for all commanders throughout the Company's trading life. Nominal though this sum was, it began as soon as the ship came afloat and continued all the while she was being equipped and provisioned at Blackwall or Deptford and at Gravesend. Captain Braund of the *Boscawen* received full pay of £65 during the six and a half months that she was fitting out for her first voyage, though he probably visited the ship infrequently.

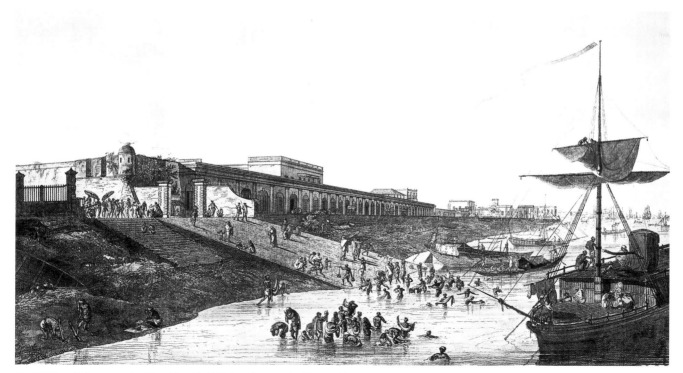

Fort William, Calcutta, on the River Hooghly. This later became the Custom House.

(BL OIOC)

Primage, a percentage of the total earnings made during the voyage, traditionally shared by the master and mariners, had developed into the captain's preserve in the Company's service. £37.8.6d was received by the commander of the 499-ton *Grantham* in 1750 but sums in the region of £100 were common later for the 1200-ton China ships. During the voyage the commander's pay was supplemented by expenses for his stay in port equivalent to 5s a day and an allowance for his table of 5 guineas. Traditionally generous contributions of food and wine came also from the Company, dating back to the early days when its own ships were victualled and provisioned at the bustling Deptford yard. The Company continued the custom after the change to the freighting system in order to provide for its factors and supercargoes who travelled on the ships at no extra charge. Usually the provisions were far in excess of the requirements for the voyage and it was customary to sell any surplus on arrival in the east, the commander, officers and chief personnel receiving shares in proportion to their status. This custom partly gave rise to Hickey's friend Bob Pott's unkind description of a commander as a 'vendor of cheese, ham, porter, and other filthy articles for lucre of gain.'[1] By the end of the eighteenth century fixed amounts were laid down for each class of ship and the amounts to be allocated to the various members of the ship's complement defined. The liquor allowance for all ships consisted of 13 ½ tons of 'Ale, Beer, Wine, or other liquers in Casks or Bottles, for the use of the Commander's Table, allowing 252 Gallons, or 36 Dozen Quart Bottles to the Ton',[2] and there were plenty of hams, cheeses, and a variety of 'pickles' or preserved foods.

The commander's income from passengers, negligible in the early days, increased appreciably as thriving towns grew up around the forts at Madras, Bombay and Calcutta and the Company's control in Bengal spread, necessitating an army of administrators, lawyers, military officers, officials of every kind, not to speak of the ladies, wives and children who followed them. These spelt profit for the commander. The roundhouse, traditionally the captain's preserve, could be divided up to accommodate them; so could any space remaining in the great cabin after the Company's supercargoes had been settled, the price rising appreciably if the passengers wanted a seat at the captain's table. Captain Wordsworth wrote jubilantly to his cousin and namesake before sailing for Bengal in 1804, 'I have every confidence that this voyage will turn out very good if not very great. In the first place I shall have a *whole cargo* of passengers.'[3] The governing council in Calcutta monitored the rates the commanders demanded from the private passengers by taking testimonials from those arriving in Bengal.

In the latter part of the eighteenth century, when the Company's ships were to all intents and purposes passenger ships, the Company regulated the price the commanders

could demand.[4] Until then no limitations were imposed and the charges fluctuated wildly according to the degree of avarice of the commander. Captain Waddell of the *Plassey* asked William Hickey for 50 guineas for a voyage from London to Madras in 1769; less than ten years later Captain Arthur demanded exactly double for similar accommodation on the *Sea Horse* when Hickey approached him for a passage to Bengal.[5] In 1770 William Hickey approached a Captain Haggis, 'a strange rough sort of tarpaulin,' for a berth from Madras to England, and was told he might be able to spare him 'a small cabin in his steerage for three hundred guineas' or six times the amount Hickey had just paid Waddell for half the roundhouse which he had shared with only two other passengers.[6] The unscrupulous commander milked the returning Anglo-Indian, especially the *nabob* who was anxious to get out of India with his fortune before the fever claimed him. When Hickey finally returned to England in 1808 he paid about £1000 for the starboard side of the great cabin. Few were as fortunate as the commander of the *Kent* who received £5000 from Warren Hastings for accommodating his wife in the great cabin on her return to England in 1785, but large sums were frequently made.

Another perquisite came from the large fees people were prepared to give to the commanders to secure midshipmen's berths for their sons or protégés, or simply as a 'guinea pig' – making a voyage with a place at the captain's table to 'learn the sea' and improve his chances of obtaining a midshipman's berth later. The Company limited these supernumeraries to five in 1791, imposing a penalty of three years' suspension on those commanders who abused this practice.

These not inconsiderable sums swelled the commander's total earnings, but the reason he was willing to pay a huge sum for his command was the privilege of private trade. The Company's attitude to the ancient custom of the master and mariners using part of the ship's hold for their own ventures was characterised, particularly in the early years, by a mean watchfulness. The early generals and commanders had had a share in the whole venture, most of them being subscribers to the separate voyages and the joint-stock voyages, but they were not expected to trade on their own account. Joseph Salbank, that 'ancientest servant' who objected so strongly to the wide powers given the generals, fulminated with equal vigour against the 'lucre of gain' displayed by these men who 'strained all the sinews of their endeavours to enrich themselves and amplify their fortunes by the most indirect and dishonest courses that their working brains could contrive; and wherehence cometh it to pass,' he asked, 'that they cram their purses so full with money after they come home, and raise themselves from a mean degree to an estate far surmounting both their merits and the obscurity of their plebeian parentage?'[7] The Court shared Salbank's attitude but they were forced to bow to the necessity of allowing some share in the trade to those who risked their lives bringing home rich cargoes. By King's Proclamation in 1631 a list of permitted goods was drawn up and remained in force, with variations, for fifty years; but the company returned to its niggardly attitude in the last years of the seventeenth century. Many commanders shared Captain Knox's disillusionment when, in 1696, the company withdrew all indulgences and introduced the permission system whereby those who wished to trade privately paid eighteen per cent for the pleasure, 'like the Pope who cannot Dispose of his pardons to eate flesh in Lent etc, without Money . . .'[8]

The broader based, less elitist United Company of Merchants trading to the East Indies of 1708 adopted a more realistic policy, but continued jealously to guard its interests. In an attempt to eradicate illicit trading activity, the Company sent two officials to Portsmouth in January 1710 to:

examine the Waiters Books who belong to each of the outward bound Ships to see what Private Trade Goods have been put on Board each Ship And that they take out such Goods as they shall find on every of the said Ships which have been brought aboard without due Licence And advise the Company from time to time of their Proceedings.[9]

From small beginnings – the reintroduction of the 5 tons outward and 3 tons homeward allowance before the permission system was introduced – there are signs that this was soon exceeded, partly because the ships increased in burthen considerably. In the charter parties of several ships of the mid-century, 25 tons outward and 15 tons homeward were allowed for private trade, the commander taking about one half, the rest being divided amongst the mates, surgeon, purser, petty-officers and tradesmen. By the end of the century the tonnage allowed was four times as much.

The commanders of the regular ships felt the first cold draft of the free market in the 1770s when the increasing numbers of Company servants in India began to find difficulty in getting their fortunes back to England for their retirement. There were two means by which they could 'remit' their wealth to Britain: Company bills drawn on London, the supply of which always fell short of demand; and the commanders' and officers' measured tonnage, which was expensive and slow. They instead invested their money in the Houses of Agency, such as David Scott in Bombay, Lambert & Ross in Calcutta, with their affiliated London bases, who handled the remittance trade. The commanders sent a memorial to the Court of Directors in 1775 on hearing that French ships were loading at Lorient destined for Madras and Bengal with goods which included those prohibited to the commanders.[10] It was only five months later that the commanders formed the Society of East India Commanders, and shortly afterwards they were petitioning the Court again. This time, they were

stressing their anxiety at the quantities of Europe goods flooding into the settlements in India on a variety of European ships – Dutch, Danish, Swedish, French, Portuguese – pointing out that this would continue while they offered opportunities of shipping home the servants' personal fortunes, ultimately reducing the petitioners 'to beggary and distress'. They complained about the duties charged on their goods at the settlements and begged the Court to remit them. They also wanted permission to bring home any number of goods as they were forced to barter them outward for anything they could get. They asked permission to pay into the Company's treasuries in India up to £8000 'on better terms than at present', and receive bills of a shorter date. They also asked for a restoration of the permission to bring up to five hundred bags of saltpetre back from Bombay and Bengal. The commanders rationalised these requests into a series of concrete proposals shortly afterwards. Though these were substantially met their situation did not improve. After the end of the American War of Independence large numbers of American ships with 'most favoured nation' status joined the other foreign ships supplying the burgeoning markets in India and joining in the remittance trade. David Scott's tireless campaign against the company's blinkered monopolistic culture and his fight to increase British exports and get the remittance trade back to London in English bottoms benefited the commanders, though they were never grateful. As he wrote to William Fairlie:

The Commanders and officers of ships when ! came onto the Direction seemed to be oppressed by Custom House officers and driven to smuggling goods out by necessity. I spoke often on this, wrote upon it, published pamphlets to open the proprietors' eyes against the Court of Directors' ill-judged restrictions of monopoly, and at last in spite of the Ships' Husbands, Custom House officers, and the majority of the ignorant Court of Directors, carried the following resolution, 'That in future the captains and officers should be allowed to fill up all the vacant tonnage outward not occupied by the Company.' There could be no smuggling after this . . .[11]

Only copper and cloth were prohibited.

Profitability of the commanders' indulgence varied considerably according to the voyage. A St Helena and Benkulen voyage yielded little profit – commanders jokingly chided their colleagues who flouted Company regulations with the warning 'If you aren't careful you will get a Benkulen voyage.' Next in unpopularity for much of the period was Bombay, with its small English population. Coast and Bay voyages, with their growing market for Europe goods, were the better ones for much of the seventeenth century, but Bengal in the latter half of the eighteenth century was for some time the best voyage.

There was little in the way of English goods to appeal to the

Wine bottles recovered from the site of the wreck of the *Earl of Abergavenny* in Weymouth Bay.

(Photo Edward M Cumming)

Indians, but the growing Anglo-Indian population were entirely dependent on the Company's ships for practically everything necessary for a civilised, European existence. The Company left this to private traders, prohibiting only woollen cloth and warlike stores. Naval supplies were the captain's preserve and always comprised a profitable cargo outward. England was the only source of woollen and leather goods – William Hickey noted at the end of the eighteenth century that leather goods usually yielded one hundred per cent in Bengal. Cutlery, scissors, razors, pencils and stationery were procurable only through the private trade: the *Halsewell*, which sailed for Coast and Bay in 1786, was carrying hides, trunks of stationery, iron nails, hoops and handles and other iron products.

Captain John Wordsworth, commander of the *Earl of Sandwich*, which arrived at Madras Road in the summer of 1783 en route for China, was carrying an investment of over £5000.[12] He had 'Four Setts Illustration of Natural History, consisting of three Volumes each Sett, bound in Calf Gilt and Letterd' at a cost in London of £35; hundreds of prints – 'Alfred the great dividing his Loaf', 'Admiral Parker's Engagement off ye Dogger Bank'; bundles of violin strings, bridges, pegs, bows and cases; hundreds of sheets of music – Davauz Concerto, Lydells Quintets, Wainwrights Duets – and, for the children, tins of peppermint drops. He was also carrying the staples of Anglo-Indian life: firkins of butter, whole Gloucester and Cheshire cheeses, hams in canvas and oat casings, and the porter, pale ale, claret, port, sherry, lisbon and old hock which the high society, particularly of Calcutta, spent so much of its time drinking. Anyone wanting to impress his guests had to produce a case of the most excellent hock – or claret or burgundy – what he had just, with great good fortune, obtained from a very special source. Huge

quantities of glassware to serve all this liquor figured largely in Captain Wordsworth's investment, as in that of all the commanders' stock for the Indian market. Riding was a very popular leisure activity in the company's settlements, so saddlery and equestrian equipment formed another significant proportion of his stock. As the Anglo-Indians slavishly followed the London fashions there was a ready sale for his 'two white satin waistcoats' and his 'fashionable hats and cockades'. Haberdashery was an important item: pages of buttons of every shape and size, ribbons and braid of every shade appear in his account book. At the other end of the scale were his stuffed horsehair couch, a mahogany dining table with chairs, a sideboard and bureaux.

There was always the chance of making a profit in the port-to-port trade. Captain Wordsworth called at Batavia after leaving Madras en route for China. There he bartered some of his prints, hats, weighing machines and furniture for plate glass and camlets for sale in Canton. By 1794 the council of supercargoes at Canton were complaining that imports of camlets in the private trade were depressing the already low price. The situation was exacerbated in 1800 over the smuggling of watches and camlets. As a result the Company came down hard on the import of camlets into China in the commanders' investments. Captain Wordsworth, brother of the poet, complained bitterly to his sister Dorothy in 1803 that he and others were called before 'those vile and abominable monsters at the India House, who will finish me by making me pay 300 guineas for my sins during the voyage.' They 'attacked us for smuggling camblets (sic) to China. One captain of our fleet is fined 1050 guineas. You must know that this (is) all new business. Though smuggling these camblets has never been allowed in the service, yet it has been so constantly done for years by every one in the service that we began to consider that we had a *right* to smuggle them. We are the first that they have fined & of course we think it very hard and unjust.'[13]

Captain Wordsworth also bartered some of his Scotch and pearl barley, saddlery, music, drugs and pickles for some rabbit and otter skins which were beginning to seep into the eastern seas from the Hudson Bay Company via outlets on the north-west coast of America and were a substantial part of the private trade by the end of the eighteenth century. In 1787 two Company ships called there before proceeding to Canton, probably for the benefit of the commanders and officers, and in 1791 over 100,000 rabbit skins, over 36,000 beaver skins and several thousand otter, marten and fox furs were brought to Canton in the private trade. Seal skins also made their appearance at this time.[14]

A China direct voyage was only moderately profitable, but as silver was more highly valued than gold a profitable exchange could be made by an enterprising commander; as early as 1732 the records show that four commanders each

A dinner plate decorated in underglaze-blue, a very typical Chinese export market product of the 1780-90 period.　　　*(Godden of Worthing Ltd)*

took out £4000 in silver bullion and changed it into gold. As the eighteenth century progressed the Company permitted the commanders to take out £3000 in silver for exchange and £2000 for the purchase of coral, amber and precious stones. As there was little in the way of goods which appealed to the Chinese, they were also allowed to make up their private trade goods to £3000 in value in silver, provided the chests of bullion were counted as part of their permitted tonnage. Flints, which the Chinese needed in their manufacture of porcelain, were taken out as ballast in the private trade.

The only English products in demand in China were chiming watches and clocks and musical boxes. Captain Wordsworth had in his investment on the *Earl of Sandwich* in 1783:

one pair high finish'd Horizontal Second Stop Watches Musical and Chime, Cap'd and Jewell'd they do not stop whilst winding up they Chime the Quarters and strike the Hours as they go and play a Tune at every Hour they also repeat the Tune at pleasure by pushing the pendant.

These seemingly innocent articles in the officers' private trade – generally termed 'sing-songs' – bedevilled the Company's trade with China for a hundred years. The Emperor collected them, and so they were highly sought after by the mandarins for bribing their superiors. On the slightest pretext the mandarin in charge of the customs, the hoppo, stopped the trade, threatening the Company with huge demorage bills until a

bribe was exacted – of which the sing-songs constituted the most important part. Extortion was facilitated by the system of trade with the Europeans. A handful of Chinese merchants paid heavily to be a member of an exclusive guild, the Co-Hong, which had a monopoly of the trade with the Europeans. Each member of the Co-Hong was appointed security merchant to a few European ships and dealt with every aspect of the trade with the ships' supercargoes and later with the council of supercargoes resident in the season at Canton. It was therefore the security merchant who was forced to purchase the 'sing-songs' to placate the hoppo. Captain Wordsworth's chiming clock, at £150, was relatively cheap; the more sophisticated – with figures dancing minuets, jigs and gavottes, birds singing and waterfalls cascading – were extremely expensive, frequently bringing the security merchants to the verge of bankruptcy and so threatening to increase the already unhealthy monopoly of the Hong merchants.

The problem of the 'sing-songs' was recognised as early as 1759 when the supercargoes asked the commanders of the season's fleet to forbear showing any to the 'hoppo's people'. Twenty years later the Court of Directors, on the advice of the council at Canton, prohibited 'the carrying out to Canton without their special licence any Clock, Watch, Temple or Toy, or other curious article whatever' though this appears to have been singularly ineffectual.[15] There was no love lost between the English and the Chinese; the official term for the chief of the supercargoes' council was 'Red-haired Devil' and all Englishmen were the 'Red-haired Devil's Imps', an attitude reflected, not without grounds, no doubt, by the meanest Chinese. Affrays were therefore common and in 1809 a Chinese was stabbed, probably by some seamen from the *Royal Charlotte*. The 'grand chop' giving permission for the ships to depart was refused and the security merchant thrown into jail until the bribe was forthcoming. The council recognised this as all part of the game of 'sing-songs'. The ships

A Chinese porcelain punch-bowl decorated in Canton with two views of the *Earl of Elgin* off the Cape of Good Hope in August 1764.

(Godden of Worthing Ltd)

The Canton factories at the height of their development.

(National Maritime Museum)

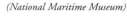

The type of 'sing-song' that the officers carried in their private trade investment. They were the cause of much aggravation and stoppage of trade.

sailed at last, but the following season it was brought up again and the chop withheld. Mr Browne, chief of the council, informed the Company on 31 January 1811 that it was not the murder that was the cause of the trouble, but the inability of the security merchants:

> to satisfy the extortion and continually increasing demands of the Hoppo for the purchase of the various articles of Clockwork and Mechanism imported in our Ships and usually denominated Sing-Songs and which it seems are now become the established vehicle of corruption between the Officer and his Superior at the Capital.[16]

The Company compromised in the early years of the nineteenth century, limiting 'sing-songs' to £100 value. They continued to number among the many aggravations of the English trade with China until Britain acquired what the Company had sought for over a hundred years – a place of its own, Hong Kong.

A series of disastrous famines in China in the last decades of the eighteenth century heralded the beginning of high noon for a favoured few among the commanders. A massive change over from cotton production to rice by Imperial edict created a huge demand for raw cotton in China. At the same time, the reduction in the duties on teas swept aside all the foreign East Indiamen which had earned a living smuggling tea into Britain, leaving the trade clear for the Company's

The English factories at Canton in the eighteenth century flanked by those of the other European trading nations. *(National Maritime Museum)*

ships. Suddenly huge amounts of silver were required in Canton to finance the greatly increased tea investment. It was not considered good policy to raise the necessary bullion in London, and Bengal's surplus was soaked up by the Indian wars. The Houses of Agency in Bombay seized their opportunity, building large fleets of country ships equal in size to the largest Company ships, to carry the raw cotton to Canton. There they deposited the silver received from the Chinese in the Company's treasury in exchange for bills drawn on London which were sent to their metropolitan branches. The Company failed to enter the trade itself to any great extent as its Bombay government was heavily in debt to the private merchants such as David Scott and was unable to find the money for the investment, filling up only one ship a year. Again David Scott overcame the directors' narrow mercantilist attitude, and secured to the captains the tonnage of their own ships from the different presidencies to China at such a low freight as ensured them great gains, especially from Bombay to China. The Chairman and Deputy Chairman of the Court of Directors appropriated the allocation of the Bombay/China voyages, usually about five a year, to make sure their 'friends' benefited. As Henry Dundas said, this voyage was 'the greatest thing in the gift of the chairs, and being no less than . . . a probable fortune to the man who got it.'

By 1799 up to 750 bales were allowed to the commanders and officers freight free: credit was available to them for a further 2000 bales provided the proceeds were paid into the treasury at Canton in exchange for bills drawn on London, and a further 2667 bales allowed at a very low rate of freight. In 1804 the freight-free allowance was increased to two fifths of the tonnage of each ship, the commanders and officers being allowed to bid for the remaining three fifths if the Company did not require it.

The other great source of money for the tea investment was opium. The best quality was grown in Bengal under a government monopoly. It was sold by public auction in Calcutta and carried to China mostly in Portuguese ships bound to Macao – never in Company ships as the risk of stoppage to the trade was far too great. The opium was sold to a specialist opium merchant and the proceeds deposited in the Company's treasury in Canton in return for bills drawn on Bengal. The Company periodically felt obliged to remind their commanders of the gravity of being found with opium on board. In 1796 the sailing orders issued by the governor and Council of Bombay to the commanders of ships from Bombay to Canton directed that:

> You must take most particular care that no opium is laden on board your ship by yourself, officers or any other person, as the importation of that article at China is positively forbid and very serious consequences may attend your neglect of this Injunction.[17]

There is no doubt the commanders dealt in opium. Captain

Alexander Montgomery, brother of the Earl of Eglington, commander of the *Bessborough*, bought opium in Calcutta in January 1779. Captain Wordsworth complained on returning to England from Canton in 1803, 'Opium and quicksilver were the only things that sold to any profit.' But they probably shipped it to Canton by country ship.

There was never any shortage of goods to bring home from China. Tea, which enterprising commanders had been bringing home for some years, did not appear in the Company's investment until after 1700. An attempt was made to limit the private trade in tea as the Company's investment increased in the first decades of the eighteenth century. There is evidence of a slackening of restrictions by the 1740s, since the Company concentrated on the cheaper teas and were willing to leave the finer teas to the private trade. A complete reversal took place after 1760, when the supercargoes found the prices of the fine teas rising as a result of competition from the private trade and suggested that the latter should be channelled into the cheaper teas, where the quantities were so vast that the effect of competition would be minimal. In 1794 the amount of finer teas purchased in the private trade accounted for one fifth of the total amount imported. In 1806 1,750,000lbs of the total 28,000,000lbs of tea sold at the Company's sales had come in through the private trade. Tea filled every crevice.[18] Several commanders were fined for stowing teas in the powder room.

With the great increase in tea imports following the reduction of duty in 1784, the Company found it needed every last silver dollar to finance its tea investment, and was only too pleased to leave the other goods to the private trade. In fact, the Company positively encouraged the commanders and officers to trade in those goods needed to protect the tea cargo – dunnage – by allowing trade in these goods in addition to the normal tonnage allowance. The Company withdrew from the trade in chinaware in 1786 and left it to the commanders, 'provided it is used as a "flooring" for the teas and does not exceed in height thirteen inches'. Round the chinaware, which was stored in boxes and filled with sago to extract maximum profitability, and amongst the chests of teas, the commanders put the rest of the dunnage: mother of pearl, turmeric, sugar, bamboos, rattans, whangees, canes and sapan, a wood which yielded a red dye. Their enthusiastic response was so great that the Company was forced to limit it to ensure keeping the midships and limbers free, as large quantities of these goods had been brought home in the Company's ships 'far beyond what is necessary for the protection of the cargo and stores, occupying tonnage to the exclusion of goods, or lumbering the ship, the Court have resolved, that unless what is brought home of these articles appear, absolutely and bona fide, necessary for, and used as, dunnage . . . any exceedings of such requisite quantity shall be charged against the tonnage of the commanders and officers . . .'[19]

A dinner plate from a typical Chinese export market dinner service with underglaze-blue borders, and an enamelled crest added in Canton to special order, c1790. *(Godden of Worthing Ltd)*

By 1799 it was agreed that dunnage up to two and a half per cent of the total cargo could be brought home on addition to the tonnage allowed for private trade. Just over half Captain Wordsworth's investment from China consisted of tea; cassia and cassia buds accounted for a further quarter, the rest comprising taffetas, turmeric, chinaware, silk handkerchiefs and lacquer ware.

Full details survive of Captain Stevens' private trade investment on the *Godolphin*, which returned from Canton in November 1749, except for the chinaware, the document which lists these remaining in only fragmentary form.[20] Camphor formed nearly half the total value of his investment, but ten years later its export was prohibited, the Company warning the commanders not to admit on board their ships 'any Camphire or Musk least the scent spoil your Tea.'[21] Next came tea, about one seventh of the total value. Benjamin, a fragrant resin obtained from trees in Java, comprised a substantial part of the remainder, with oranges, tamarinds, arrack and rattans completing it.

All private trade goods had to be deposited in the Company's warehouses for sale at the company's auctions 'by inch of candle'. On Captain Steven's total receipts from sales of £7740 he paid £1710 customs duties, £500 as discount for cash payments, £360 duty imposed by Parliament, £140 'indulgence' on goods not included in the list of 'indulged' goods issued by the company, £150 warehouse charge, £30 to the almshouse at Poplar for the six pence per gallon charge on his arrack, and £90 clearance through customs. The full details of his venture can be seen in Appendix 5.

Not all the tea reached the Company's warehouses before the duty was reduced in 1784. William Hickey recorded in

An English East Indiaman c1720 by Peter Monomy, 1681-1749, displaying the Company flag.

(National Maritime Museum)

Inset: Puankhequa (1714-1788), a
merchant of the Co-Hong which
conducted all the trade between
the Chinese and the Europeans.
(Goteborgs Stadmuseum, Sweden)

Main picture: From a modest though well-appointed terrace on the river outside Canton in the early eighteenth century, when the Chinese government first permitted the supercargoes of the European ships to live ashore during the trading season, the factories developed in size and magnificence.

(National Maritime Museum)

A view of Calcutta from Garden Reach and shipping on the Hooghly in the eighteenth century.

(National Maritime Museum)

Ships of large burthen arriving at Madras had to anchor well out to sea beyond the Coromandel shoals. Deep *masulah* boats, the planks sewn together with coir rope, transported all personnel and goods over the treacherous surfs to the shore at Madras.

(National Maritime Museum)

An Indiaman in a fresh breeze. By C Brooking.

(National Maritime Museum)

The system of a paddle steamer towing a chain of barges initiated by 'Peacock's iron chicks' in the early 1830s revolutionised the transportation of bulk cargoes and passengers up and down the great rivers of north India.

(BL OIOC)

Left: This splendid coat of arms was first granted to the 'New' or 'English' Company in 1698 and later to the United Company of Merchants of England trading to the East Indies, or the United East India Company. The crest, a lion rampant holding a crown, distinguished all the Company's uniforms and appurtenances.
(BL OIOC)

Right: The *Sampson* in stress of weather, 25 April 1794, one of over a hundred superb water-colour paintings with which Edward Barlow illustrated his *Journal*, providing a unique record covering half a century of the ships in which he served and the places he visited.
(National Maritime Museum)

William Daniell's aquatint of Brunswick Dock, Blackwall, dated 1803. Built in 1789 to provide security for the valuable cargoes of the returning East Indiamen, it was later incorporated in the East India Docks. The ships' cargoes were transferred in secure convoys under Customs supervision to the East India Company's warehouses, mainly in the City.
(Museum of London, Docklands Collection)

y Lower Doune a topsaile coming on to tears and blowing so dreadfull as
the first very moment it had giuen ould to haue blowen vs into Eternety makeing our very
er to Quake in our head it all being so very dreadfull as the the very Blast of god
Displeasure had come vpon vs to Confound vs eff in a moment and had it pleased god that
our saile had beene open and driuen and our Mast and Rigging then it had sertainly fused
the sea to haue Swallowed vs vp in the twinkling of an eye the sernes of it being past
discription at that time and in what Condition were we in god grant before the Judgment
seat of Christ being taken vpon such a sudden alarme we may haue the time grieuatie the
Lord show as his decrees he put into mind of our Liues and Conseruation and of that
so Remember we are But Dust and do preserue our selues for such a doom
Change as this might haue proud had it not beene for gods great Mercy who are the
god of heauen and Earth the feare of all that it is there to prepare our harts and minds
that he may alwayes Liue in his feare that when Euer we die we may be receiued in
his fauour and grace which god of his infinet Mercy grant and at the first cruizing
vpon that feare we lost all our saile spelt on Most of them Blown away our foretop beeing
new Broke our yard and the Mast cut haue Beene might haue Bene vs in a most
Lamentable Condition all vpon a sudden we being not able to lie agenst the wind tore
away Before it Bareing north sail Back agaire till such strift of the wind abated
which was in halfe an hour before and in two houres the wind vered to South ward
But wee were in Great feire of Losing our passage about the Cape being
in such a Condition as you may see here Before Being surprized as well as beene
Being cut on Indifrent Morality yet it pleased god at our great Mercy and act for had the
Mast word one hurled our thin the ditch vay again flashing what saile we suth with
our staysaile and spritsaile and Bending More saile for the doom of them that were
spelt and Blown away But we had not made an End in 3 or 4 dayes after with oure
fore yard But Made a main topsaile yard and maintop sail Serue for a fore saile and
Sterting our Leues west north west to need and to north the winds Continuing prety
faire for vs in 11 dayes after we had sight of the maine Land of Ethiopia
sailing about seuenty leagues to the Eastward of Cape agulas or the Southeparts of the Cap
of Good hope or Cap Bonesprance.

The East India Company had exclusive use of a significant proportion of the Legal Quays between London Bridge, top left, and the Tower of London, bottom right, the only stretch of the River Thames where all dutiable goods could be unloaded. The Company had the use of most of the quays between the Bridge and Billingsgate, whose set back wharf can be seen in the centre of the picture. Part of the Rhinebeck Panorama, so-called after Rhinebeck, a small town in Canada where it was discovered.

(Museum of London, Docklands Collection)

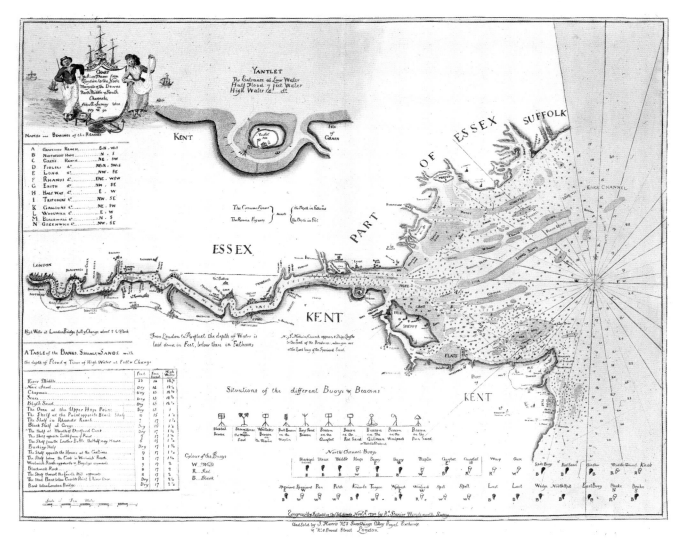

Above: Richard Stanier's 1790 chart of the River Thames reveals the difficulties of the first stage of the voyage. A north-east gale, so necessary to get the ships away down-Channel from the Downs, made navigating the bends of the River and the shoals of the estuary a slow and hazardous business, sometimes taking several days.

(National Maritime Museum)

Left: The Director's Court Room, East India House, London. By Thomas Hosmer Shepherd, c1820.

(BL OIOC)

The East India fleet leaving St Helena, July 1830. The ships shown are *Inglis, Windsor, Waterloo, Scaleby Castle, General Kyd, Farquharson, Lowther Castle*, being escorted by HM Frigate *Ariadne*. By William John Huggins, Marine Painter to King William IV. *(Trevor Hearl)*

Opium Ships at Lintin by William John Huggins, 1824, published 1838. From about 1820 when men-of-war and East Indiamen awaiting pilots began anchoring off the island of Lintin, it became the accepted rendezvous for the country ships carrying opium and the receiving ships operated by Chinese merchants specialising in this forbidden trade. *(National Maritime Museum)*

East India House, Leadenhall Street, London. By Thomas Hosmer Shepherd, c1820. *(BL OIOC)*

North East view of Bentinck's Buildings, the Beach, Madras. By John Gantz, 1822. *(BL OIOC)*

The rocky, inhospitable island of St Helena in the South Atlantic, acquired by the company in 1673, was a compulsory port of call for all homebound East Indiamen on whom the islanders depended for all their supplies of grain, which could not be grown on the island. After 1815 the possibility of catching sight of Napoleon provided added interest for the officers.

(Trevor Hearl)

A View from the waters of Messers Barnard and Dudman's Shipyard, Deptford by John Clevely, 1774.
(Sotheby's Picture Library)

East India Company officer's maritime
service uniform, probably undress.
(Museum of London, Docklands Collection)

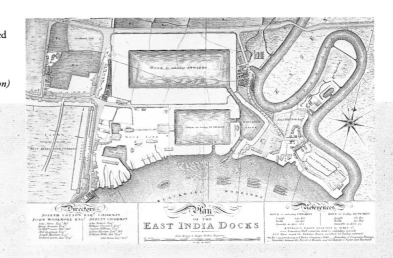

Main picture: The Brunswick Dock became the Export Dock and a new, much larger Import Dock was contructed to the north. A view by William Daniell looking towards Greenwich.
Inset: Plan of the East India Dock opened in 1806.
(Museum of London, Docklands Collection)

Above: The reconstructed *Batavia*, a Dutch East Indiaman which was wrecked off the north-west Australian coast on her maiden voyage in 1628. Shipwrights studied the remains of the hull in the West Australian Maritime Museum, Fremantle, historical records and traditional craftmanship before building the 160ft long ship at Lelystad between 1985 and 1992.

(Jean Sutton)

Right: Modern blocks tower above the quays between London Bridge and Old Billingsgate where the Company's hoys unloaded the produce of the east in the early days.

(Bryan Sutton)

Left: This brightly painted cotton produced in Jaipur is similar to those on which the first East India Company's success was built. With their vivid, fast colours they took Europe by storm, alarming British weavers and dyers. Laws were passed prohibiting their import and use.

(Jean Sutton)

A view of the River Hooghly from Garden Reach, Calcutta, today.

(Jean Sutton)

The General Court Room where all imports were auctioned by the candle.

(BL OIOC)

his memoirs how a man 'of a Herculean form' came off a cutter and boarded the *Plassey* in the Channel, asking Captain Waddell, 'Well, Captain, how is tea?' He disputed Captain Waddell's price as there were 'a great number of China ships this season.' He proceeded to buy all the Captain's and officers' stock which was hoisted out of the gun room and other places in which it had been stowed and loaded on board the cutter within sight of a custom-house schooner but outside the limits.[22]

The tonnage permitted for the use of the commanders' and officers' private trade investment in the China ships increased generally towards the end of the century with the adoption of the larger ships. In 1805 the commanders of four 1200 ton ships arriving in Canton each had between 56 and 62 tons for their own private trade, while one ship had a total of 133 tons for the commander and officers. The privilege homeward had also increased: in 1795 as an encouragement to the commanders to take as large a surplus of the Company's tea as pos-

sible, an additional 30 tons was allowed 'to a commander on account of himself and his officers if he shall not have refused any of the Company's cargo . . . but in no case whatever, the whole allowance to the commander and officers of any ship shall exceed 99 tons including their privilege.' In the last years of the eighteenth century the tonnage allowed to the commanders and officers on the outward-bound ships to India was similar to that on the China ships – between 90 and 100 tons. However, their privilege homeward was limited to 30 tons for the commander, the rest in proportion.

The problems of the commanders of the regular ships to India increased as the century came to a close. In England the Board of Control and David Scott encouraged the opening up of the India trade, convinced that the Company's monopolistic policy would result in London losing its position as the premier port for oriental produce, a view held equally by Lord Mornington, the Governor-General, in Calcutta.

The partial opening up of the India trade in 1793 with the

The mysterious Orient – the European anchorage at Whampoa from Danes Island.   *(National Maritime Museum)*

3000 tons made available by the Company was a drop in the ocean as far as the remittance trade from India was concerned. Government continued to promote the importation into London by any means. In 1802 the regular ship commanders memorialised the court of directors, pointing out that the committee set up to decide on the sum to be donated by each commander to the fund to recompense their colleagues made redundant through the change in the shipping system in 1799, had over estimated their profits on a voyage. They claimed these had been much reduced by the great number of ships sent to India for rice, loaded with Europe goods; by the India ships which had loaded Europe goods on their return; and by the permission to the owners of extra ships to carry out 100 tons of goods to compensate them for having no troops to transport. They asked that the £500 penalty be remitted for the present voyage.[23]

Just how many commanders succeeded in making a fortune from their private trade is difficult to assess. Certainly there exists a great deal of evidence to suggest that they did so. Even Captain Knox, serving during the period of greatest restriction, admitted to have 'gotten an Estate', though he felt he had to thank God more than the Company for it. Captain Wordsworth and his contemporaries were more fortunate. The value of his investment, at £5000, was about average at that

time: the total investments averaged £120,000 per annum in the 1780s. A good profit could be expected from this original outlay, and as Captain Wordsworth went on to become a successful India shipping husband he presumably was not disappointed. In 1789 investments totalling £118,310 realised £930,930 at the Company's sales.[24] Between 1785 and 1793 goods sold at the Company's sales on behalf of the commanders and officers fetched over £6,000,000. This did not include interest on certificates and profits on bullion and precious stones.

The commanders' unceasing complaints that they were allowed insufficient tonnage, and their objections to a system which prevented them sending home their goods in foreign bottoms, also suggests that many found their private trade very profitable. They grasped at any opportunity to increase their tonnage, buying that of their officers whenever possible: the commander of the *Surat Castle* paid £40 a ton for his second officer's allowance of 6 tons in 1810. There were frequent disputes over the 30 extra tons granted in 1795: the commanders claimed it all for themselves but this was disputed by the surgeon and second mate of the *Atlas* in 1817 and the council at Canton upheld their claim to a share. In the following year, the commander of the *Regent* brought out an authorisation from the Company granting him the whole of the extra tonnage;

this was overruled by the council in Canton which stated that the commander should have only 19 of the 30 tons, the rest to be divided between the officers and the surgeon.

Captain Eastwick had a good idea of the state of affairs at the end of the eighteenth century:

> Of course, much depended on the skill and good management of the individual commander, the risk of the market, his knowledge of its requirements, and his own connections and interest to procure him a good profit . . . In short, the gains to a prudent commander averaged from four to five thousand pounds a voyage, sometimes falling as low as two, but at others rising to ten or twelve . . . and three or four voyages assured any man a very handsome fortune.[25]

The risk of the market was paramount, and something over which the commanders had little control. Although the Anglo-Indians were entirely dependent on the officers' private trade for everything they required, all information about articles in great demand at any time was at least a year out of date. Further, all the commanders acted on this information at the same time, so that glut succeeded scarcity all at once. The commanders returning from Madras early in 1768 brought news of a great shortage of glassware, with the result that all the commanders going out that autumn invested in large quantities of that article. All the ships arrived in Madras within ten days of one another 'bringing so great and sudden a supply of European articles as to overstock the market, and in consequence there were no purchasers for many of the investments . . .Glassware in particular . . . sold at a loss of sixty per cent.' Much of the profit on private trade investments probably went to agents like Mair and Cotton of Madras who bought up the officers' investments and held them until a more favourable price could be exacted.

It was a case of 'Who Dares Wins'. The most successful commanders were probably those who were willing to invest large sums when they saw an opportunity for big returns. Captain John Clements of the *Royal Charlotte* took advantage of the glut of tea in London in 1773 and the consequent fall in the number of ships required for China that season by renting his own ship. She was taken up for Bombay, sailing in February 1772, and from there Captain Clements freighted her at a daily demorage of £18.5s, returning to the Downs in August 1775. Captain John Pascal Larkins rented his ship the *Warren Hastings* for a year in 1787 and was known to have freighted country ships from India to Canton to take advantage of the terms offered by the Company with a view to filling the treasury at Canton to finance the tea investment.

Captain Wordsworth was ecstatic at obtaining the best voyage in the history of the Company in 1804: the directors decided to send a ship to Bengal and China, even better than Bombay/China. He wrote to Dorothy that he was sure he would do well with his Bengal investment as returning ships reported good profits: 'These ships have sold for forty or fifty percent all round . . . There is no doubt but that I shall get as much cotton upon freight as I like to take in and at better terms than at Bombay. And with the probability of taking on my own account three times as much as the Bombay captains I shall also have a chance of making by opium and rice, etc, . . .' [26] But his investment of £20,000 – four times that of his cousin in 1789 – was made up of borrowed money and a windfall the family had received. He had made losses of up to £1000 on his first two voyages as commander of the *Abergavenny* and now he was staking all – his own and his family's future – on one throw of the dice. His ship never got away from the English coast. She struck the Shambles off Portland and sank with great loss of life, including that of her commander. Fortunately he had insured his investment.

Notes:
1. Hickey, *op cit*, Vol 3, 297.
2. Hardy, *op cit*, 64 and 83.
3. Rand, F. P.: *Wordsworth's Mariner Brother* (Mass 1966).
4. BL OIOC. Company's despatch to Bombay 5 April 1776; v Bombay District *Gazetteer*, 26, Part 2, 11. Rates varied between £50 for a cadet and £200 for a General Officer, the commander paying the owners £10 per passenger until the end of the eighteenth century when it was raised to £15. In 1810 the rates for company servants were between £95 for a cadet and £250 for a General Officer.
5. Hickey, *op cit*, Vol 1, 118 and Vol 2, 98.
6. *Ibid*, Vol 1, 181.
7. BL OIOC (Foster): *op cit*, Vol 4, 228.
8. Knox: *op cit*, 374.
9. Thomas, James H: *Portsmouth and the East India Company in the Eighteenth Century*, p13.
10. Guildhall Library: Memorandum Book *op cit*, 25 October 1775.
11. Scott: *op cit*, Vol I, no. 26, 30 March 1795.
12. Cumberland, Westmoreland and Carlisle R.O: Papers of John Wordsworth, D/BS.
13. Rand: *op cit*,
14. Morse: *op cit*, Vol II, 158.
15. *Ibid*, Vol II, 37.
16. *Ibid*, Vol III, 155.
17. Morse: *op cit*, Vol II, 28 November 1796.
18. Hardy: *op cit*, 80: By the end of the eighteenth century the company permitted the following amounts of tea to be brought from China by:
    a: paying 7% on sale value: commanders 688lbs, officers 432lbs
    b: paying 17% on sale value: commanders 8648lbs, officers 5464lbs
19. *Ibid*, 80.
20. Berks R.O., Papers of Richard Benyon: D/Esy, f8.
21. Morse: *op cit*, Vol V, 87 .
22. Hickey: *op cit*, Vol 1, 248 and 249.
23. Guildhall Library: Memorandum Book, *op cit*, 30 January 1802.
24. Parkinson: *op cit*, 204 and 205.
25. Eastwick: *op cit*, 43.
26. Rand: *op cit*,

CHAPTER 6

THE $\mathcal{S}$HIP'S $\mathcal{C}$OMPANY

It was along the banks of the Thames from Wapping to Deptford that the naval lieutenant or the chief mate found the crew for a man of war or a ship bound for Barbados or Canton, Malaga or Riga, or simply along the coast to Newcastle. Here lived the seafaring community, dissolute and improvident ashore, absolutely dependable and hard-working at sea; a distinct community in speech, dress, even physical appearance. There were no uniforms to distinguish them, but nevertheless there was a distinct uniformity about their dress: their striped or flowered waistcoats, trousers and knee-length petticoat breeches peculiar to their trade, and their canvas jackets, all gaily decorated with coloured braid, ribbon and bright buttons set them apart. The attractions of a crew uniformly dressed had not escaped notice: the captain of the *Plassey*, arriving in 1770 at Whampoa where there was always a spirit of rivalry among the crews of the different European ships, was conducted up to Canton in his barge 'jack, ensign and pennant flying, the crew all in clean white shirts and black caps.'[1]

This community comprised a wide range of ability and experience. There were the able-seamen whose parents had taken out indentures for them to be apprenticed to ships' masters for seven years. Others, as boys 'chargeable on the parish', had been herded into a life at sea by Queen Anne's law providing for them to be apprenticed up to the age of twenty-one. At the other end of the scale were the landsmen with little or no experience, some, like the parish boys, swelling the seamen's pool as a result of Queen Anne's act providing for the increase of seamen and the better navigation of the coal trade by legislating for 'lewd, disorderly menservants, . . . Rogues, vagabonds and sturdy beggars' to be sent to sea. Others were previously unemployed, choosing a seafaring life simply as an alternative to starvation.[2]

East India ships' companies were by far the largest among merchant ships, with fewest tons served per man. There was great disparity in the early years between the large, heavily armed ships and the smaller vessels used for seeking out a trade: the *Charles II*, 816 tons, sixty-four guns, had a crew of three hundred men while the 130-ton *Tonqueen Merchant* had only twenty-six men. During the eighteenth century one hundred men became the standard; one hundred and thirty for the large China ships later.

Large numbers of midshipmen and officers accounted for a substantial part of the complement, a feature which distinguished the Company's ships from other merchantmen and brought them into affinity with the Navy. Even naval terminology was adopted, the term 'midshipman' being preferred to 'apprentice' used in the rest of the merchant fleet, though the term 'mate' persisted in East India shipping circles despite the Company's official address of 'officer'. By the end of the eighteenth century the uniform introduced for mates at the same time as that for commanders added to their distinction from the rest of the merchant fleet.

Six mates were usual on Company ships, at least from the end of the seventeenth century. The first four mates, like the captain, were Company servants though they were appointed and paid by the owners. In the latter part of the eighteenth century the Company renewed its efforts to ensure that experienced navigators were in charge of its valuable cargoes. No one was to be appointed to the position of chief, second or third mate who had not performed one voyage to India in the Company's service. Four years later new regulations required chief and second mates to be at least twenty-two years old and to have performed one voyage as third or fourth mate; third mates had to be twenty-one and to have done two voyages; the fourth mates twenty with one voyage to their credit.[3] These rules with minor modifications continued for the remainder of the Company's trading life.

Although Eastwick had obtained his master-mariner's certificate and served as chief mate on a merchantman and master's mate on a naval vessel by the time he took his first berth on an Indiaman, he was 'unable to ship in a higher capacity

Cruickshank's cartoon 'Saturday Night at Sea' shows the confined space between the guns that was home for the seamen for two years or more.

(National Maritime Museum)

than that of fifth mate' as it was his first voyage to India. Henry Meriton had been at sea since the age of nine and was appointed third mate of the *Pigot* at twenty years of age. He claimed to have been an apprentice in several ships in the West Indies' trade, then a gunner, progressing from second mate to first mate and master of a brig. Towards the end of the eighteenth century mates were required to provide proof that they were 'qualified in the Lunar method of finding the Longitude at Sea'; those not so qualified were obliged to take themselves off to Mr Lawrence Gwynne of Hackney. The first four mates had to produce an authenticated certificate stating their date of birth and experience to date each time they applied for a post. An example is given in Appendix 11.

There appears to have been a gentlemen's agreement among the officers to give a helping hand to those who had suffered a disaster. Henry Meriton and John Rogers returned to the Thames after serving as third and fourth mates on a prolonged voyage plagued by disease and death on the *Pigot*. Within a few days they signed on as second and third mates on the *Halsewell*, obviously displacing officers who had been sworn in earlier. After the wreck of the *Halsewell* some days later, both men transferred to the *Bridgwater*, which sailed in April, in a higher capacity. Thomas Gilpin, fourth mate on

the *Earl of Abergavenny* which sank in February 1805 sailed soon afterwards as second mate of the *Comet*.

Midshipmen and mates were generally drawn from that class of people termed 'gentlemen'. Eastwick said of his brother officers on the *Barwell*, 'they were one and all gentlemen by education and family.'[4] There were many instances of seamen eventually achieving officer status but their chances were limited by lack of education and money. Few seamen could read or write, which precluded their achieving a position higher than that of quartermaster or petty-officer. Instruments and uniforms were expensive: Eastwick estimated that a capital of £500 was necessary until an officer achieved the position of second mate, by which time he could reasonably be expected to live on his income.

In a printed resolution opposing the opening up of the India trade in 1811, the Society of East India Commanders stressed the excellent reputation of 'the Company's Naval Service' which had enjoyed national esteem for more than a century. It had employed the sons of reputable families, and the time served in it had been accepted by the navy as part of the six years required to be served in the Royal Navy to qualify for a lieutenancy. Great numbers of young men reared in the East India Company's service had therefore gone on to be distinguished officers in the navy, while many paid-off naval officers had entered the Company's service. The officers in the Company's service were well educated which 'had benefited the nation in the perfection of discoveries, navigation, geography, wind and currents.'[5]

Whenever peace was resumed several paid-off naval officers obtained berths on India ships. On the *Halsewell*, bound to Coast and Bay in 1786, were twenty-four year old Mr Pilcher, fourth mate, lately lieutenant on board the *Scipio* guardship, and Mr Brimer, serving as a supernumerary mate on the passage to Madras where he had relatives who were in a position to forward his career. Captain Timmins of the *Royal George* had been a naval lieutenant.

Six midshipmen were usual though the large China ships had more, especially in wartime. In a letter to his girlfriend Mary Hutchinson in 1801, Captain John Wordsworth exalted: 'The midshipmen are the finest lads I ever saw. We have eight . . .'[6] A good general education was essential: David Scott advised a friend whose son was not progressing as a midshipman, 'he should be sent immediately to a school where he can be taught his own language to read, to speak and write it as also mathematics and navigation'.

Travelling as a 'guinea pig' was a respectable way of experiencing a first voyage to the east; but according to an authority, if he were old enough, 'he would make a better seaman in a shorter time by going as midshipman, and being obliged to do a certain line of the ship's duty . . . young gentlemen going out with that appellation are . . .generally rated as Ordinary Seamen or Captain's servants and proceeded on their next voyage as midshipmen.'.[7]

With the boom in the country trade – which had passed almost completely into British hands by the last quarter of the eighteenth century – the demand for young British men to officer the ships was insatiable. The directors had a quota of 'free mariner' licences to award to young men with experience, but influence was needed to obtain these and the numbers were totally inadequate. A Court order of 1782 limiting the number of midshipmen had only succeeded in shifting the problem. The Court tried to clamp down on the excessive numbers after a survey of twenty-five ships sailing in 1790

The fortified town of Surat on the River Tapti where the Company had its first factory.

(National Maritime Museum)

revealed the number of officers and seamen exceeded the regulations by seventy-nine, an average of eight per ship, excluding the permitted allowance of five supernumeraries per ship.[8] This was probably a gross underestimate. When fourteen year old John Pope signed on as seaman on the *Francis* in 1786, he was one of forty seamen who were all to disembark in Bengal to go into the country trade with the full connivance of the captain. All received the full wages, contrary to Company regulations. There is no indication in the Rate and Wages Book that they did not serve on the passage home and that they were replaced by Lascars. The Directors fumed in vain against the practice 'which must be very expensive to owners and injurious to freight' and determined to enforce the order more firmly.

The posts of surgeon, purser and captain's clerk were the other 'gentlemen's' posts on board ships in the Company's service. The surgeon's qualifications were rather suspect in the early period but became more dependable during the eighteenth century. In 1769 surgeons were required to be examined by a physician in the presence of two Directors, bringing Company practice into line with that of the Navy. In later years a diploma had to be produced by the candidate. Nevertheless, as late as 1800 David Scott could write to a friend, 'The lowest medical officer in the Company's employ is Surgeon Mate of an Indiaman then Surgeon,' and not 'at all equal to a Surgeon's appointment in the Company's service.'[9] It is evident that mutual compatibility between officers and professional men and the captain resulted in a long association. Sam Baggot served as fourth mate on the *Earl of Abergavenny* under Captain John Wordsworth in 1796, second mate in 1798 and first mate under the latter's cousin John Wordsworth when he assumed command in 1800, remaining in that position until her wreck in 1805. C H Stewart served both commanders as purser for three voyages, as did the surgeon, John Laing.

East India ships were alone among merchantmen in carrying all the tradesmen: gunner, cooper, caulker, sailmaker, joiner, armourer, poulterer, butcher; even tailors were listed in the complements of early ships. Assistants made up the total: the first and second mates, the surgeon and the petty-officers – the boatswain, carpenter and gunner – each had his own servant. The captain had two servants, a clerk, a steward, a cook and a tailor. The boatswain and carpenter each had two mates, the surgeon and cooper had one.

The seamen made up only half the Company on an India ship. One or two of the more experienced were promoted to quartermaster and received a few extra shillings a month. Music was very important on board and the commanders usually ensured that a few men proficient in playing a musical instrument formed part of the Company. In the early years one of the most highly paid was the trumpeter, whose job was to add dignity to the commander's approach. There are fre-

quent references in journals and diaries to captains' bands. William Hickey never heard anything that pleased him more than the wonderful music that woke him on the morning following the *Plassey*'s arrival at Whampoa in 1769. Each of the foreign ships had an 'excellent band, consisting of every description of wind and martial instruments, the whole striking up the moment the sun appeared above the horizon, continuing to play for an hour. The same thing was done in the evening, an hour previous to sunset.'[10]

The pay was determined by the free market: it was slightly higher than that operating in short safe voyages, lower than that in ships where unhealthy conditions prevailed such as the slave trade. The normal peacetime rate varied little during the whole period, apart from a rise after about 1650, chiefly because seamen had to be lured from serving in Dutch ships at a time when the supply was still very limited. The higher rates were maintained for the rest of the century but fell slightly in the following hundred years. Edward Barlow's pay as chief mate during the last thirty years of the seventeenth century was consistently higher than that of chief mates in the succeeding century. By 1770 it was up to 26s in the Company's service, the same as that paid in the brief lull in hostilities in 1803. What appears to be incredible stability in wage rates is illustrated by comparing those on Samuel Braund's ships in 1746 and the Company's own ships in 1813, in each case inflated by war. Apart from the pay received by the surgeon and his mate and the butcher who all benefited from a gradual rise in status the rates are exactly the same. Since food and accommodation were found the rates compare very favourably with a weekly wage of 6s for a farm labourer and 14s for a London artisan.

The day before the ship sailed from Gravesend the crew received two months' wages in advance, a practice adopted early in the Company's life; by the end of the seventeenth century other merchant ship owners were constrained to follow the Company's lead. Before sailing the crew made arrangements for their next of kin or a friend to receive one month's wages for each six months the ship was absent. Absence money was paid to the person designated through the medium of the Company's paymaster, to whom the husbands of the ships made available the necessary sums.

At first sight it is difficult to understand why men signed on in the ships employed in the Company's service. Certainly the pay was no better than in other trades, and all the disadvantages of a seaman's life in those days were magnified on long voyages: long periods at sea living on salt victuals rotting in the barrel in the tropics, the likelihood of death from shipwreck or from malaria or the 'bloody flux' prevalent in the eastern seas. Until long after the Company's exodus from trade, seamen had few rights and those on long voyages suffered far more from the complaints common amongst seamen in those days. In the last years of the old Company, service in

Company ships was not popular. When Captain Knox threatened to take action against the securities of some of the seamen who had run off with his ship, the *Tonqueen Merchant*, at St Helena, the Committees tried to persuade him 'earnestly to forbeare prosecuting for this reason, that the Company had a very bad name already and that this would make theire name so bad that they should have no seamen to serve them hereafter.'[11]

Chief among the seamen's complaints was the dependence of their wages on the safe return of the cargo, even though its loss or damage was in no way due to their negligence. Another complaint was the long delay – often up to five or six months – in payment of wages while the cargo was checked. This was one of the grievances dealt with in the Act for the Better Regulation and Government of Seamen in the Merchant Service of 1729, providing for the seamen to be paid on their final discharge or within thirty days of the ship's entry at the Custom House, whichever was earlier. This act also provided for contracts to be signed by the seamen stating the voyage for which they were taken on, thus avoiding the prolongation of voyages such as that of the *Return* discussed earlier, and the pay they were to receive. Seamen lost all their wages if the ship was captured, which most affected those undertaking long voyages. All that Edward Barlow received for his voyage on the *Experiment*, taken by the Dutch in the Straits of Banca in December 1672 on her return from a voyage to Formosa, was his two months' advance pay, the absence money paid to his sister and 55s charity money – a total of seven months' pay for sixteen months' work. Taken as a prisoner to Holland he finally arrived back in England in September 1671, three years and two months after his departure from the Downs.

The same applied if a man was dismissed during a voyage. Barlow signed on in the *Delight*, commanded by Captain Smith, bound to China in January 1683. While loading at Achin the captain threatened Barlow with a carpenter's adze during a disagreement, and when Barlow stayed his hand Captain Smith sent him off the ship. He was left to fend for himself in a place seldom visited by European ships, dependent on the charity of the natives and European captains of country ships until he managed to get a passage as far as Bengal. From there he shipped back to London as chief mate on the *Kent*, the former chief mate having assumed the command on the captain's death. On his return Barlow approached the Company for redress but all the advice he received was to take his case to court, a course he had insufficient means to pursue.

Despite the obvious disadvantages of serving in ships employed in the long voyages to the east, there were also many compensations. The lure of the east and the desire for adventure and seeing strange lands were powerful attractions; for every month spent at sea on salt victuals there was at least a fortnight in port on good fresh beef to compensate. The

eastern trade offered the opportunity of combining adventure and profit: the officers, purser, surgeon, petty officers and some of the tradesmen were included in the list of those allowed a portion of the permitted private trade and it was an unimaginative seaman who could not find a corner in his chest to hide away a few articles that would 'answer' in England.

Adventure went hand in hand with possible enrichment. East India ships were always taken on 'in Trade as also in Warfare' and carried the King's commission. With the exception of two very brief interludes, naval ships never ventured round the Cape of Good Hope until the commencement of warfare with France in the mid-eighteenth century. The Company's ships and men had a dual role: to open up the trade and also to defend it. Within a few years of the Company's foundation seamen were engaged in war with the Dutch in the tiny Banda Islands which by geological accident were the sole producers of the coveted spices nutmegs, cloves and mace which the Dutch were intent on monopolising. Two ships were sent to occupy the island of Run and to 'stand up to the "Flemings" to the utmost of their powers . . . even to the loss of lives and goods.' Pulo Run's surrender was accepted and Dutch ships coming to inspect could not produce anything to countermand it, but later the *Swan* was attacked and captured with loss of life. The reason given that the Dutch 'could not suffer any other [nation] under any other circumstances to enjoy the traffic of spices acquired at such cost in Banda, Amboyna and the Moluccas' and were under orders 'forcibly to drive them out of Pularoon and Banda.' A survivor recorded that after the *Defence* fell into Dutch hands; 'they kept twelve of us in a dungeon where they pisst and shatt upon our heads and in this manner we lay until we were broken out from top to toe like lepers, having nothing to eat but durtie rice and stinking rain water.'[12]

Although the Company was notoriously tight-fisted it recognised that rewarding those who put themselves out to protect its property was in its own interests, and it had the advantage of large metropolitan establishments where victims of such efforts could be placed. The Company had an excellent record on the welfare of its employees. Typical was the situation in which the men of the *Morrice* found themselves on arrival at Bombay from Surat in 1718. A full-scale attack was being launched by the Company's Marine on the stronghold of a neighbouring local ruler with whom the Company was engaged in a struggle for control of the Konkan seaways. The President of Bombay told the men of the *Morrice* 'that if any would go Volunteers for the next Days Service, that they should be paid at their Arrival at Bombay 40 Rupees, which is about £5 Sterling, and whoever should lose a Leg or Arm in the said Expedition, should have £30 paid by the Company at their Arrival in London and be employed in their Service during Life.'[13] Forty volunteers offered their services, cheered by the promise of £30 for their widows and 10s for each child should they perish during the battle. John Steele, carpenter's mate, almost cut through the bar of the gate before being cut down himself. An officer was killed leading the seamen in the day's attack, and by the following morning sixty men had lost their lives and many more were wounded before the attacking force could be landed on shore under covering fire from the Company's frigates. Clement Downing, who served in the Company's Marine in this and other actions, felt that the East India Company were 'worthy to be served above all the merchants in Great Britain for the care they take of those who receive Damage, and also for the widows of those who are killed in the Service.'

The rewards offered to the men of the *Morrice* were standard. The United Company recognised that a sailor loves a fight and encouraged him to indulge his natural instincts to the Company's advantage, an enlightened attitude singularly lacking in the old Company which frequently failed to reward men who had put themselves at risk defending Company property. The charter parties laid down that before the ships' departure from the Hope an order 'for the Encouragement of all the Mariners', written in 'large legible characters' should be displayed 'in the most Visible Place' throughout the voyage. John Deane was rewarded with a pension of £100 per annum, his wife to receive £50 per annum if she survived him – which she did – and eventually the position of foreman in the Company's drug warehouse for his efforts to save the *Sussex*. Her commander, Captain Gostlin, ordered the crew to abandon ship during a storm off the Cape of Good Hope in March 1738, but Deane and a handful of men refused, determined to 'stand by the ship at all hazards.' Their efforts were unsuccessful, the ship striking the Bassas de India, a dangerous shoal in the Mozambique Channel, while they were attempting to run for St Augustine's Bay. Only Deane survived to return to London in the autumn of 1739.

The Poplar Fund, from which pensions and compensation for those maimed or killed in the Company's service were paid and an almshouse built (Poplar Hospital), was started as early as 1619 with the fortuitous bequest of the ill-gotten gains of a Company factor together with 'some other remaynders of old accompts'. Two pence in the pound was levied on all Company salaries and gradually odd sums were added to swell the fund. A contribution was at first taken from the seamen's wages but this caused such an outcry it was discontinued in 1633. By the time Cromwell's Naval Commissioners were seriously putting their minds to the thorny question of pensions for the state navy the Company's fund amounted to over £2000. By 1679 it was over £3500, fifty years later four times as much; by 31 December 1827 it had risen to £163,000. In 1734 men employed in the Company's service were exempt from paying the seamen's six pence per month to support Greenwich Hospital, and the two pence in the pound contri-

John Deane, the only survivor of the *Sussex*, was one of the many seamen rewarded by the Company for their efforts to save valuable property and cargo. *(BL OIOC)*

bution was renewed. In answer to the Board of Control's request in 1784 for details of the Fund's sources of income, the Company stated that it was:

> supported by subscriptions of gentlemen on their being elected Directors, by some few voluntary contributions, by a duty of sixpence a gallon upon arrack, 2 shillings per ton upon ships taken into the service, 1 ¼% poundage on the amount of the wages of the commanders, officers and others employed on board them, exceedings of purserage, fines for the breach of charter parties, and various other mulcts.[14]

Out of this there was an annual expenditure of £3666.[15] Soon after the fund was started a house was purchased with room for twenty poor men. It got off to an inauspicious start with the first two inhabitants: one of them was drunk and disorderly, the other, showing more ingenuity than moral fervour, when told that he could not take his wife to live with him, took another man's wife and cohabited for six years before his deception was discovered. These premises were pulled down in 1802 and replaced by improved dwellings with twelve better class houses for commanders or mates and their widows; a

The East India Company almshouse at Poplar.
(*London Borough of Tower Hamlets Local History Library and Archives*)

further six were added six years later. All were pulled down in 1866 and the inmates pensioned off.

Whatever it was that attracted men to serve in the ships hired by the Company, there was little difficulty manning outward-bound ships in peacetime, but the outbreak of war brought all sorts of problems in its wake. As naval lieutenants trawled the banks of the Thames for seamen, wages increased immediately: on the commencement of hostilities in 1740 they rose sharply, rocketing to an all time high in the late 1750s during the Seven Years' War when seamen were demanding and receiving up to 70s. On the sudden renewal of the war with France in 1803 seamen already taken on at peacetime rates refused to weigh anchor until their wages were stepped up to the wartime rate of 45s. Henry Bonham, husband to several East Indiamen, resorted to the distribution of a bounty of £342 amongst the crew of the *Essex* and £264 amongst that of the *Lord Melville* as a means of persuading the crews to sail. Down river at Gravesend other husbands were agreeing to the full wartime rate to get their ships away. Letters from the husbands to the Committee of Shipping on the commencement of war in 1793 with its attendant sudden shortage of manpower are litanies of extra costs: bounties, 'crimpage' paid to the men who recruited the down and outs along the River by fair means or foul, extra wages, expense of replacing pressed men.

The problem was exacerbated by the need to take on more men to serve the extra guns the company exhorted the owners to ship. In November 1803, soon after the Company had agreed to meet the expense of shipping more men, John Pascall Larkins suggested to the Committee of Shipping that the *Walmer Castle* should have additional armament as she was sailing a single ship from St Helena to Benkulen. The Company sanctioned twenty additional men on the voyage out, their names to be sent to the Company, but stipulated that during her stay in China any men exceeding her compliment should be sent to other Company ships by the supercargoes. Ten guineas were to be allowed for the additional seamen in addition to their wages and 1/- per day diet money but the Company were to be at no expense for the voyage home for any men not left in China. The owners pressed for £20 per man to be paid in advance within two months of the ship leaving England.[16]

The sudden resumption of peace could have its problems too as is shown by a hastily scrawled note written on 14 March 1783 by John Mavor, husband Robert Williams' accountant, to Stephen Williams, captain of the *Sullivan*, at Portsmouth. He enclosed a list of men including the surgeon, gunner, several tradesmen, the fifth mate and midshipmen who had signed on at the India House at the war wages, begging him to get them to sign a new contract at the reduced peacetime rates which he had not managed to get done at Gravesend. 'You will see that it is of moment as unless this is done they will have it in their power to claim the original wages they have signed the contract for and by that means bring a heavy expense on the owners. Be so good as [sic] be careful of the contract as it must be lodged in Mr William's hands as security against the seamen's claims.'[17] There were also problems with men running away after receiving their

Bombay by George Lambert and Samuel Scott, 1732, with East India Company ships in the Harbour and the Custom House in the background.

(BL OIOC)

two months' advance wages at Gravesend, the official commencement of the voyage. 'You can have no idea of the trouble I have had in procuring men for the ship, of the tricks that have been played on me by running away . . . If we lose not more than 500£ in the manning of our ship I shall be satisfied,' Captain John Wordsworth wrote to his sister Dorothy in March 1801.[18]

Ships were in danger of losing their passage for want of men, since they were in direct competition with the navy for the best seamen. There was no restriction on pressing in the Channel in the early days. Shortage of men through pressing contributed to an eight month delay in the departure of the *Septer* in 1695. She sailed from Gravesend on 28 September but was immediately ordered to Spithead to rendezvous with a large merchant fleet and await convoy. While there a 'hot press' arose on the news of a threatened French invasion backed by the exiled James II and a large number of the *Septer*'s men were taken to man Admiral Russell's fleet. The *Septer* put in at Portsmouth to find hands but with little success. Some were returned early in May from the King's ships as the crisis evaporated but she was still short. Captain Phenney went up to London with orders to fill up with Danes and Dutch and it was not until 19 May that she eventually sailed in convoy with ninety merchant ships and nine men of war.

On the outbreak of war with the American colonists, the Company managed to persuade the Admiralty that it was counterproductive to delay the departure of Company ships dependent on the monsoon, thus possibly causing them to lose their passage. In 1776 the Admiralty granted protections not only to the crews of Company ships but also to its pilot boats, hoys and watermen. Only when the navy was in the most desperate circumstances, as in the late 1770s and after the renewal of war in 1803, were men pressed out of outward bound Indiamen; even then they were usually returned by Admiralty order.

There was no protection from impressment in the Channel for the men in homeward bound India ships. Men who could already glimpse the cliffs of Dover frequently mutinied when the pressing sloops approached. The log of the *Halsewell* records that on Sunday 28 October as she approached the Nore on her return from Bengal:

At noon came on board two of His Majesties Lieutenants to impress our men which they resisted and armed to defend themselves. At 5pm weighed and at 1/2 past 9 pm past the Conquistadore at the Nore, was fired at by several ships but could not bring our ship too. The people refusing to clew the sails up or let go the anchor. His Majesties frigate the *Albermarle* Captain Nelson kept firing shot at us one of which struck off the chick [sic] of the main mast another through the main topsail several overhead. When the officer came to let go the top sail halyards found them ripped aloft. At last with difficulty the Chief and Fourth mate let go the anchor the ship being head right on for the shore and having fresh weigh when brought up found ourselves in ½ fathom. The lights of the Nore SE. Came on board Captain Nelson with offers to our people which they all refused.' On the following morning 'came on board again Captain Nelson who told the people if they refused serving His Majesty he must bring the frigate alongside. After much Trouble and difficulty they got all our people and left only the foreigners and servants promising to bring men in the evening. At 8pm came a lieutenant with 24 men to work the ship up to her moorings.[19]

On their part, the commanders were ordered not to take on board deserters from naval ships; naval captains suspected Company commanders of positively enticing men from their ships, a suspicion fuelled by the commanders' frequent refusal to allow search. They were sorely tempted as they viewed their third-rate wartime crews but were deterred by the dire consequences. Writing to his cousin on the eve of his departure from Portsmouth in January 1805 Captain Wordsworth described his crew as 'trash' but conceded, 'bad as we are I believe we are better than any ship of the season. I could get men here and very good men, but if I was caught shipping men that belonged to the Navy I should be dismissed the service.'[20] The previous March, the Commander-in-Chief Portsmouth threatened to impress the whole company of any ship harbouring deserters.[21]

No protections were extended to India ships' companies on

In his *Days at the Factories*, published in 1840, George Dodd recorded the crafts he had witnessed on his visit to Green, Wigram and Green's shipyard. Here a shipwright uses an auger to bore trenail holes in a ship's planks.

(Museum of London, Docklands Collection)

eastern stations when naval squadrons appeared from the mid-eighteenth century. From this time on there was an ever present possibility that men would be pressed out of India ships at Madras or Bengal. 'We are sorry to find,' wrote the Governor at Fort St George to the Council at Canton by the *Winchelsea* which arrived 17 June 1759 'that the Company's ships of last season are likely to be so much distressed by the want of men who were taken out of them for the Service of His Majesty's Squadron, it was done by the Admiral's own authority, and it is not in our power to prevent it.'[22]

Captains frequently complained to the Indian governments that they were not able to proceed to Calcutta because of loss of men through pressing. Captain Kymer of the *Lord Castlereagh* wrote on 27 February 1807 that his surgeon had died and his surgeon's mate had been taken out, leaving him with no medical assistance on board.[23] The capture of the *Warren Hastings* by the French frigate *Piemontaise* on 21 June 1806 when returning from Canton shows the dangers to which ships carrying valuable cargoes were exposed. Eighteen of Captain Larkins' seamen, probably his best, had been pressed into naval ships at Canton, and forty Chinese had remained there, leaving only one hundred and thirty-eight to sail the ship and man the guns against Captain Epron's three hundred and eighty-five.

Company ships frequently carried out men for HM ships in India but nevertheless had more men pressed out. Company lists based on the commanders' ledgers showed that, for instance, in 1808 fifty-seven ships arriving back in England had had one thousand one hundred and seventy-seven men pressed in India, leaving an average of one hundred and sixteen men. Incomplete records for 1809 showed that thirty-seven Indiamen had had six hundred and twenty-six men pressed in India leaving an average of only one hundred per ship on arrival in England.[24] The situation in which the *Castle Eden* found herself returning to the Channel from Bengal in 1808 with several other Indiamen in convoy of HMS *Monmouth* revealed the dangers. Before land was sighted the fleet was ordered to heave-to and a lieutenant sent on board the *Castle Eden* with orders to take five men there and a further twenty-five on anchoring in the Downs. Only a few days previously the French prisoners on board the *Castle Eden* had rioted and the motley wartime crew had appeared more disposed to support the prisoners than their officers. Order had only been restored by the bravery of the petty officers who had stood up to the prisoners despite being threatened with clasp knives and managed to put them under restraint. Captain Colnett assured the lieutenant that he would protest as he was already undermanned, having fifteen men less than his complement and scarcely a real seaman amongst them. The lieutenant contented himself with three men and on arrival in the Downs no further men were taken, but another lieutenant in a yawl from a sloop of war came on board and

A caulker drives oakum into the seams between planks of a ship's hull using a caulking iron to make the hull watertight.

(Museum of London, Docklands Collection)

A sailmaker reinforces the edge of a sail with rope.

(Museum of London, Docklands Collection)

called for the ship's company to be mustered. He took off twenty-two men, Captain Colnett impressing upon him that in doing so he made himself responsible for upwards of £200,000, the value of the ship and cargo, but all the answer he received was the usual: 'Let them look out that's got the watch.' Following the heavy losses of 1809 the Admiralty introduced regulations confining impressment to the Indian stations and the Channel and limiting it to specified proportions of men and petty officers.

The commanders of Company ships made up their crews depleted by sickness, desertion or pressing with Chinese and Lascars, an Arab people who settled on the west coast of India and formed a distinct race of seamen in a non-seafaring continent. Notoriously cowardly and prone to cold by reputation, they were considered a necessary evil to maintain the numbers of seamen required by the charter party. Recruiting of Lascars was a highly organised system.[25] A *ghant serang* in the port contracted to furnish a crew for an agreed sum, making his own bargain with individuals. His agent on board ship was the *serang* who acted as boatswain, seeing that the men carried out the officers' orders, maintained the level of discipline required by the captain and paid out the money given by the owners. The commanders were given very detailed instructions on the diet, management and care of Lascars in their charge. On the ships' arrival at Gravesend a surgeon reported on the men's condition. After disembarking the Lascars were handed over to agents who contracted to lodge them and feed them in barracks until berths could be found for them on returning Indiamen. By the early nineteenth century the con-

dition of the Lascars particularly was causing concern and the House of Commons appointed a committee to consider if the Act 54 Geo III cap 134 which regulated the treatment of Lascars and Chinese required additions. In their report to the House, the committee pointed to the frequent overcrowding at the barracks, one thousand to one thousand one hundred often arriving at the same time. There was no separate accommodation for the sick so disease spread rapidly. However, the cold climate appeared to be the cause of most deaths, exacerbated by the men's habit of selling their bedding and clothes to finance a dissolute and licentious life. The Chinese fared better as they were naturally cleaner, though the accommodation was very overcrowded on the arrival of a large China fleet. The committee concluded that agency was no longer the best method of dealing with them now that they were so numerous: a properly instituted establishment was needed away from the populous quarter of London. The committee were satisfied that there were no abuses by the English or the *serangs*, but in 1814 following this report new regulations were brought in.

Lascars and Chinese were shipped back to the east on the outward bound ships at the Company's expense. Their conditions were not necessarily improved when they were taken on board. William Docker, Master Attendant, reported in a letter to the Committee of Shipping on 28 May of the generally ill state of the Lascars on board the *Walmer Castle* and the *Glatton* due to scantiness of bedding, which they had probably sold, and ordered rugs to be given out, to which the husband John Pascall Larkins agreed. A few days later William

Docker complained that though several Lascars on board the *Admiral Rainier* had mortified feet, they were receiving no medical attention. He directed the owners to get medical assistance to them and see that care was given.[26]

Few commanders had a good word for either Lascars or Chinese. Samuel Braund did not mince his words: 'The Owners recommend to ye Captains to avoid Shipping of Lascars if possible on any account, they choosing to pay ye Company for what is brought home short of ye Compliment[sic].' During the protracted discussion on whether or not to bring charges against the owners of the *Nottingham* for breaking Company regulations it was revealed that she had sailed from Canton with only one hundred and four instead of the charter party regulation number of one hundred and twenty-seven. Captain Anderson produced written instructions from the owners not to enter any Chinese while he had one hundred men left. The Shipping Committee questioned whether the owners could give premeditated orders before leaving England in direct contravention of charter party requirements. Captain Dale of the *Streatham* reported to the Governor of Prince of Wales Island, following an action early in September 1809, that his defence was confined to the main deck so he had sent an officer below 'to encourage the people at the guns'; however, he had been unable to keep the Chinese and Portuguese to their stations. In the same action Captain Gelston of the *Europe*, which had struck, said his Lascars were 'only in the way' though Captain Campbell of the *Caroline* was more charitable: he had had every support from the officers, passengers and the people – 'especially the people as mainly foreigners and native seamen – indeed only four British subjects before the mast remaining.'[27]

The Company's tireless efforts to get some satisfaction from the navy on the thorny question of impressment were matched by its persistent attempts to persuade the government to codify the obsolete requirements of the Navigation Acts. Passed during the middle years of the seventeenth century to create the conditions in which a strong maritime force could develop, these acts laid down that three quarters of the crew should be Englishmen and that this proportion should be maintained throughout the voyage. This was patently absurd in wartime since the English seamen's pool was not sufficient to man both Navy and merchant fleet. It was not possible to fulfil these conditions on leaving England – let alone maintain them during the voyage. The *Earl of Abergavenny*, which sailed for Bengal and Canton in 1805 had only sixty-three Englishmen in her crew of one hundred and fourteen. Of the rest about one third were Portuguese; there were several Italians and Irish and the rest were from Russia, America and every country in Europe. Yet Cornet Burgoyne, travelling on board to Bengal, could agree with her captain that 'Her crew was by no means a bad one, she was much better off than many Indiamen that sail from England in wartime.'[28] Eventually the government conceded the point by reversing the ratio, allowing three Lascars to one British seaman. Even this was not sufficient: not until a few years before the Company's exit from trade removed the problem did the government really meet the Company's demands. 'Whereas Lascars and other natives of the east are not deemed to be equal in strength and use to European and other seamen' the Act of 1823 at last admitted, it was henceforth permissible to ship as many Lascars as was thought necessary, provided there were four English seamen to every 100 tons of the ship's registered burthen. Even this clause was modified since it was not always possible to find four English seamen for every 100 tons: the governor of the settlement to which the ship was consigned was permitted to give the ship a licence to proceed even if she did not carry the required number.

Notes:

1. Hickey: *op cit*, Vol 1, 198.
2. 2 and 3 Anne, c6.
3. BL OIOC L/MAR/C644.
4. Eastwick: *op cit*, 60.
5. Guildhall Library. Memorandum Book: op cit, 21 May 1812.
6. Rand: *op cit*,
7. BL OIOC. L/MAR/C325, 23 May 1795: Letter from James Caggan.
8. BL OIOC. L/MAR/C531 f496, Committee of Shipping, 19 October 1791.
9. Scott: *op cit*, Vol II, no. 305: Scott to Sir William Grant, 29 August 1800.
10. Hickey: *op cit*, Vol 1, 197-198.
11. Knox: *op cit*, 339.
12. Keay: *op cit*, 43-47.
13. Downing Clement: *A Compendious History of the Indian Wars* (1737).
14. Foster, Sir William: *John Company* (1926) 169.
15. By the latter part of the eighteenth century pensions of £18 per annum for midshipmen to £100 per annum for commanders were paid, depending on pensioner's income and capital, and between £18 for a midshipman's widow and £100 for a commander's widow. Eight years' service was necessary to qualify for a pension but this was waived if the claimant had been maimed or wounded defending his ship and was incapable of further service at sea. Seamen's pensions were from £4.16s.
16. BL OIOC. L/MAR/C27(2), 25 November 1803, f34-36.
17. BL OIOC. Eur Ms D1051/1
18. Rand: *op cit*.
19. BL OIOC. L/MAR/B Log of the *Halsewell*,
20. Rand: *op cit*.
21. PRO ADM 1/3915, 14 March 1804.
22. Morse: *op cit*, Vol V, 73.
23. BL OIOC.L/MAR/1/23.
24. *Ibid*
25. BL OIOC. L/MAR/C902: problems presented by recruitment and care of Lascars.
26. BL OIOC. L/MAR/C27(2): numbers 109, 110, 111 of 9 December 1803.
27. BL OIOC. L/MAR/1/23: commanders' reports to governor of Prince of Wales Island.
28. Rand: *op cit*,

CHAPTER 7
PREPARING
FOR THE
VOYAGE

Every year between early September and late February successive fleets of ships taken up by the Company anchored first in Long Reach then at Gravesend to take in supplies. Scores of lighters – some belonging to the Company bringing cargo and treasure from its wharves in London, some hired by the husbands or suppliers carrying stores and provisions – plied up and down the twenty or so miles of river between London and Gravesend. For about six weeks a couple of mates and the boatswain, aided by a skeleton crew, loaded and stowed hundreds of chests, bales and casks on each ship in preparation for the departure.

All the stores and provisions were carefully vetted by the Company. A complete list of all the ship's supplies was submitted by the husband of each ship to the Company's waiters or inspectors who in turn passed it on to the Court of Directors for their approval. Husband Samuel Braund's papers include an order of the Court dated 25 November 1742:

A view of Blackwall looking towards Greenwich, 1750.

That ye following Articles being Certified to ye Company's Waiters by ye Husband of each ship to be Stores for ye Ship's use in the common and usual Package, may be received on board the respective ships without sealing, ye said waiters being ordered to take such Examination and Inspection as they shall think fit.[1]

Before the ships sailed the waiters spent several days checking that the goods on board tallied with the list earlier submitted. Provisioning the ships in the very early days, before the company established settlements in the East where ships could restock with essential supplies, was a daunting task: ships bound for Bantam were provisioned for two years and those for Surat for eighteen months. By the mid-eighteenth century owners' instructions to commanders stated that seven months' provisions should be sufficient for a voyage.

Amongst the most essential consignments brought down by lighter to Long Reach were guns, the gunner's and armourer's stores, barrels of powder, a forge to make ammunition of various types during the voyage, with a supply of grenade shells, moulds for bullets and shot, with lead and soldering copper. The Company required the owners to provide a chest containing specified small arms and weapons for hand-to-hand fighting in case an enemy boarded the ship. Those supplied by John Bunford, gunsmith, for the *Boscawen*'s stores in 1748 included blunderbusses but otherwise differed only in quantity from those carried by the *Sulivan* in 1783, the *Hindostan* in 1787 and the Company's own ship HCS *Buckinghamshire* in 1821. These weapons comprised a whole sub-category of arms which came to be known as 'India ship store': muskets, bayonets, musquetoons, swivels, pistols, poleaxes, cutlasses with scabbards, together with all the necessary materials for servicing them and making the ammunition. Each of these weapons had to be submitted prior to the voyage to the Company's 'viewer' who stamped it to show that it came up to the specified standard.[2]

The gunner's standard stores included all the paint required for repainting the ship prior to her return voyage. Little is known about the colours of these ships before the latter part of the Company's trading life; the paints included in the *Boscawen*'s stores in 1749 – Prussian blue, copper, vermilion, ochre, red and white lead – suggest bright but tasteful colours.

All essential supplies for maintenance and repair work had to be carried on board. Large quantities of timber, oak and deal plank, sheathing board and treenails were required by the carpenter. The caulker's stores included several hundredweight of 'old junk' – old cable for shredding to make oakum – with barrels of pitch and tar for caulking and paying the lower masts and the rigging and tallow, turpentine, oil and rosin for paying the upper works and the upper masts and yards. Several tons of spare cordage was the chief item in the boatswain's stores. The sailmaker needed up to twenty bolts of

THE "SILENT HIGHWAY"-MAN.

The East Indiamen's supply of drinking water, taken from the River Thames below the capital, was always notoriously fetid. Londoner's growing concern at the polluted state of the river is forcefully expressed in this cartoon from *Punch*, dated 1858. *(Museum of London, Docklands Collection)*

spare canvas, as well as spare suits of old and new sails. Sheet lead, iron and hides were shared by the carpenter, gunner and armourer; billet wood and chaldrons of coals were needed for the galley fire and the armourer's forge; tallow, cotton and oil for the lanterns, and fodder for the livestock.

By far the most important item in the ships' provisions was water. The *Durrington*'s victualling bill (see Appendix 7) states 'what shall be thought fit but not less than forty tons', which appears to have been general for ships carrying a crew of a hundred men. The water was taken straight out of the Thames, filthy and stinking. The most fastidious passengers carried their own filtering machines to remove the noxious scum, but they could do nothing to improve the colour or diminish the foul odour emanating from it. The character of the water underwent a series of changes during the voyage and eventually sweetened and cleared considerably. Thames water was generally considered to be the best for sea store amongst seafaring folk, a view which was shared by the company's servants in India. Francis Rogers, visiting Surat in 1703, noted in his diary: 'Thames water highly valued by the Factors after having purged so often in our passage'.[3] Oddly enough, its ultimate purity lay in its initial extreme foulness, as John Bostock discovered when he carried out experiments in 1829.[4] Thames water contained so much organic substance, chiefly animal, that a type of fermentation was set off without the addition of any other element. During the fermentation process the organic substances discharged gases, leaving the valuable salts behind. Unfortunately, the people on board were obliged to drink it during its many stages of depuration, adding to the general discomfort of the passage.

In 1803 the Court of Directors recommended to the owners that they 'carry on board a machine for purifying water and a still'.[5]

Of course, water was no more the staple drink at sea than on land in those hard-drinking days. Small beer was the chief thirst-quencher, water being used only for tea. Cases, casks and bottles of a variety of alcoholic liquors cluttered the ships. The *Durrington*'s list of stores for 1746 included 1 ton of ale, strong beer, cider or rum; 40 tons of small beer; 250 gallons of brandy or strong English spirit; 6 tons of wine in casks, and for each seaman, a cask of brandy or strong waters not exceeding 6 gallons. By the time the ships reached the Eastern seas the beer, which travelled badly, was probably undrinkable, but arrack was available. In Edward Barlow's time the seamen were allowed a pint of arrack a day when the beer was done. The most popular variety of arrack, which was distilled from sugar-cane, the juice of the coconut tree, or rice, came from Batavia. Opinions differ on its effects, probably because the arrack itself varied enormously; some contemporary accounts suggest it was similar to beer, and quite wholesome; others attribute the high death rate at Batavia and Benkulen to the great consumption of arrack.

Next in importance to the water and other beverages came

the bread, actually biscuit – bread baked at least twice – hard and usually full of weevils. Young Hickey, going out on the *Plassey* in 1769, recorded 'There was nothing I felt the want of so much as bread', especially as the biscuit on the *Plassey* was 'uncommonly hard and flinty'.[6] One of his fellow passengers bet another that he could not eat one in four minutes without a drink and lost his bet by only a few seconds. In fairness to the biscuit baker it should be noted that when Captain Waddell rewarded some natives on the Coromandel coast with a bag of these same biscuits they were overjoyed, ship's biscuit being considered a great delicacy among them.

It was the following year that Alexander Dalrymple asked his correspondent the French hydrographer D'Après de Mannevillette, 'As I much wish to introduce the custom so laudably pursued on board the French India Ships of baking bread for the Sailors, I shall esteem it a very great favour if You will procure for me a Baker who has been a Voyage to India, with some description of the Oven you use . . .'[7]

Rivalling the biscuit in unpopularity among the crew was the 'salt horse' or 'hard salt junk' as the salt beef and pork which formed the crew's staple diet during the voyage was called. The Indiamen's crews were luckier than many, however, as only the best parts of the beasts were allowed. There

One of Cruikshank's well-known exaggerated representations of life aboard a Company ship – but the reality was often no less amusing.

(National Maritime Museum)

were several incidents of commanders exchanging their good quality provisions for poor and taking the balance. A total of 25 tons of salt beef, salt pork, suet and tongues were carried on the *Durrington* in 1746, the pork and beef costing on average 22 shillings per hundredweight. Large quantities of bay, or sea, salt and saltpetre were carried for salting down beasts for the return voyage. 1lb of meat required 2oz each of salt and saltpetre for the salting process. The cooper must have been fully occupied in tending the water casks and the saltmeat casks to stop leaks caused by the movement of the ship. One of the many uses for the large amounts of vinegar carried on these ships was culinary, as it helped to make rancid meat palatable. Dried fish was served to the crew on meatless days. This was chiefly stock-fish – Norwegian haddock or hake, beaten flat – with smaller quantities of ling, and red and white herrings. The other staples of the crew's diet at sea were dried peas and beans, used to make stews, and cereals for puddings and porridge. Cheese and butter were shipped in fairly large quantities in casks for the crew; the 13 double Gloucester cheeses and 25 Cheshire cheeses supplied to the *Boscawen* in 1749 were no doubt for the captain's table.

In the first voyage, while the crews of the other ships in the fleet were badly affected by scurvy, James Lancaster kept the disease at bay in the *Red Dragon* by administering daily doses of lemon juice to the crew. In 1612 the company's surgeon-general advised the ships' surgeons that 'The use of the juice of Lemmons is a precious medicine and well tried . . .'[8] Lemon juice appeared on the victualling bills of Company ships one hundred and eighty years before it was made compulsory by the Royal Navy and lemon or lime juice continued to be included after the Company changed to the freighting system. In 1803 the Court of Directors recommended that the ships carry one gallon of lemon juice for every four men both out and home, though limes bought in India could be substituted on the return passage.[9] Raisins, currants, fresh bread, mouthwashes with vinegar and salt water, and watercress crushed in ale were also considered cures for scurvy until long after James Lind's definitive experiments in 1747 proved beyond all doubt that oranges and lemons effected an immediate cure for those sickening from the disease. This probably accounts at least in part for the huge quantities of raisins and currants carried on the ships in the Company's service.

The livestock, chiefly for the use of the captain's table, were the last part of the provisions to be loaded for the voyage.

Shoal waters presented a hazard from Cape Comorin to the mouths of the Ganges. A French ship is shown aground at False Point on the delta of the Mahandi.

(BL OIOC)

A view of East India Company ships at Blackwall.

With the great increase in passengers towards the end of the eighteenth century the East Indiamen became floating farmyards, but a fair number of beasts and large numbers of poultry were carried from the very earliest times. They led a wretched existence on board, the sheep crowded into the longboat, the poultry in pens on the poop . . . the first victims in a gale. Supplies were replenished wherever the ship touched: bullocks were plentiful in most ports, sheep at the Cape, hogs and poultry at ports in India and at Canton.

Several commanders cultivated garden plots on the poop on which they grew vegetables and salad stuffs.

While the ship lay at anchor at Gravesend, the passengers appeared on board to arrange for their berths, adding to the general chaos. 'The ship was in so lumbered a state we could scarcely crawl into the great cabin and the quarterdeck was covered in packages', William Hickey wrote of his visit to the *Plassey* anchored at Gravesend in 1768.[10] There were few passengers until the latter part of the Company's life. Forty passengers sitting down to dine at the captain's table while their children played 'tag' in the steerage was a very late phenomenon.

For almost a century the great cabin, traditionally reserved for company servants, housed an exclusively male society.

Chief among these were the supercargoes, a handful of merchants who travelled out and home with the ship, conducting the Company's trade in the destined ports. Long after the established settlements in India made the supercargoes on India-bound ships superfluous, they remained a feature of those ships bound to the Red Sea and the Persian Gulf and to Canton, since the Company had no settlements there. Although the Chinese permitted the European traders to have splendid factories outside the walls surrounding Canton, they would not allow them to reside there between seasons. Until 1715, the supercargoes on each ship conducted the trade from their ship alone, but after that the supercargoes of each small fleet of ships were grouped together to form a council, one of the supercargoes being appointed chief. From 1761 onwards a nucleus council was resident in Canton throughout the season, migrating to Portuguese Macao after the fleets' departure.

The foremastmen, as their name suggests, inhabited the area forward of the mainmast. The crew's quarters and routine were similar to those found in naval vessels: the hands messed and slung their hammocks in groups between the guns on the main deck. Recruits for the Company's army and royal troops messed and slept in the steerage, the area forward of the bul-

The cot was the most practical berth in rough weather – once you had managed to get into it.
(National Maritime Museum)

warks of the great cabin enclosed by the cabins on either side. Returning Lascars and Chinese must have frequently been herded together like cattle.

Officers and passengers were accommodated in the stern. The captain's cabin was usually in the roundhouse. The officers, surgeon, purser and petty officers had cabins in the steerage, most of which were simply partitioned off by canvas sheets lashed to cleats on the decks above and below. In the last part of the eighteenth century, Company rules forbade the erection of any permanent bulkheads forward of the great cabin, though we know that in earlier ships there were at least four substantial cabins in the steerage. Writers and cadets were accommodated in the great cabin, which was divided up by means of canvas partitions to form as many cabins as were necessary. Important company servants sometimes had the whole of the great cabin to themselves. Captain Sutton of the *Duke of Portland* expressed his regret that he could not accommodate William Hickey in 1777, the whole of the accommodation being engaged by Mr Wheler. On his previous voyage to Madras in 1769 Hickey and two other cadets had shared two thirds of the great cabin and a factor had had the rest to himself. At the end of the eighteenth century when writers and cadets were carried in large numbers on each ship, they were forced to share cramped dormitory accommodation in the steerage, though they often paid up to £100 for their passage if they had a seat at the captain's table. Thomas Twining, a young boy of seventeen travelling out at this time, described going on board ship to find his berth, fighting against the nausea brought on by the indescribable 'smell of the ship'.

Parents took advantage of the vastly increased need for clerks to serve the new government in Bengal and cadets to man the Company's army to get rid of their profligate sons. Their spinster daughters were sent out in increasing numbers to seek advantageous marriages with the wealthy 'nabobs' who were enriching themselves in Bengal. Following close behind were members of the legal profession like William Hickey.

Outnumbering them all were the military, who were shipped out in ever-increasing numbers to fight the numerous wars of the eighteenth and nineteenth centuries. In January 1805 the *Earl of Abergavenny*, Captain John Wordsworth, bound to Bengal and China, anchored on the Motherbank close to the new depot on the Isle of Wight where recruits waited to embark. She took on board twenty-five recruits from the 8th and 24th Light Dragoons and twenty from the 22nd Regiment of infantry, all King's troops, and one hundred and eight recruits for the Company's army in India. Wives and children were not listed in the ships books but the list of survivors of the wreck includes several. There were twenty-six cadets, who, according to the new regulations, were to have a place at the captain's table from the moment of their arrival in Portsmouth to protect them from the multitude of parasites that lay in wait for them in this premier port: 'on no account' were they to sleep out of the ship 'without express orders in writing' from the Committee of Shipping.[11]

As the number of passengers carried on board India-bound ships grew, the roundhouse was increasingly brought into commission to provide passenger accommodation by means of canvas cabins erected in the same manner as in the great cabin. The roundhouse was traditionally the captain's station, as well as the dining area for those who ate at the captain's table and the social centre for the officers and passengers. The great cabin, which had always been considered the best accommodation on board, began to lose favour towards the end of the eighteenth century as the relative peace it afforded in earlier years was eroded by increasing numbers of soldiers and young children carried on board. The ill and ageing William Hickey, returning to England from Bengal in 1808, agreed with Captain Colnett, on the latter's advice, to take the starboard side of the great cabin in preference to the roundhouse, as being on all occasions much quieter, but he regretted his choice. He complained of the perpetual 'horrid screeching and crying' of children going to England for their education, and found their 'vociferous mirth when playing their gambols in the steerage' no better. Added to this there was the constant 'music' of the rudder working and the 'perpetual creaking of the bulkheads'. On the main deck one was always 'half-poisoned by a variety of stinks' and frequently set afloat by the sea breaking in despite the deadlights. Hickey would never recommend anyone to have the lower accommodation if upper was available, the annoyances of the roundhouse being few in comparison with those of a berth between decks.[12]

His view was shared by Emma Roberts, who recommended the upper accommodation especially to the ladies. The roundhouse and cuddy could be reached in a few steps without having to climb stairs, often a difficult operation because of the rolling of the ship. Ladies were also saved the 'offensive circumstances' arising out of having to pass sailors going about their business. Cabins on the upper deck were less likely to be infested with rats and could be kept clean more easily. The noises that had to be tolerated were certainly a disadvantage: there was the constant trampling overhead of men on duty and passengers enjoying a walk on the poop; ropes dragging; blocks falling; and the perpetual cackling and squawking of the poultry – an irritation so universal that by this time many captains had banned the hen coops from the poop – but upper accommodation was on the whole the lesser of the two evils.

Officers and passengers had to provide their own furniture and so travelled in as luxurious or spartan a manner as they wished. William Hickey never saw so handsome an apartment in a ship as the cabin of 'Count' Douglas, third mate of the *Plassey*:

> It was painted of a light pea green, with gold beading, the bed and curtains of the richest Madras Chintz, one of the most complete dressing tables I ever saw, having every useful article in it; a beautiful bureau and book case, stored with the best books, and three neat mahogany chairs, formed the furniture.[13]

Hickey had an eye rather to utility than elegance when he asked a European carpenter to make his cabin furniture for his final voyage back to England in 1808: it consisted for four large and strong teakwood chests, a bureau with writing desk and apparatus attached to it, a 'capital cot' for sleeping on, a table and a few other articles. Hickey attached more importance to 'a chest of claret and another of Madeira of a very superior quality' to help him tolerate the tedious voyage.[14]

Outward bound passengers usually provided themselves with a couch, often with drawers underneath, which served as

a bed in calm weather, and a cot, a shallow wooden tray to take a mattress, which could be swung in bad weather; a wash-hand stand, table and chair completed the furniture.

For Mrs Sherwood, arriving at Spithead in 1805 with her husband, a captain in the 53rd regiment, to find a berth on the *Devonshire*, the comparison of the advantages of accommodation in the roundhouse and the great cabin was an academic exercise. By the time they arrived the other passengers had taken all the accommodation. Captain and Mrs Sherwood were lucky to secure the carpenter's cabin amidships. This 'worse than dog kennel' they shared with a gun, the muzzle of which faced the port. Their cot was swung over the gun at right angles leaving neither space enough to sit up in bed nor room to pass on either side, so that on entering and leaving the cabin they were forced to duck underneath the cot. There was just enough room for one chair and a small table at the side of the gun. When the pumps were working, the foul-smelling bilge water passed through their cabin to the scuppers. Worst of all, Mrs Sherwood had to go down to this shocking place early every evening before the soldiers who filled the steerage settled down for the night.

To add to their discomfort the ships were kept riding at anchor in a naval port – Portsmouth, Plymouth, Torbay – until the next convoy. The *Devonshire* sailed from Portsmouth on 25 April in company with seventeen other Indiamen and no doubt a bevy of West Indiamen and brigs bound to Newfoundland or simply as far as Cork – the whole unwieldy fleet came afloat together, shepherded by a couple of naval frigates.

Notes:
1. Essex R.O. Papers of Samuel Braund: D/Dru, B20.
2. *Ibid*, B11 and Harding, D.F: *Smallarms of the East India Company*, Vol. IV, pp575-578.
3. Ingram, Bruce: *op cit*, 185.
4. Cruden, Robert P: *History of Gravesend in the County of Kent* (1843), 45.
5. BL OIOC. L/MAR/C(27)2, 46.
6. Hickey: *op cit*, Vol 1, 150.
7. *Les Flottes des Compagnies des Indes 1600-1857*: Andrew S. Cook: *An Exchange of Letters between Two Hydrographers*, 178.
8. Roddis, Louis H: *James Lind, Founder of Nautical Medicine* (1951), 55.
9. BL OIOC L/MAR/C27(2), 46.
10. Hickey: *op cit*, Vol 1, 133.
11. Rand, *op cit*,
12. Hickey, *op cit*, Vol 4, 358.
13. *Ibid*: Vol 1, 121.
14. *Ibid*: Vol 4, 370.

CHAPTER 8
THE *V*OYAGE

The East Indiaman has settled into maritime lore as a superbly built and equipped ship but, with her bluff bows and ample beam, rather slow, a quite different image from that of the clipper of later decades. But as Henry Wise's *Analysis of a Hundred East India Voyages* between the years 1791 and 1834 shows, there was little to choose between them. The average miles per log from India or China to England was 13,398 and the average length of the voyage was one hundred and fourteen days, which compares very favourably with the performance of most of the clippers. Equally erroneous is the belief that all the ships made snug for the night. Commanders bound to Benkulen or China – where there was no market for European goods – had little incentive to arrive in the shortest possible time. On the other hand, the many instances of commanders endangering ship and cargo by parting company with the fleet, or putting at risk the health of the crew by refusing to stop to pick up fresh water and supplies, in order to arrive first at their destination with their private trade goods belie the traditional view.

Four ships managed by Samuel Braund sailed for various destinations in the east in the mid-eighteenth century. They were the *Edgecote*, bound to Coast and China; the *Boscawen*,

One of the finest of the later East Indiamen, the *Herefordshire*, seen off the North Foreland. She was built of teak in Bombay.   (*Science Museum*)

bound to Bombay, the Persian Gulf and the Red Sea; the *Warren*, bound to Bombay and Bengal; and the *Grantham*, bound to Coast and China. Braund exhorted his commanders to report to him on the progress of their voyages by returning ships whenever the opportunity offered. Their letters provide a window through which we can glimpse the many problems encountered on the Company's standard voyages.

The charts were still rudimentary: hazardous shoals and reefs were not accurately marked. The commanders probably used the charts in John Thornton's *Oriental Navigation* comprising the third book of the *English Pilot* started by John Seller in the 1670s, and some by Henry Cornwall. Charts of much greater accuracy were being produced by the Dutchman van Keulen and the French hydrographer d'Après de Mannevillette but were not yet available in translation. The mercantilist philosophy that determined commercial policy extended to all the means of prosecuting trade: charts were jealously guarded to give advantage to the author's nationals. To compensate for the inadequacy of the charts the commanders would have built up a great fund of shared experience over glasses of hock in the Jerusalem Coffee House and in the various ports in the east. They knew they were on the Cape Bank when they saw 'Gannets . . . and Trunk Weeds, which are infallible Signs of it' and an abundance of red crabs

as they approached Cape Comorin warned them that they were being pushed into Tuticorin Bay.

Until the precise longitude of hazards in the eastern seas was known, their position on the charts could be only an approximation. However, since ships' navigators were unable to compute their exact position until the latter part of the eighteenth century the margin of error in the charts was not as serious as it might have been. The navigation instruments available were by this time quite sophisticated: in skilled hands latitude, or the north/south position, could be determined to a very great degree of accuracy using Hadley's quadrant, introduced in 1731 – a great improvement on the old Davis's backstaff and the earlier cross-staff. The means available to navigators for estimating their longitude, or east/west position, were crude and the results only an approximation. Dead reckoning remained the basis of their calculations for much of the eighteenth century: the common sea log gave them the ship's speed in knots; the Azimuth compass their direction; adjusted for winds and currents the resulting 'dead reckoning' gave them their 'position by account'. The basic rule at this time for commanders of ships approaching port was the same as for the previous four hundred years: to get into the right latitude then sail east or west, making sure they took in sail at night, and heaving the lead to take soundings

A splendid painting by Dodd showing an East Indiaman weighing at the start of the 13,000 mile voyage from the Downs. *(National Maritime Museum)*

when they judged they were approaching the shore. The four "L"s – the log, the lead, the latitude and the look-out – were the mainstay of navigation.

The *Edgecote*, Captain Pearse
In November 1747 the *Edgecote*, in common with several other Company ships, sailed under convoy of Admiral Boscawen and a naval squadron from Spithead, the departure point for all Company ships in time of war. Each ship carried a detachment of royal troops, the first ever to be sent to India, for the relief of Fort St David at Cuddalore, where the Company's staff had retreated following the fall of Madras in 1747 to the French Company's troops under Dupleix. Admiral Boscawen's instructions were to deliver the troops to Fort St David then blockade the French Company's head-quarters at Pondicherry.

At the beginning of January 1748 the fleet put in at Madeira for water and provisions, an unusual stop for Company ships. A further stop was made, presumably on the admiral's orders, at Santiago, the largest of the Cape Verde islands. Since before the turn of the seventeenth century, commanders had been instructed not to stop at the Cape Verdes because the tropical fever picked up there was 'the greatest cause of the death and losing of many of our men'.

The *Edgecote* lost company the night she sailed from Santiago, and on arriving at the Cape found the rest of the fleet had been there seventeen days. In a letter written on 17 April at the Cape, Captain Pearse reported he had arrived three days earlier after a voyage of just under twelve weeks from Santiago. He expressed anxiety on a number of issues:

> Are at Great Expence, ye Soldiers by ye Admiral's orders have fresh provisions on shore. The Cordage exceeding bad. In our passage from St Jago to ye place had a great deal of sickness. I hear that four of ye fleet are bound to China am afraid we shall loose our passage.

The fleet arrived on the coast of Coromandel on 28 July by a new route, which came to be known as the Middle Passage and was adopted by the Company from 1750. This involved passing to the east of Madagascar and following a course through the thousands of islands lying between Madagascar and the Malabar coast. Many variations on the Middle Passage developed during succeeding decades, all lengthy, but a greatly improved route – the Degree and a Half Channel, saving more than a thousand miles – was learned from a French manuscript in 1811.

Captain Pearse wrote from Fort David one month later, on 25 August:

> we were in great hopes of subduing Mauritius but Mr Boscawen feeling it not practicable with out ye loss of a great

many men which were wanted for Pondicherry, after being there five days thought proper to proceed. Soon after our Arrival ye Admiral gave Captain Cook of the *Admiral Vernon* & Self orders to get all our Stores out yt we might proceed on our Voyage to China.

It was certainly very late in the season to attempt a voyage to Canton. Sickness added to Captain Pearse's worries. He and many of his officers and men had been ill, and he was eleven men short through death and desertion, forcing him to ship ten Lascars. A menace of a different nature threatened his continued voyage to China, especially in view of his weakened condition:

> About 6 weeks ago by our Men of War in this road Twelve sail of French Ships w[hi]ch ye Gov[erno]r has advice landed men at Madras, we all imagine as they have not been at Bengal that they're gone to wait for the China Men in ye Straights of Malacca if so I hope gone before us am afraid will be poorly off.

The *Edgecote* succeeded in avoiding the French ships as a letter of 11 November, written at Benkulen, explained:

> Sailed from Fort St Davids 29th last Augt. Rec[eive]d my orders and despatches from Gov[erno]r Hayer to proceed to China & in our passage to stop at Quida in ye Straights of Malacca for Intelligence from a Small Vessel w[hi]ch ye Gov[erno]r had sent there for ye purpose. Arrived there ye 14th sepr not finding ye s[aid] Vessel Sent my boat and Officers Ashore with ye *Admiral Vernon*'s to inquire whether she had been there or if there were any letters for Europe Ships The King said he had no letters nor had ye said Vessel been there; but that ye *Hardwick* & *Wager* had touched there & on being informed of French Ships being on ye Coast of Malacca Saild Immediately it is believed for China . . . we suppose ye Vessel from w[hi]ch we was to have our Intelligence is taken . . . we thought it most prudent to make ye best of our way out of ye Straights and proceed to this place for Better Intelligence . . . the Gov[erno]r here has not heard of any french Ships being in ye Straights of Sunda, we are obliged to stay here a few days our people being ill of ye Scurvy.

Benkulen, 'the most sickeley place in the known world', seems an odd place to recover from sickness. This was the chief settlement on the Company's 300-mile pepper plantation on the west coast of Sumatra. For Marlborough, a fortified storehouse with living accommodation for the governor and his staff, was built on slightly elevated ground. Both the staff and the crews of visiting ships were prey to the two scourges of that coast: the 'bloody flux' – amoebic dysentery – and malaria, then known as the fever or the ague. It was not at that time realised that mosquitoes carried malaria, but it was evident

Though this painting of the East India fleet at sea is dated 1803 it appears to represent the battle of Pula Auro, 1804.

(National Maritime Museum)

that the danger came from the marshy land, particularly in the evening. Commanders of ships loading pepper along the coast were ordered to moor their ships well offshore, keep the ports shut and bring off all shore parties before sundown.

Captain Pearse concluded his letter from Benkulen with an account of the state of affairs on board. His bowsprit was sprung and needed repair; both standing and running rigging were bad and he needed more cordage. He needed fresh salt provisions to replace some salt pork that had turned bad, and he had procured some puncheons of beef and flour. The Lascars he had shipped at Fort David had been discharged and the governor at Fort Marlborough had reimbursed him for half their cost, presumably since he had had to ship them while on government service.

After spending nine days at Benkulen, the *Edgecote* weighed and sailed through the Sunda Strait to Batavia where she anchored on 6 December. There the Dutch governor informed Captain Pearse that 'he had heard of ye French Ships . . . if we had proceeded should have run a Great risque'. In a letter brought back by the *Godolphin*, Captain Stevens, Captain Pearse reported he intended to sail for Canton in

company with the *Admiral Vernon* on 1 May. She arrived safely at Canton and sailed with 160 tons surplus on 1 November, arriving at St Helena on 17 March 1750.

The *Boscawen,* Captain Braund

While the *Edgecote* was at Batavia waiting for the onset of the south-west monsoon to take her up to Canton, two more of Braund's ships were at the Hope preparing to sail: the *Warren*, Captain Glover, bound to Bombay and Bengal, and the *Boscawen*, Captain Braund, bound to Bombay, the Persian Gulf and the Red Sea. On 18 March, in company with the *Salisbury*, also bound to Bombay, they attempted to get over the 'flatts', the shoals between the Goodwin Sands and the Kent coast, into the Downs, always a hazardous business. The *Warren* and the *Salisbury* succeeded, but the *Boscawen* was forced to put back owing to a change of wind, and in so doing went aground for nine hours, though she received no damage. Four days later, with a fine gale at east-south-east, she was under sail, and by sunset on 29 March was off Start Point, Devon, from where she took her departure.

James Barlow, a young writer going out to the Company's

presidency at Bombay, joined the ship at Deal with the purser and three other young writers.[2] Passengers frequently embarked there to avoid the dangers of getting over the 'flatts', often the worst part of the voyage, and the chaotic conditions which reigned on board ship during the first few days. At the Captain's table were Mr Mann and Mr Peisley, supercargoes who were to conduct the trade when the *Boscawen* left Bombay for her tour of the Persian Gulf and the Red Sea; the chief mate, Mr William Larkins; the second mate, the surgeon, the purser, the Captain's clerk, five other young writers, and two 'guinea pigs', boys going out on their first voyage. The other officers sat at the third mate's mess in the steerage.

> We assembled fifteen of us . . . Eight every Morning to Breakfast in the Round-house, when we had always Tea, and sometimes Chocolate; with Biscuit and Butter in Plenty; neither did we want Milk, having a fine Goat that supplied us with it all the Passage: at Twelve we dined, the Table being always served with four to six Dishes of fresh provisions, and equally well in regard to Drink, having Wine, Punch and Beer; In short, we had every Thing we possibly could have, or the Shore could afford, except Greens and Fruit: At four every Afternoon there was Tea and Coffee . . . Then at Eight we all met again at Supper, when we had generally one Dish warm, with some remains of the Dinner; and, before we separated from Dinner and Supper, we drank these three Toasts; To all our absent friends; To the Continuance and Encrease of the Wind, if it was Fair; or to a fair One, when it was not so; and To a happy Sight of the next Land we intended to make.

The fare at the captain's table was rather superior to that of the crew who messed in groups between the guns in the fore part of the main deck. For breakfast they probably had 'burgoo', a porridge made of oatmeal and water with a few pieces of salt meat in it. The main meal of the day was dinner: this invariably consisted of a stew made from salt beef thickened with oatmeal, or salt pork thickened with peas, served with biscuit. The stew was served in a leather mess jack, which contained the ration for the number of men in that mess. On meatless days the crew had fish, or cheese with butter or edible oil. Puddings were made with flour and suet. No other meals were catered for, but the cook would make a hash of anything returned by a mess for their supper. After such meals the men were probably grateful for their brandy and the tobacco ration which was always included in the list of stores for each ship.

James Barlow spent his time on board walking on deck or reading and writing in his cabin, though 'it was seldom her Pitching and Rolling would admit the latter with any Pleasure'. In the evenings, some of the officers and passengers played whist over a bowl of punch, though there was no gambling. On other evenings, some played the violin and others sang. Prayers were held on fine Sundays, the purser officiating, but on this voyage it turned out to be their 'foul-weather day' and they had only two services throughout the voyage.

On 12 April they passed the Canaries, and three days later the Tropic of Capricorn, where they picked up the north-east trade wind, 'much the most agreeable Part of the Voyage'. It was insufferably hot when they passed the sun a few days later, and they were 'obliged to shake off our Cloth Waistcoat, worsted Stockings, Blankets, etc'. The *Boscawen* averaged 130 miles a day until 23 April when the north-east trade failed in the latitude of the Cape Verdes, and she found herself in the calms, with squalls and heavy rain and a great deal of thunder and lightning. A strong south-east current threatened to drive the ship so far to the eastward that she was in danger of being driven into the Bight of Benin with the possibility of being becalmed for weeks. They were able to make only 20 to 30 miles a day, and the exceptionally large number of sharks indicated that they were dangerously close to the coast of Guinea. There was a horrifying incident when some of the crew on the poop hooked an eight-foot shark which resisted their attempts to haul it over the taffrail; it jerked and writhed within inches of about a dozen who were watching from the balcony underneath. Dozens of bottles cluttering the balcony impeded their attempts to reach the door to the roundhouse, but fortunately some of the windows were open and they forced themselves through to safety.

On 3 May in longitude 14° 9'W from Start Point they crossed the equator with the usual ceremonies: those who had not crossed before forfeited a bottle of brandy and a pound of sugar or submitted to a ducking from the main yard-arm. The latter procedure filled Barlow with dismay until he realised that the victims considered it a huge joke. At the line they picked up the south-east trade, but it proved very disappointing, the wind being so southerly they were in danger of not clearing the coast of Brazil. As Barlow commented, 'so, though in such a vast Ocean, yet found it hardly wide enough for these ships to traverse'.

They reached longitude 23° W from Start Point before they began to steer a south-easterly course in the region of the Island of Trinidad; as Barlow said, 'when bound to the East Indies, we must go one half of the Voyage to the Westward'. As expected at this point in the voyage the weather became unsettled:

> we bent the best suit of sails, set up the Rigging, reeved a new Tiller Rope, hung the Chains to secure the Rudder, put up the dead lights, shut in all the half Ports which made us as dark as a Dungeon, lashed all the Moveables, and in every shape prepared for encountering the boisterous Gales and large Seas we expected to have in running down our Easting.

By the end of May they were in latitude 35° 20'S, with a

The *Essex* East Indiaman in Bombay harbour c1800, with the Custom House in the background.   *(BL OIOC)*

north-easterly wind, and kept the ship between that and 34°S, running 150-200 miles a day for the Cape in cold, stormy, boisterous weather, the ship rolling so much they had to hold fast all the time. 'We were forced at Meals to sit upon the Deck with every one his Plate in his Hand, and had generally some Diversions from our being tossed from one side to the other'. At night they were kept awake by the sea beating in, or the ship's violent motion. As they drew nearer the Cape they were surprised to find more moderate weather and smooth water, and were in high hopes of getting past 'this Corner of Land, so famous for bad Weather, very quickly, tho' it was the Depths of Winter'.

There was great excitement on 6 June when a sail was sighted ahead and everyone thought they had caught up with the *Warren* or the *Salisbury*, but it proved to be a Dutch ship bound for Batavia. The Dutch Captain said they were 720 miles from the Cape but Captain Braund was sure his estimate of 430 miles was nearer the mark.

They hauled up to make the land and sighted Cape Aghulas on 10 June, after which they steered south-east by east running 194 miles in twenty-four hours. Suddenly a storm arose at noon on Sunday 11 June and from then until four o'clock the following afternoon, with only the spritsail, foretopsail and foresail treble-reefed, they scudded helplessly before a strong west-north-west wind that carried them 214 miles. On the Sunday afternoon six men were thrown from the helm when they shipped a sea on the starboard quarter; it carried away the starboard quarter-gallery and the yawl was wrenched off its hooks and dashed to pieces against the guns, wounding many passengers and crew. Fortunately the quartermasters were able to steer from the gunroom. At seven that evening, another sea carried one of the guns overboard and demolished all the coops on the poop. The last sea came in right aft at eight on the Monday morning, driving in one of the deadlights in the great cabin and shattering the larboard gallery. They hauled to the north to get out of the bad weather and steered a course for the Mozambique Channel, the Inner Passage usual during the south-west monsoon. About this time a seaman jumped from the tops in an attempt to be first down, but missed the backstay he had intended to grab hold of. Within a few hours he died and was quickly committed to the sea, the purser officiating at the funeral.

For some days they had contrary winds and made little headway against the strong southerly current in the Mozambique Channel. On 27 June they sighted land and hauled up to make what they thought was Madagascar, but which proved to be the dangerous shoal the Bassas de India, the graveyard of many ships.

> It is extremely well laid down in the chart as to its latitude, but not properly described, as from it we imagined the Bassas de India to be nothing but a Rock; whereas it is a pretty large Island, extending from North to South, at least six or eight miles. It is very low next the Sea, and but a very little Rising anywhere, has a large Range of Trees along the Coast; and, by what we could perceive with our Glasses, the Ground had a tolerable Verdure; but a very great surf, almost all round it.

During the time they thought it was Madagascar, a seaman had sighted smoke rising from the island; he forgot this later, when it was realised that the land was in fact the Bassas de India, and did not recall it until the *Boscawen* was well clear and could not turn back. This was the cause of much regret on board because it was thought that the smoke might have been a sign of the survivors of the *Dolphin*, a ship which had that year gone missing.

On 5 July they anchored at Johanna, now called Anjouan, one of the four islands in the Comoro group lying between the north-west coast of Madagascar and Mozambique, and soon after 'had the ship as full of Black People as ever she could hold, who came off in Canoes, with Oranges, Limes, Etc, Fruit, which we eagerly devoured . . .' The *Boscawen* stayed eight days at Johanna, during which there was 'a constant fair' on board, with state visits by the king, and the exchange of poultry, goats, monkeys, greens, fish and fruit for tobacco, small knives and other trifles beloved by the people of Johanna. Before sailing they took on board twenty-five small bullocks and plenty of wood and water, as well as large stocks of fresh provisions.

On Friday 14 July the *Boscawen* weighed anchor in beautiful weather. With a steady gale at south-west and a favourable current she ran 135-200 miles a day up to a short distance off Cape Bassas on the coast of Ethiopia. When in the latitude of Bombay a course was set to eastward. During this time many of the crew went down with the fever and three died. Barlow noted that 'no ship ever left Johanna without suffering in this manner', but none of those who had a seat at the captain's table suffered. They set all the sail they had and reached Bombay harbour on 1 August, one day before the change of the moon which was always attended by bad weather, European captains holding off the land at this time. They had made a remarkably quick passage of just over four months, and were the first to arrive, acquainting the governor with the news of the peace with France and the exchange of Madras for Louisburg.

Captain Braund, having sold his private trade goods at a very good profit, reported on 13 September that he was 'now under sail for Surat and Persia with freight Bales for ye Company from whence we are to be back time enough for Mocha'. On 18 November he announced his arrival at Gombroon. Between early September and April thousands of ships plied between the Malabar coast and ports to the westward. Although the Company ships approached the Malabar coast during the south-west monsoon months – Bombay particularly seems to have been accessible at all times – native shipping was laid up from the end of May until Coconut Day (the festival marking the end of the rainy season on 1 September), during which time insurance cover ceased. The best time for a voyage to the Red Sea was February to March. Ships attempting to sail after this had to run south across the line until they picked up the south-east trades, and even then they had variable winds and a huge swelling sea to contend with. The south-west monsoon was the time for the return voyage from Mocha to Bombay or Surat; after the beginning of September it was impossible to get out of the Red Sea, as Sir Henry Middleton had discovered in 1611. The *Boscawen* arrived back at Bombay in the autumn of 1750 and sailed for England in November. She probably returned via the Mozambique Channel, the usual route during the north-east monsoon, and arrived at the Cape on 16 January 1751. By 24 February she was at St Helena and reached the Downs on 26 May, a voyage of six and a half months.

The *Warren*, Captain Glover

After a good start the *Warren* met with nothing but trouble. Captain Glover's first letter after leaving England, written at the Bay of All Saints, Brazil, on 18 June 1749, reported that the *Warren*'s foremast had sprung after passing the Cape Verdes, and he had been forced to put into the Bay for repairs. Ships endeavouring to avoid the dangerous currents off the West African coast frequently failed to correct their south-westerly course in time, coming to grief on the coast of Brazil, particularly on the Albrolhos reef, and were forced to put into Rio de Janeiro or the Bay of All Saints for repairs. Captain Glover requested a survey by the Master of Attendance and his carpenter at the Bay, together with his own carpenter and officers; they confirmed his opinion that 'ye Masts in general are bad'. Captain Glover must have lost some of his hands, probably through desertion, for, before sailing on 21 June, he had to ship ten Lascars.

There was no more news of the *Warren* until sixteen months later, when Captain Glover wrote from Bombay, where the *Warren* had arrived in June 1750. Approaching the Cape he had had trouble with the main yard-arm, and two days after rounding the Cape, his main topmast sprung. Illness added to Captain Glover's problems: off Madagascar the second and third mates, a passenger and one of his Lascars died. Shortly afterwards, the chief mate and the surgeon 'were ill of the same distemper . . . and several of ye Co begg'd to put in at Johanna'.

The crews of East India ships were usually suffering to a greater or lesser extent from scurvy by this stage of the voyage. Their breath was foul, their gums bleeding, swollen and spongy, their teeth in many cases actually falling out; their legs and arms were swollen and their general condition so weak they were incapable of carrying out their duties. It is a mystery how scurvy persisted in the Company's ships when lemon or lime juice were compulsorily included in the victualling list. It can only be assumed either that both commanders and men regarded the Company's insistence on its administration as a bureaucratic rule to be ignored, or that the method of preservation was so imperfect that the curative elements were ineffective. References to serious outbreaks of scurvy on various voyages never include any suggestion that lemon or lime juice were administered in an attempt to cure the sick. There was certainly a general realisation that scurvy resulted from a lack of fresh provisions, and that salvation would come when the ship touched land. Even so, as late as the end of the eighteenth century, fifty years after Lind had proved beyond all

doubt that oranges and lemons effected an immediate and infallible cure, commanders of ships arriving at Canton with crews suffering from scurvy demanded fresh meat, not fresh fruit.

Seamen suffering from scurvy were convinced that a call at Johanna would cure them. For more than two centuries the sick from Company ships were carried ashore there to recover. Even the soil was believed to have curative properties. As late as 1769 a traveller noted the practice of burying the sick up to their necks and leaving them all day. Another common treatment was to lay them on the earth under a tent of spare canvas and spars.

Captain Glover did not say to what extent the problem of sickness was assuaged by the call at Johanna, but it reoccurred before the *Warren* arrived at Bombay. They sailed from Johanna on 15 September 1749, crossed the line a week later and got as far north as Socotra, but the change of the monsoon had already set in; the wind came round to the northeast and they lost ground. On 2 November, Captain Glover called a consultation of his officers: the general opinion was that they should return to Johanna until the north-east monsoon was over. They could not make Johanna, but they man-

The animals were frequently victims when high seas washed over the decks, the hen coops usually being the first to go by then board.

(National Maritime Museum)

aged to get to Mohilla, where many of the ship's company died. At the end of February 1750 they went on to Johanna and remained there until mid-March when they sailed. On 19 May they had soundings in latitude 18° 35'N,

> when a violent storm arose at NW & increased to such a hurricane that between 9 & 10 in ye Morning all ye Masts went by ye Board, nothing left but Bowsprit, at ye same time had 5ft 9in Inches Water in ye hold & between 2 & 3ft in ye tween decks, tho' all ye Hatches was well Secured, had much to do to keep her above water, being obliged to have all ye Pumps at work & could not gain on her till 12 o'clock at night . . .

The sea continued to run high, the wind veering to southwest, and, unable to get jury masts up, they lay to for three days, drawn to the north-west coast of India. There the *Warren* 'rode out in ye open sea a violent hard Gale, w[hi]ch obliged me to heave 19 Guns overBoard all 9 pounders to prev[en]t foundering'. She was forced to put in at Diu for repairs, and finally reached Bombay early in June after a long and costly voyage, and with 'the greatest part' of the cargo damaged.

Captain Glover laid most of the blame for his bad voyage on the mastmaker, 'ye Occasion of all our Misfortunes. Ye builder likewise has behaved Extremely ill, our Lower Deck is worse than I ever saw a Ship on her first Voyage.' He had requested a survey by a few India commanders and their carpenters, with the master builder, all of whom agreed with him. He also complained of the boat builder, the biscuit baker, and the stock-fish supplier; the ropemaker he declared 'indifferent', and his only praise was for the suppliers of the salt provisions and sailmaker.

The *Warren* was still at Bombay preparing to continue her voyage to Bengal when the *Boscawen* returned from her year's tour of the Persian Gulf and the Red Sea to take in cargo and provisions for England. The *Boscawen* sailed on 17 November, taking Captain Glover's letter back to Samuel Braund.

Fear of losing his passage yet again plagued Captain Glover. Under orders to keep company with the *Britannia*, Captain Sumner, from Bombay to Calcutta, he felt obliged to leave her during the voyage as she was making such slow progress. The two ships sailed on 11 October 1750 when the north-east monsoon was setting in. During the south-west monsoon, according to the Bombay Calendar, the voyage could be made in fifteen to twenty days, for though the Malabar coast was very dangerous, ships standing out to sea were fairly safe and once round Cape Comorin, the south-west wind took the ship quickly up to Bengal. During the north-east monsoon, however, the voyage was far longer: ships had to keep well over to the east side of the Bay of Bengal, as the Coromandel coast, with its treacherous reefs extending from Cape Comorin to Point Palmyras, was extremely dangerous, especially during the period from mid-November to mid-December when insurance cover ceased. After passing to the east of the Nicobars and Andamans, ships usually steered a north-westerly course across to Point Palmyras, avoiding the Sandheads, shoals stretching out of the mouths of the Ganges like the prongs of a fork. The ships anchored in Balasore Road, a deep bay with shoal water where ships could lie in only 8 fathoms surrounded by breakers and yet be out of sight of the shore. However, it was well-buoyed and there were plenty of pilots to guide the ships safely over the flats and shoals up to Kedgeree or Culpee where they discharged their passengers and cargo and took in stores and provisions for the return voyage.

The *Warren* arrived in Bengal on 25 January 1751, a voyage of one hundred and six days as opposed to the two to three weeks possible at the right time of year. However, there were compensations in arriving during the north-east monsoon months, even though it was difficult to beat up the Hooghly against the strong north-easterly wind and the extremely swift tide. The south-west monsoon brought rain and thick weather with poor visibility which was very dangerous with all the shoals and sandbanks. In very poor conditions pilots had the habit of skulking in the creeks pretending they had not seen the ships arrive. Health hazards were fewer too, during the north-east monsoon. The low-lying marshy banks of the Hooghly swarmed with mosquitoes during the summer months, while the sudden drop in temperature in September caused chills that precipitated malarial attacks.

On 19 February Captain Glover wrote 'Have got all my salt-petre on b[oar]d, am now taking in Bales. Believe shall be dispatch by ye 28th Inst shall use all diligence to gain my passage', concluding that the *Britannia* had arrived only the day before. The *Warren* actually sailed on 1 March, very late in the season. She probably had to steer an easterly course, picking up the south-east trade to get over to the Natal coast where the strong southerly current in the Mozambique Channel would get her round to the Cape. Captain Glover reported a fine passage round the Cape up to St Helena, where he arrived on 24 June. There were only two ships as it was the depths of winter; in the summer months – January to March – many Company ships were anchored there as it was a port of call for all homebound ships. In wartime, it was a recognised rendezvous for ships awaiting convoy or seeking company when no convoy was available. Special precautions had to be taken by ships approaching St Helena in wartime in case the island had changed hands since the commander last received news. Secret orders, in sealed packets not to be opened until the ships were to the westward of the Cape, directed the commanders how to proceed to be certain the island was still in English hands. An abstract of the Secret Committee to the Governor of Bombay of 12 March 1758 during the war with France directed the commander:

The *Bridgewater* was one of the many victims of gales at the onset of the south-west monsoon. She is seen here under jury rig entering Madras Roads, 10 April 1830.
(BL OIOC)

in order to be more certain of the island being in safety, to give directions to the Officer in his boat, that at some distance from Bankes's Platform he do hoist a Waft and fire two musquets which signal will be answered from Bankes's by likewise hoisting a waft, and firing three musquets, the Waft will be kept flying on the Platform until that in the Boat is struck, on this the Boat may venture on shore, but if they at Bankes's do not answer the Signal, the Boat must immediately return on board, as he may then conclude the Island is in the Enemy's Hands.

St Helena's barren appearance on approaching from the sea was in marked contrast to the luxuriance of its many deep valleys. The town and anchorage for the ships was in St James' valley almost at the northern end on the leeward side of the island, so the strong south-west wind rushed down from the head of the valley laying on her broadside any ship that had not all mainsails well reefed. The islanders supplied the ships with beef and huge lemons which soon had a beneficial effect on sufferers from scurvy, earning for St Helena the same name among homeward bound mariners as Johanna had among those outward bound. In return the ships supplied the islanders with grain, which would not grow there. The charter parties included clauses enabling the Company to load supplies for St Helena in the lazaretto or any other corner of the ship not required for cargo, at half freight.

The *Grantham*, Captain Walter Wilson

The *Grantham* sailed from the Downs on 20 December 1749 in company with the *Duke of Cumberland*, Captain Osborne, both bound to Fort St David and Canton. While the *Grantham* lay at anchor in the Downs waiting for gales to subside, a total of thirty-three Lascars were brought on board from the *Godolphin*, Captain Stevens, just returned from Canton, and the *Exeter*, to be taken back to the East.

The first letter received from Captain Wilson – the content of which has unfortunately not survived – was written at Goru on the west coast of Africa on 25 January 1750, reporting the total loss of the *Cumberland*. In setting course for the Cape Verdes from the Canaries, the two ships had got caught up in the hostile currents off the Guinea coast and the *Cumberland* had foundered. Fortunately there was no loss of life, the *Grantham* taking all the *Cumberland*'s people on board. On 5 March, just to the north of the equator, the *Grantham* fell in with the *Durrington*, Captain Crabb – another of Samuel Braund's ships – which had sailed in company with the *Edgecote* and Admiral Boscawen's fleet in December 1747 and was returning to England. Captain Crabb took on board Mr Torriano, one of the *Cumberland*'s supercargoes for Canton, to make a report on the wreck to the owners and to the Directors in Leadenhall Street. He also took back a letter from Captain Wilson:

refer you to Mr Torriano who comes home on ye *Durrington* I am in a bad state of health Mr Misenor another supercargo and all ye *Cumberland's* Lascars on b[oar]d am afraid must put into some place for water before we reach Fort St Davids.

The next letter received from the *Grantham* was written by Captain Oliver, who had gone out first mate, on 27 July 1750, reporting the death of Captain Wilson nine days after the meeting with the *Durrington*. While they were rounding the Cape, one of the seamen had fallen overboard and drowned, and another had died, but otherwise the ship's company was well. On 23 May the *Grantham* put in to St Augustine's Bay, where she found the *Fort St George*, Captain Mortimer, which had sailed with the *Edgecote* and Admiral Boscawen's fleet in December 1747. Although Captain Oliver does not mention this, an account of the meeting is included in a letter from Captain Burdett, who went out as third mate of the *Fort St George*. Her movements after her arrival at Fort St David in July 1748 are not clear, but she sailed from there on 11 November 1749 bound to Madagascar to pick up slaves, arriving at St Augustine's Bay on 4 January 1759 with:

a very sickly Ships Company who continued so till ye latter end of May our Extreem weakness obliged us to stay at St Augustine's bay till ye 25th March when we sailed for Tullear Harbour where we got ye same day & continued so very Sickly were obliged to stay there till ye *Grantham* Captain Oliver arrived who spared us an officer and thirty Lascars & Some Stores, w[hi]ch enabled us to sail June ye 10th for Young Owl & Mathalege . . . where we arrived June ye 30th & proceeded thence July ye 26th for this place with 115 Slaves Men & Women for acco[mp]t of ye Co.

Apart from Captain Mortimer, who had died on the voyage from Mathalege to Fort St David, twenty-two of the ship's company, including the chief and second mates, had been buried.

Captain Oliver reported that the *Grantham* had sailed from St Augustine's Bay on 2 June and arrived at Fort St David on 14 July. He intended sailing for Canton at the end of the month but feared he would lose his passage.

The usual route from the Coromandel coast to Canton during the south-west monsoon lay through the Straits of Malacca. The end of July was quite late to attempt this route, however, as typhoons could be expected in the China Sea at the change of the monsoon from the beginning of August. When the north-east monsoon was fully established it was impossible to beat up the China Sea and ships were forced, like the *Edgecote* in 1748, to await the south-west monsoon. About this time, however, commanders losing their passage began to try out routes which avoided the China Sea: in 1740

a China bound ship arrived on 13 October at Canton by standing to the eastward of Pula Sapato and up to the Philippines under the direction of one of her supercargoes on board who had made several voyages to Manila and so become familiar with the route. In succeeding decades a variety of routes entailing passing between New Guinea on the east and the Celebes on the west were tried out. These were generally referred to as Pitt's Passage, after the *Pitt*, Captain William Wilson, which in 1759, leaving Fort St George too late in the season to sail up the China Sea, followed a route east of the Celebes, through the Moluccas to the Pacific Ocean, and east of the Philippines, reaching the Chinese coast between the Philippines and Formosa. For a long time the eastern passages were not favoured by commanders, who were deterred by the wear and tear on anchors and sails resulting from lack of knowledge of the conditions of those parts, but later, when the Canton council sent charts to Fort St George, these alternative routes became more widely used, especially by the China fleets sailing without convoy in wartime. A new variation on the eastern passage was added in 1794 by Captain Thomas Butler, who parted company with the India ships off the island of St Paul on 7 October and steered a course south of New Holland between that continent and New Zealand, arriving at Macao on 1 January 1795.

The *Grantham* reached Macao in mid-September after a short passage from the coast. At the Grand Ladrones, a cluster of islands at the mouth of the Canton river, she had to wait for the sea pilot to steer the ship through the Bogue, the narrow fortified channel separating the sea from the river, which spread out to a great width on the other side. The sea pilot left the ship in Macao Road, where it was necessary to wait for the 'chop' or permit to proceed in the charge of the river pilot over the two dangerous bars up to the European anchorage at Whampoa, about fifteen miles below Canton.

Before the 'chop' was granted, the ship was measured for custom's duty by the 'hoppo' – who held his appointment annually and so had only a limited time to squeeze as much as he could out of the foreigners. The ship was measured between the foremast and the mizzenmast: this figure was multiplied by the extreme width and the product divided by ten. In addition to the basic fee based on this measurement there was a fixed fee called 'presents'. Since 1727, after thirty years of arguments, this had been fixed at a standard 1950 taels for each ship 'being for the presents to the Toyen, Juntuck and other Great Mandarins for our Ship's Present; which are now by custom looked upon to be as much their due as the Measurage'.[3] The *Grantham* paid 1401 taels measurage for 188 Chinese units, making a total of 3351 with the presents, or just over £1100.

There were five other English Company ships at Whampoa that season and several huge ships belonging to the other European companies. Whampoa was a pleasant place. Near the anchorage were two islands that the Chinese put at the disposal of the Europeans during their stay. On Danes Island the crews of each ship erected long sheds, or bankshalls, about 100ft long, to accommodate the upper masts, yards, spars, sails and rigging; before the voyage home they were all put in good repair and the ship overhauled and repainted. The bank-shall was also used as a place of recreation for the crew, being fitted out with tables, chairs and cots. French Island was where the crews relaxed, played games and generally took their exercise. During the many years of hostility between England and France, fights frequently broke out between the English and French seamen, and they had to be restricted to separate islands. In normal times, the presence of the different nationalities brought out the competitive spirit in the crews. Every effort was made to smarten up the ships: brasses were polished, decks scrubbed, and everything kept ship-shape. The twice-daily playing by the ships' bands, at dawn and dusk, added to the pleasant atmosphere. Above all the plentiful supply of fresh food after so many months on salt victuals was an agreeable change: bullocks, hogs, boars, a variety of fresh and salt fish, rice, fruit and vegetables were all available.

By November, the *Grantham* already had all her chinaware and Bohea tea on board and was expecting to be dispatched early in December, leaving Messrs Misenor and Palmer to stay over till the following season and bringing home three other supercargoes. In December Captain Oliver wrote 'have buried one man . . . some of ye Ship's Co have been down with fluxes but are now on ye mending'. Her dispatch must have been very much delayed, as it was not until 3 February that she sailed through the Straits of Sunda in company with four French ships. In squally weather in the Strait she fell foul of one of the French ships which carried away the *Grantham's* head, forcing her to put in at Batavia for repairs.

Returning to England

From St Helena the ships steered a course for Ascension, an uninhabited island where the more enterprising passengers and members of the crew formed shore parties to turn turtles which came ashore during the night to lay their eggs in the sand. The turtles were collected the following day to add variety to the ships' victuals. From Ascension a north-north-west course was steered, the ships passing to the west of the Cape Verdes and the Azores until they picked up the south-westerly wind to take them up the English Channel. The first ship

to arrive back was the *Edgecote* which sailed from St Helena on 22 March 1750 and arrived in the Downs on 1 June. The *Boscawen* reached the English coast almost a year later in company with the *Fort St George* to which the *Grantham* had lent a helping hand at Tullear in Madagascar in May 1750. The *Grantham* and the *Warren* arrived many months later.

In the Downs the pilot went on board to guide the ship up to Erith where she was lightened before continuing up to Blackwall or Deptford. Once more the lighters plied up and down the River, carrying away empty casks, anchors, guns and shot, cables and rigging. The crew was paid off and a ship-keeper went on board to guard the ship against the variety of River thieves that were such a menace until the East India Docks were opened at Blackwall in the early years of the nineteenth century.

The valuable cargo was transferred to the Company's hoys under the eyes of the revenue officers and the ship's mates and taken up to the Company's wharves in the City. From here, the goods were transported to the appropriate warehouses which increased in numbers and size during the following decades: the tea and chinaware brought back by the *Edgecote* and *Grantham* were taken to warehouses in Fenchurch Street, Crutched Friars, Whitechapel or Tower Hill; the *Warren's* saltpetre from Bengal to a special warehouse on Cock's Hill; the bales of cotton, chintz, raw and wrought silks from Persia, China, Coromandel and Bengal to Cutlers Lane and Houdsditch; spices from Malabar to Leadenhall Street; drugs from Persia and China and all the baggage and private trade goods to Lime Street and Billiter Lane. Eventually, all the goods were sold at auctions held in the Company's sale room 'by inch of candle'; those goods for home consumption found their way to the China shops, the rest were sent by the Liverpool merchants to the West Indies and the American colonies or transhipped to Europe by the Company.

Empty and silent once more, the ships were taken up to the mooring chains at Blackwall or Deptford where their kintledge was taken out and all the rest of the equipment removed before they went into dock for repairs in preparation for the next voyage.

Notes:
1. Essex R O. Papers of Samuel Braund, D/Dru B20.
2. BL, OIOC. Tract 133, Barlow.
3. Morse: *op cit*, Vol 1, 185.

CHAPTER 9

A *Voyage* TO *China* *Direct*

On Monday 7 February 1803 the *Exeter*, 1200 tons, Captain Henry Meriton, bound for China direct, came afloat at Deptford.[1] Born and bred into the seafaring community of Rotherhithe, Meriton lacked the influential friends in the Court of Directors who might have secured him a more profitable Bombay/China voyage.

The ship was surveyed before the water butts, kintledge and flints, billet wood, pitch and tar, deals, dunnage and old ship's stores were taken on board. On 25 February the *Exeter* moored abreast of Tower Key, Gravesend. Throughout the following week, in gales with rain and snow, hoys brought down the Company's bales, long ells and cloth. A skeleton crew took in the ship's provisions and the lumpers heaved aboard twenty-six guns and carriages. Ship's stores, the commander's and officers' private trade goods and treasure, Company bales, store sails, cordage and dry provisions were taken in and finally the ship's boats were hoisted aboard. Twenty-seven Chinese boarded the ship to return to China and by the end of the month the whole ship's company was on board. The rigging was set up, sails bent, and on the first day of April the sea pilot joined the ship and the *Exeter* sailed for the Hope where the ship was paid. On 3 April the gunpowder was hoisted aboard and early on the following day the *Exeter* weighed and ran over the 'flats' in stages, dropping anchor in the Downs at 6pm on 5 April, 1803, with a cargo valued at £117,717.16s.9d.[2] She carried no bullion for the Company, but eight ships of the season carried a total of £570,960.3s.4d in silver for the tea investment. The next morning she weighed in company with the *Lady Castlereagh*, bound to Bengal, and the *Warren Hastings* bound to China direct. For the first time in ten years there was peace and the ships could sail in small fleets without convoy. Thirty-eight Indiamen, an exceptionally large number, had been taken up as many were bound on circuitous routes to pick up garrisons from Dutch possessions that had been occupied during the war. Twenty-six extra ships were also taken up in subsequent

months to cope with all the circumstances brought about by the Peace of Amiens. This was Meriton's seventh voyage to China, his fifth in the *Exeter*. On his first voyage as captain he had distinguished himself by taking the *Medée*, a French frigate, by the ruse of burning lights in the ports to deceive the enemy into thinking he was a ship of the line. He must have been relieved to be able to decide on his route and be spared the indignity of subordinating himself to the orders of a naval commander whose knowledge of the eastern seas was probably inferior to his own.

Captain Meriton benefited from revolutionary advances in navigation which Captain Pearse and his fellow commanders over half a century earlier could not have dreamed of. Hadley's quadrant had been developed and improved to evolve as a sextant, beautifully constructed by John Bird and later reduced to a fraction of its size without losing any of its precision by Jesse Ramsden. Used in conjunction with Mayer's lunar tables, transcribed and presented as the *Nautical Almanac* in 1767 by the Astronomer Royal, Nevil Maskelyne, longitude could at last be calculated to within 30' accuracy. The tables gave the distance of the sun and certain bright stars from the moon for every three hours Greenwich time, adopted as the prime meridian in England that same year, for every day of the year. The improved instruments enabled the navigator accurately to compute the local time and by comparing it with Greenwich time the longitude could be estimated. The calculations involved were very lengthy and complicated. No doubt Henry Meriton had been to school to learn the method twenty years earlier when he joined the *Pigot*, in line with Company rules. The changeover did not happen overnight: the new instruments were beyond

Right: A mid-nineteenth century chart of the South China Sea showing the dangerous Paracel Islands and shoals on which many ships came to grief. From William Herbert's sea atlas *A New Directory for the East Indies* first published in 1758. *(National Maritime Museum)*

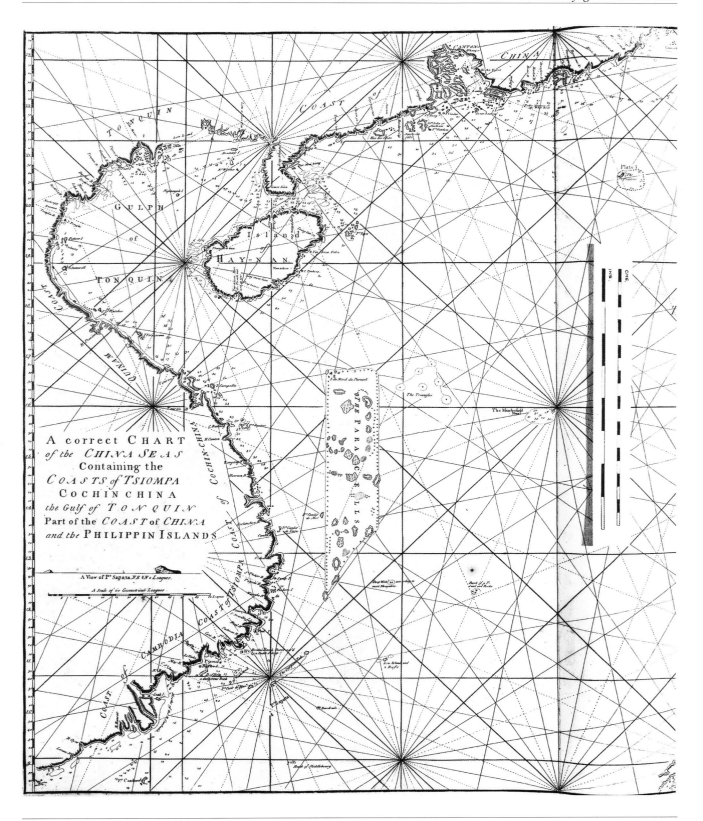

A View of P.º Sapata. *N.E.&N. 2 Leagues.*

A Scale of 60 Geometrical Leagues.

A correct CHART
of the *CHINA SEAS*
Containing the
COASTS of TSIOMPA
COCHIN CHINA
the Gulf of *TONQUIN*
Part of the *COAST of CHINA*
and the *PHILIPPIN ISLANDS*

Alexander Dalrymple, explorer and cartographer, was the first official hydrographer of both the East India Company and the Admiralty.

(BL OIOC)

the pocket of most mates, while they had to cope with a mountain of bigotry and prejudice on the part of the old school of commanders who derided the new methods.

Dead reckoning and finding longitude by taking lunar observations continued to form the basis of estimating a ship's position at sea until a final step enabled navigators to achieve much greater accuracy: carrying Greenwich time in a box. For a long time after Cook had successfully proved the accuracy of Harrison's instrument the high cost of chronometers restricted their use. It was not until the last decade of the eighteenth century that Arnold and Earnshaw were producing excellent instruments at a very reasonable price. It was the latter's chronometer number 245 that Captain Meriton carried with him on the *Exeter*'s fifth voyage to China.

His charts were far more reliable than those available to Captain Pearse. In tandem with the revolution in navigation was the transformation of the charts on which the commanders relied for their safe arrival in eastern ports. Alexander Dalrymple had become fascinated by the routes to the east while working as a writer at Madras, where he had gained practical surveying experience charting the Sulu archipelago, Borneo, Hainan and the China coast. Returning to England

he began publishing charts and in 1779 at his own suggestion he was appointed official hydrographer to the East India Company. He pored over the commanders' logs and sought the help of captains of country ships with their vast knowledge of the eastern seas. He became a prolific publisher of charts, both his own and other people's, together with *A Collection of Plans of Ports in the East* accompanied by detailed explanations, in his unremitting striving to making the seas safe for mariners.

After 1784 the whole emphasis of the Company's trade shifted to the China Sea. Large fleets of ships carried immense amounts of treasure to Canton for the tea investment and returning with cargoes of tea on which the survival of the Company – and to some extent the country – depended; equally large fleets of country ships from the Bay of Bengal took cotton and opium to boost the supply of silver in the company's Canton treasury; all served to concentrate the minds of those involved on the need to improve the safe navigation of the China Sea. Dalrymple was helped by James Horsburgh, whose own country ship had been wrecked off the China coast through an error in the charts. Both he and H M Elmore, another mariner in the country trade, were in Canton working on charts when Meriton arrived in 1803 and he and his fellow commanders would have been able to draw on all their findings during their stay in Canton on this and previous voyages. Horsbough succeeded Dalrymple as Company hydrographer two years after the latter's death in 1808 and drew on the services of leading surveyors using the latest techniques to produce his charts and the *East India Directory*.

The *Exeter* had a good voyage without incident. The quarter book of Captain Hamilton of the *Bombay Castle*, also taken up that season for a Bombay/China voyage, gives an idea of how the crew were employed.[3] They were divided into two watches, starboard and larboard, each with three or four midshipmen, a boatswain's mate and three quartermasters to work on the forecastle, fore top, main top, the waist and afterguard. Twenty-four men in each watch went aloft to reef the foretopsail yard, thirty-seven the main topsail yard, and fourteen men and four boys the less important mizzen topsail yard. The rest of the seamen remained on deck steering the ship and hauling at the braces and tackles.

Captain Meriton was obviously a strict disciplinarian. On two occasions during the voyage he ordered a seaman to be flogged: one for drunkenness and insolence while on duty and for seditious language when about to be punished, the other for drunkenness and assaulting a mate.

The *Exeter* sailed via the Straits of Malacca. On arrival at Pula Rondo Captain Meriton noted in the log that his chronometer was 2° 31' too far to the eastward, proving that its rate had been losing 7' a day and not the 1' a day given him by Mr Earnshaw before he left England. Captain Meriton

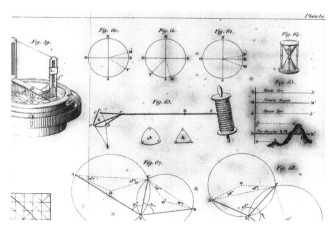

Above: The common English log (shown in centre) was the basic instrument in estimating the distance run until fairly late in the eighteenth century when the first patent log appeared. *(National Maritime Museum)*

Left: A sandglass recovered from the site of the wreck of the *Halsewell*. Each ship was equipped with a box containing at least thirty glasses of varying sizes designed to meaure denominations of time from half a watch down to a quarter of a minute.

(Photo Bryan Sutton. Courtesy Dorset County Museum)

bought rattans, betel nut, tin and sago at Penang and Malacca. There they found the *Ocean* and *Henry Addington* which had sailed from the Downs six months before the *Exeter* bound to the Cape to take off the garrison and transport them to Bombay before sailing for China.

On Saturday 3 September as the *Exeter* arrived off the Chinese coast the sky turned blood red, a sure sign of the approach of a typhoon common in those seas at that time of year. The *Exeter* made snug and rode out the storm which was accompanied by much lightning, but the *Coutts* which was in the vicinity was dismasted and completely disabled.

On 6 September the *Exeter* sailed into Macao Road. A violent squall took her aback and it blew hard with a deluge of rain so that 'the people could scarcely lay upon the yards' and there was a great deal of thunder and lightning in the night. On the following day the *Exeter* weighed and sailed past the Boca Tigris and on Thursday 8 September the ship went over the bars and anchored half a mile below the lower part of Danes Island with the other ships: the East Indiamen *Ocean*, *Earl of Abergavenny*, *Warren Hastings*, *Henry Addington*, and the *Cumberland* which had been to the Cape and Coast; a number of country ships; one Danish, two French and several American ships. Gone were the large Swedish ships which had dominated the trade twenty years earlier, buying tea which was smuggled into Britain, accounting for over half of the thirteen million pounds consumed annually in the coun-

try at that time. The act of 1784 reducing the duty on tea had eliminated this competition. Two ships at Canton in 1804, the *Rollo* and the *Atlas*, had been freighted by the English government to carry prisoners to Botany Bay and taken up on their home run by the Company to bring back teas. American ships were now evident in large numbers, having favoured nation status with the British government.

As the rigging was taken down and overhauled and got back up again the Hoppo's assistant came on board to measure the ship. The routine of unrigging, unloading, cleaning, repairing and repainting the ship during the five month stay in port began. Captain Meriton went up to Canton in one of the boats carrying his private trade goods to take up residence in the English factory with the Select Committee of Supercargoes and attend to his personal trade until the ship's departure. Established in 1779 to represent the company and buy the tea for all the ships, the Select Committee was a far different group of people from the merchants who had conducted the *Edgecote*'s trade fifty years earlier. By the time Henry Meriton arrived in 1803, appointment to this group was the greatest prize in the company's patronage, reserved for the closest 'friends' of the Chairs. The Supercargoes lived in luxurious ease while they amassed the personal fortunes that would enable them to live out their retirement in England as gentlemen. There were disadvantages: they were forced to be celibate, as women were not allowed up to Canton; they were

An Indiaman taking in her cargo at Whampoa.

(BL OIOC)

restricted to a small area around the factories where they lived a siege-like existence, perpetually on the defensive against the calumny spread against the British by the Portuguese jesuits all over China and the arbitrary behaviour of the mandarins, the Chinese officials. Lord Macartney's embassy of 1793 to secure a charter of rights for the English trade had signally failed to elicit from the Chinese emperor any relaxation of the restraints on the trade so irksome to both the company's servants and the commanders of the ships. Faced with the common enemy – Chinese officialdom – the Committee and the Hong merchants developed an excellent working relationship based on mutual trust and respect. Ponqua was the Security Merchant allocated to the *Exeter*.

There was no shortage of incidents to threaten the tranquil conduct of trade. The men had to have liberty after being so long at sea, and brawling was frequent despite the authorities' attempts to limit it by confining the different nationals to separate islands. The wounding or even death of a Chinese for

which the judiciary demanded the life of any man, regardless of whether or not he was the guilty party; the bad behaviour of the crews of the country ships over whom the Select Committee had no control but on whose opium receipts the tea investment depended; the discovery of Chinese women found on board the ships – all these circumstances could result in the withdrawal of the Grand Chop (permission to sail) with consequent delays and huge demurrage bills until an appropriate bribe was given to the relevant official – 'all part of the game of clocks and watches.'

Drunkenness was the greatest evil, as insoluble as it was persistent. Petty officials erected stills producing the poisonous 'samshu' on Danes Island within reach of the ships, in contravention of the law agreed by the Chinese and the Select Committee, while the Dutch were always a good source of supply at Whampoa. Drunkenness was the cause of a serious incident while the *Exeter* was at Whampoa, with John Cotterell the chief instigator. He refused duty while drunk

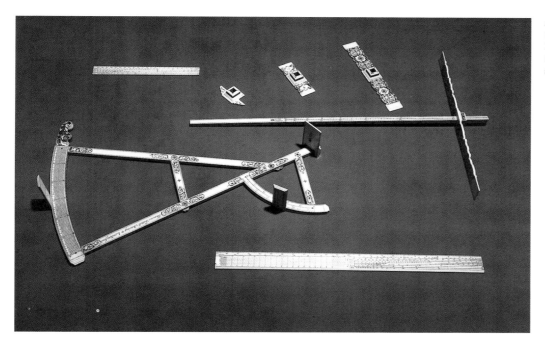

A cross-staff and a back-staff (or Davis' quadrant), for over 200 years the chief navigation instrument for measuring the altitude of the sun.
(National Maritime Museum)

and attempted to strike the second mate when he tried to confine him. The mate struck Cotterell, knocking him down. His head was injured in the fall and the surgeon sent him to his hammock. Two other seamen were confined: Moon for abetting Cotterell; Aldridge for drunkenness, riot, mutiny and tumult. On hearing about the incident, Captain Meriton judged it to be sufficiently serious to return to the ship to hold a consultation of his officers to examine the offenders. Cotterell was ordered to the gangway for punishment but was declared unfit by the surgeon and sent back to bed. All agreed that Moon should be punished and he was given a dozen lashes at the gangway. Aldridge had earlier used mutinous language and tried to incite the crew to disorder in the captain's hearing. In the incident under consideration he had quitted his night watch in a drunken state and behaved riotously, refusing to be quiet. Even after being put in irons he persisted in seditious and mutinous language, and when the second mate attempted to gag him he had torn the mate's shirt off his back 'in a most violent manner'. He was ordered to receive two dozen lashes at the gangway but a further two dozen were administered before he showed any sign of contrition or acceptance of his crime.

The Select Committee delegated powers of supervising the men to the commodore of the season. The *Exeter*'s seamen periodically took their turn in patrolling the river, rowing up and down in boats, all men being refused liberty on those days. The commanders that season were fortunate that the Hoppo 'seems to have been almost human', not 'rapacious and oppressive, filled with the insolence of low-bred ignorance.'[4]

The *Jahangir* country ship that had arrived late in July brought rumours of the renewal of war with France. If no convoy arrived in time the Select Committee faced the awesome responsibility of arranging for the safe return of the huge fleet of Company and country ships, valued at more than £7 million.

The Committee considered every aspect of the situation.[5] They were opposed to delaying the sailing of the fleet: there was a strong Dutch force at Batavia, possibly reinforced by a French squadron. Any delay would increase the danger from this quarter, while once winter set in, the passage round the Cape would combine both wartime and physical hazards. They judged that the Dutch would be disinclined to stray far from their ports and cruising ground knowing Admiral Rainier was in the area with a superior force. Britain's delay in giving up the Cape of Good Hope would equally lead the Dutch to strengthen the Straits of Bally, making the passage between Borneo and Java very dangerous. The Straits of Malacca, on the other hand, had several advantages: according to the latest intelligence Malacca and Penang remained in English possession and, warned by the *Jahangir* of the imminent resumption of war, would be preparing their defences against a Dutch or French attack. It was a good season for the Straits of Malacca, and an 'easy and expeditious' route with which the commanders were familiar; the East Indiamen would provide protection for the returning country ships, water and supplies would be available, and there would be a possibility of getting a convoy for the Indiamen as far as St Helena. Intelligence of the enemy might be available there to determine whether to go on to Achin or to return via an east-

Hadley's quadrant or octant of 1731 which replaced the less accurate Davis' back-staff and marked the breakthrough in navigational progress which took place in the eighteenth century. *(National Maritime Museum)*

Watch number 512 by Earnshaw, one of a few watchmakers who produced instruments within the financial means of the East India Company's officers in the latter years of the eighteenth century.

(National Maritime Museum)

ern passage if the French and Dutch had a formidable force in the Bay of Bengal.

Having considered the best route the Committee were faced with two major decisions: should they wait for official intelligence; and should they divide the fleet. The general opinion was that since all the fleet would be ready by the end of the month and there was no commercial need to send two fleets, a single, stronger fleet would be preferable. If it were risky to despatch the whole fleet by the eastern route it was doubly risky to divide it. To divide the fleet and send it via the Straits of Malacca would expose each to attack by a small force of frigates, while they may not attempt to attack the whole fleet. Such concentrated strength might even deter two or three line of battle ships which the 'good conduct, spirit and skill of our Commanders' would, perhaps, successfully repulse. If such an enemy force were stationed off Pula Auro, their usual station, it could successfully pick off each half of a divided fleet in turn. The India fleet had some help in the persons of two naval officers, Lts Fowler and Flinders, and twelve survivors of a stranded naval vessel had been allocated to the *Bombay Castle* to make up the numbers. Captain Timmins of the *Royal George* had himself been a naval lieutenant.

Security required involving as few people as possible. Only the three senior commanders and Captain Meriton 'in whose knowledge and prudence we have the greatest confidence and his numerous voyages to China may have enabled him to acquire more correct information on the several tracks than many others senior to him in the service' were asked to express their opinions on the Committee's conclusions in writing.

Captain Meriton read the Committee's report 'repeatedly with the greatest care and attention' before replying that the fleet '. . . would combine a force so respectable *in reality* and from their numbers much more in *appearance* that no part of the Enemy's Squadron detached (particularly of Frigates) would succeed in Capture, if they even attacked – the chance of falling in with the whole of the Force in India is scarcely probable and therefore I do not think the risk equal to combining the force.' He came down strongly in favour of returning by way of the Straits of Malacca, not doubting that Malacca and Penang were in British hands, so precluding a French and Dutch rendezvous there, 'and surely the British fleet will be watchful of that navigation.' The only danger he envisaged was approaching the Straits from Pula Auro, but felt the French Admiral would expect the fleet to avoid the eastern tracks.

Apart from anxiety about the voyage home, Captain Meriton and his officers were plagued by a high sick list, due mainly to diarrhoea, which varied between twenty and thirty-six over a long period. The situation was not helped by the surgeon's death just before the fleet sailed. The other major problem was the ship's persistently taking in water, necessitating the employment of Chinese constantly working the pumps.

While final preparations for the voyage were made – taking in the St Helena stores and the last of the tea – the *Exeter*'s crew spent a good deal of time making boarding netting and were exercised in the use of small arms and the great guns. Captain Meriton obviously took the company's new instructions to the ship owners in 1801 seriously: they were to provide netting to deter boarders and were to 'post a sufficient number of Men in the tops either with swivels or Musquetoons and pole axes' to fire down on the boarders trying to climb up the nets.[6] There was also great attention paid to exercising the topgallant yards.

On 29 January Captain Meriton came back on board together with seventeen Chinese hired for the return voyage. The same day the *Exeter* was surveyed and despatched. At daylight on Tuesday 7 February, she weighed in company with the *Earl Camden*, Captain Nathaniel Dance, commodore, *Warley, Alfred, Royal George, Coutts, Wexford, Ganges, Abergavenny, Henry Addington, Bombay Castle, Hope, Dorsetshire, Ocean, Lord Castlereagh*, East Indiamen, and the *Shaw Nisera, Jahangir, Minerva, David Scott, Ardecier, Neptune* and *Gilwell* country ships and the *Ganges* brig. The *Warren Hastings* and *Cumberland* caught up later.

The following days were squally with rain, strong gales and a following sea and the fleet was often scattered. On Tuesday at daylight, finding the *Exeter* alone, Captain Meriton mustered the people to quarters, examined them and cleared for action. The *Exeter*'s log records:

Wednesday 15
Soon after noon perceived the *Alfred, Hope, Royal George* and *Bombay Castle* out chasing with the signal for an enemy. Soon saw five strange sail – at half-past two the commodore made the signal to form line ahead 2 cables; also to keep in close order. At 4pm signal to conceal all lights and keep hammocks up; people at quarters during night; at 3pm could see the enemy: one 74 gun ship, two frigates, one corvette and a brig standing for us; at 8pm they hove to on our starboard quarter, our fleet lying to on starboard, the country ships on our starboard bow. Lay to all night with everything in the most perfect readiness for action.

Captain Hamilton's Station and Quarter Book give us an idea how the *Exeter*'s company would have been deployed. Captain Meriton and his chief mate were on the quarterdeck with the purser to take notes. The captain was in charge of three carronades on each side with three men and boarders with pikes. The third mate commanded the four foremost

guns, the gunner commanding the gun deck fore and aft. A midshipman was in charge in the light room on his own, with one to pass the magazine, two to fill with powder, two to carry the powder to the five aftermost guns and the foremost guns and one to carry powder to the two after guns – presumably the stern guns which were of such importance in the defence of the ships. The fourth mate, with nine men, was in charge of the small arms on the poop and elsewhere, with two midshipmen on the poop and braces. Several men were allocated to the braces as it was essential damaged rigging should be knotted and spliced immediately to ensure the ship remained manageable. They were also necessary for making major changes to the ship's course. One was allocated to the 'will and wings' to look out for damage between wind and water. Each man had his station in case fire broke out and the boat crews knew which boat to man in case of abandoning ship. Had there been a chance to board the enemy the company were to get pikes from round the capstan and prepare to act in conjunction with those with small arms. The boarders would come up from below on receiving the order armed with cutlasses and tomahawks and pistols to repel the enemy, but the captain of the guns would remain at his station.

The *Exeter*'s log continues:

At daylight saw the enemy lay to about 6 miles to windward, the different boats passing to their large ship. At 6am the commodore's signal to amend the line ahead. At 8am signal for the order of sailing. Seeing they did not come down the commodore showed his colours and made easy sail and steered our course . . . at half-past 8 signal to steer SWbyS at 9 the enemy made sail after us. *Ganges* signal to go within hail. At 10 same

The sextant, developed in 1767, combined the best features of the quadrant and the reflecting circle. *(National Maritime Museum)*

Days.	Stars Names.	12 Hours. ° ′ ″	15 Hours. ° ′ ″	18 Hours. ° ′ ″	21 Hours. ° ′ ″
1	The Sun.	40. 59. 11	42. 34. 44	44. 9. 51	45. 44. 35
2		53. 32. 7	55. 4. 24	56. 36. 16	58. 7. 45
3		65. 39. 18	67. 8. 27	68. 37. 14	70. 5. 39
4		77. 22. 36	78. 48. 58	80. 15. 1	81. 40. 46
5		88. 45. 20	90. 9. 27	91. 33. 21	92. 57. 0
6		99. 52. 6	101. 14. 34	102. 36. 52	103. 59. 1
7		110. 47. 42	112. 9. 6	113. 30. 25	114. 51. 40
6	Aldebaran.	50. 36. 10	52. 4. 5	53. 31. 57	54. 59. 44
7		62. 17. 43	63. 45. 10	65. 12. 34	66. 39. 57
8	Pollux.	31. 25. 48	32. 53. 11	34. 20. 40	35. 48. 12
9		43. 7. 5	44. 35. 4	46. 3. 8	47. 31. 15
10	Regulus.	17. 51. 57	19. 20. 36	20. 49. 26	22. 18. 27
11		29. 45. 36	31. 15. 26	32. 45. 26	34. 15. 35
12		41. 48. 49	43. 19. 55	44. 51. 10	46. 22. 36
13		54. 2. 11	55. 34. 36	57. 7. 12	58. 39. 59
14		66. 26. 28	68. 0. 18	69. 34. 20	71. 8. 33
15	Spica ♍	25. 4. 34	26. 39. 23	28. 14. 26	29. 49. 44
16		37. 49. 37	39. 26. 14	41. 3. 5	42. 40. 8
17		50. 48. 40	52. 26. 59	54. 5. 31	55. 44. 15
18		64. 1. 2	65. 41. 3	67. 21. 18	69. 1. 48
19	Antares.	31. 37. 14	33. 19. 7	35. 1. 13	36. 43. 32
20		45. 18. 29	47. 2. 10	48. 46. 5	50. 30. 12
21		59. 14. 6	60. 59. 31	62. 45. 11	64. 31. 2
22		73. 23. 37	75. 10. 43	76. 58. 2	78. 45. 31
23	β Capri-corni.	33. 17. 26	35. 4. 38	36. 52. 4	38. 39. 45
24		47. 41. 9	49. 29. 53	51. 18. 44	53. 7. 40
25	α Aquilæ.	65. 57. 35	67. 29. 54	69. 2. 36	70. 35. 39
26		78. 24. 51	79. 59. 9	81. 33. 29	83. 7. 45

A page from Tobias Mayer's lunar tables, which were published in England in 1770. (*From* Navigation in the Days of Captain Cook, *Maritime Monograph no 19, 1794, National Maritime Museum*)

Captain Nathaniel Dance.

signal to *Royal George*. At halfpast 9 signal to prepare for action, for *Ganges* to shorten sail, at noon enemy coming after us in line ahead under all sail our fleet in order of sailing under easy canvas at 10 past 1pm *Royal George* signal to tack, and *Ganges* and *Warley*. Commodore tacked and intended fleet to tack in succession. At halfpast 1pm enemy line of battle ship (a rear admiral French) opened her fire on *Royal George*. The fleet tacking as fast as possible but unfortunately the manoeuvre not being commenced soon enough many of our ships got foul of each other and prevented others from tacking in which time the *Royal George* lay exposed to a heavy fire from the enemy's

line when *Ganges*, *Alfred*, *Commodore* and *Warley* got up, the enemy made all possible sail from us. The *Royal George* made signal of distress – in want of immediate assistance. The whole fleet in chase of the enemy under all sail. From 2-4pm the *Hope* and ourselves were gaining on them fast, but from the unlucky circumstance of our running to leeward of the Strait's mouth, were obliged to tack and give over chase and had the mortification of seeing them escape when no doubt if *all* the ships came into action we should have given a handsome account of them *all*.

At 3.30pm the commodore made the signal to tack and by 5pm they had found the country ships. The *Royal George* had three men wounded, one of whom had subsequently died, and had received a good deal of damage to her hull and rigging. At sunset the enemy ships were just in sight standing to eastward. The *Exeter*'s log records for 6am the following day, 'Put all chests down and cabins up. Everything as before. Put into Malacca.'

The enemy ships were the 74-gun line of battle ship *Marengo*, flag ship of Rear Admiral Linois; two frigates, the

40-gun *Belle Poule* and 36-gun *Semillante*; the 22 gun corvette *Berceau* and a 16 gun Batavian brig, the *Aventurier*.

During the following days the fleet repeatedly anchored and weighed in squally weather with much thunder and lightning, frequently much scattered. On Tuesday 28 February HMS *Albion* and *Septer*, 74 gun ships, came into the fleet and in hot, sultry weather all made sail to the north-west. With such a large fleet, in squally conditions, it was with great difficulty that the ships kept clear of one another. On the afternoon of Sunday 18 March in excessively hot weather the commodore made the signal for the country ships to part company, while the commodore with the *Septer* and the sixteen East Indiamen hauled to windward. At daylight the highland of Ceylon lay 20 to 25 leagues to the south-west.

On Saturday 9 June the fleet arrived at St Helena and HMS *Plantagenet* took over to convoy the fleet to England. The *Exeter* had never ceased taking in water, and the other ships lent Captain Meriton twenty-nine Chinese to keep the pumps going continuously. She arrived safely in the Downs with the rest of the fleet on 8 August to the acclaim of the whole City of London.

The extraordinary failure of the powerful French squadron under Admiral Linois to damage or capture a significant number of the China fleet is difficult to explain. Linois was reportedly on his guard because a Portuguese captain had told him that three of the Indiamen had been converted into 64 gun ships. This information appeared to be confirmed when three of the large ships burned lights all night, actually in defiance of Captain Dance's orders. Linois' suspicion turned to certainty the following morning when three of the ships raised blue ensigns and pendants, the rest of the fleet raising red colours with no pendants. Linois also claimed that seven or eight of the Indiamen fired from two decks, which must have confirmed Napoleon's resigned opinion that all his admirals suffered from double vision.

From his station on the Malabar coast Admiral Rainier

applauded the Select Committee's decision: 'your disposition for the sailing of the ships and the Country Trade fully merited the success that followed that prudent and well concerted measure – the whole Country Trade reached their several points of destination without a single capture.'[7]

At a special meeting called on 22 August at the Jerusalem Coffee House the Society of East India Commanders commissioned a portrait of Nathaniel Dance and a painting of the action at Pula Auro, saying they 'had judged this Action to surpass credibility, when the intelligence of it first reached England.'[8] The East India Company awarded Captain Dance a £500 annuity for bringing the fleet safely home while the various insurance companies also rewarded him.

The *Naval Chronicle* expressed the general view of the fleet's action: 'by its unprecedented success it has added to our national fame; and by its preservation of so vast a property, at this juncture, it has added to our means of security and strengthened our sinews of war.'[9]

Notes:
1. BL OIOC. L/MAR/B138L-N, 1803-1804: Log of the *Exeter*.
2. BL OIOC. L/AG/1/6/23: Commercial Journal.
3. NMM HMN 33: Hamilton's Station and Quarter Book.
4. Morse: *op cit*, Vol II, 1803.
5. BL OIOC. G/12/268: Select Committee Consultations, 12 January 1804.
   See also *Les Flottes des Compagnies des Indes 1600-1857*, pp265-281: Wraight J.M.: *Nathaniel Dance and the Battle of Pula Auro, 1804*, for an excellent appraisal.
6. BL OIOC. E1/238, pp26-30, no. 47 of 24 September 1801, reissued 1803.
7. Morse: *op cit*, Vol II,
8. NMM. HMN/38
9. *Naval Chronicle*, Vol 12, 1804, pp345-349.

CHAPTER 10

THE COMPANY'S STEAMERS

An unusual vessel dropped anchor among the season's Indiamen in Balasore Road early in December 1825. She was the *Enterprise*. Captain James Johnston, a 500-ton paddle steamer measuring 141ft, built on the Thames by Gordon & Co, a firm of iron founders who had taken over Dudman's shipyard at Deptford.[1] Her two 60hp engines, made by Maudslay, Sons & Field of Lambeth, drove a pair of collapsible paddles that could be hoisted on deck when a favourable gale of wind enable the ship to sail by means of her lugsails.

High hopes were pinned by the merchants of Calcutta on this first major experiment in steam communication between England and India. They saw in the provision of a regular steamer service via the Cape of Good Hope a means of gaining advantage over their rivals in Bombay, who were looking to the overland route for their future salvation. *Enterprise*'s commander, James Henry Johnston, an ex-naval man who had devoted several years to promoting steam navigation, himself favoured the Red Sea route, but he had been unable to get any backing for this from the General Steam Navigation Company in London. Others promised support if he could find backers in Bengal for a relay of steamers, but in Calcutta the interest at that particular time would only extend to the opening of a fund out of which a prize of a lakh of rupees, or about £10,000, was offered to the first steamer to sail from England, to Calcutta and back to England twice, averaging not more than seventy days on each of the four passages.

It was in a bid to win this prize that a group of shareholders got together to finance *Enterprise*, but though her achievement was memorable, her time of more than double the target was disappointing. She sailed from Falmouth on 16 August 1825 and arrived at Diamond Harbour, Calcutta, after a passage of 13,700 miles, on 7 December, a total of one hundred and fifteen days. Compared with the ninety odd days achieved quite frequently by the Company's ordinary sailing ships on a good run, this was by no means an encouraging performance.

As the official in charge of public works at the East India House pointed out at a later Parliamentary enquiry into steam communication between England and India, this was not a fair trial. The coals had been badly organised and much time had been lost. The ship had not had sufficient power for her size – a proportion of 1hp to 4 tons was too low. She had had a late start and so had not found the north-east trade wind. However, at the time of her arrival in Calcutta excuses had little effect on the backers who were looking for a good chance of a return on their capital. Her soot-begrimed passengers were only too pleased to disembark and it was unlikely that anyone could be found to sail in her back to England.

Steam navigation in general in India may well have suffered a severe setback had not an emergency arisen providing the opportunity to demonstrate the utility of steam. Lord Amherst, the Governor General, had been provoked into declaring war on the Burmese king after several anti-British incidents, and launched an amphibious campaign. The *Diana*, a small 32hp river and coastal passenger steamer employed in ferrying passengers from the Indiamen up to Calcutta, (since her launch from Kyd's Dock, Kidderpore, in 1823) was purchased by the Bengal Government. She ran over to the Arakan coast where she was usefully employed in towing men of war boats into position for attack and carrying personnel up the Irrawaddy. She even captured a number of Burmese boats in one incident. Even the little 8hp *Pluto*, with paddles mounted in place of her buckets, exchanged an ignominious existence dredging the Bay of Bengal for the more glorious one of carrying troops over the reefs and shoals of the

Right, above: To the Honourable East India Company belongs the distinction of ordering the world's first iron warship, the paddle sloop *Nemesis* launched by Lairds in November 1839. Here she is seen scudding before a heavy gale on her passage from England to China.
(BL OIOC)

Right, below: The paddle steamer *Enterprise*, the first steamer to sail round the Cape of Good Hope. *(Science Museum)*

The paddle steamer *Diana* proved the value of steam power during the first Burma war.
(National Maritime Museum)

Arakan coast.[2] *Enterprise*'s arrival at Calcutta was providential. Her disillusioned owners were only too happy to settle for the £40,000 offered by the Bengal Government; as a troop carrier, under Captain Johnston's command, *Enterprise* took despatches and carried the sick and wounded for the last nine months of the war.

By the time Lord William Bentinck arrived to relieve the retiring Governor-General, Lord Amherst, in July 1828, a number of steamboats were chugging up and down the Hooghly between Calcutta and the Sandheads, towing ships, carrying mail, and ferrying passengers. The *Irrawaddy* and the *Ganges*, designed for use as river tugs and sea-going transports in the fight with the Burmese, were built in the Calcutta shipyard and fitted with engines sent out from England, with engineers to supervise their construction. Although hostilities were ended before they were launched, useful work was found for the *Irrawaddy* on the Tennasserim coast and the *Ganges* joined the *Enterprise* as an accommodation vessel and packet. A second pair were launched in Calcutta early in 1828. These were the *Hooghly* and *Berhampooter*, shallow draught vessels, also locally built, and fitted with Maudslay engines shipped out from England.

Headway in steam navigation was obviously being made, but it may well have been piecemeal and haphazard without the direction brought to it by Lord Bentinck. He was an experienced planner, used to overseeing major projects. He was also – and remained so to his death – a steam enthusiast. But for Lord Bentinck steam was not merely one more step along the road of technical progress. He considered it to be the key to improving the government of India, which in his view was

bad. By bringing England and India nearer together, steam would enable the intelligent but backward Indians to improve their culture, while English people generally would be able to keep their eye on 'those cold, selfish and unfeeling' Englishmen who ruled India for the Company. He felt that 'in proportion as the communication between the two countries shall be facilitated and shortened, so will civilised Europe be approximated, as it were, to those benighted regions'.

Symbolically, it was the *Enterprise*, in the command of Captain Johnston, which carried Lord Bentinck up to Calcutta in July 1828, a short time after the launching of the *Hooghly* and the *Berhampooter*. These were the brain-child of the far-sighted political agent on the North-East frontier, David Scott, who had seen the possibilities of employing river steamers in the wilds of Assam, just acquired by the Company following the Burma war; he had already started mining the local coal to provide the fuel. Bentinck, however, postponed their departure for a time. He took the broad view: it was necessary first of all to determine what were the problems of administering the large Bengal presidency; having decided what these were, it would be possible to see in what ways steam navigation could be employed in solving them.

So much attention has always been paid to the length of time taken by one of the Company's ships to reach India, that the fact that many Company servants and soldiers faced another three or four months voyage up the Ganges on arrival at Calcutta has been overlooked. By the time Lord Bentinck took up his post as Governor-General this problem had considerably increased. Through conquest or treaties British influence had penetrated into the northern mountain ranges of Afghanistan, the Punjab, and up to the borders of Nepal and Tibet. The Bengal presidency had become so large that its division was imminent and by 1833 had been officially reorganised into the Presidency of Bengal and the North West Provinces. A constant stream of government officials and military personnel moved slowly north-west to Agra, Cawnpore and Lucknow, whilst a continuous procession of treasure chests containing all the rents collected from these outlying regions returned, heavily guarded, to the capital. The great rivers – the Ganges and its tributaries in the east and the Indus in the west – were the Grand Trunk roads of India. The Indian government was put to great expense hiring native boats to transport personnel and prove and adequate guard for the treasure. The difficulty was that the traditional sailing craft could either barely move at all or were swept along at an incredible rate according to the state of the monsoon; the value of a steamer service which would be largely unaffected by the seasons was immeasurable.

Lord Bentinck saw in the provision of a steamer service between Calcutta and Allahabad not only a means of saving money – the absolute priority in his brief as Governor-General – but a means of controlling the activities of the junior officers, who took full advantage of the licence afforded by the customary means of transport. The traditional methods of conveyance would have to continue for the married officers with wives and families and whole households to transport, but steam vessels would be a most effective means of transporting junior officers to upcountry stations.

It was decided that one of the steamers built for service on the Brahmaputra should be used to carry out trials on the Ganges to ascertain the viability of a steamer service. In keeping with the spirit of the time, a race was held between the *Hooghly* and the *Berhampooter* along a stretch of the river near Calcutta, lined with steam enthusiasts. The outcome of the competition decided that it would be the *Hooghly* that sailed up to Allahabad on an experimental voyage, coal being sent ahead to four points along the route and to her destination. The priorities of any future steam service were revealed by this experiment: native river pilots who understood the freakish behaviour of the Ganges would need to be stationed at frequent intervals along the river, to keep their eyes on the daily shifting and changing river bed. The boats would have to be purpose built: hulls like those of sailing ships or floating baths – so common among the early steamers being built in Europe – were not appropriate to the peculiar conditions of the Ganges. A speed of more than six miles per hour was necessary for any progress to be made in the narrow parts of the river where the current ran very fast. It was important that the draught should not exceed 2ft. The *Hooghly* and *Berhampooter* would certainly not be suitable for regular service: the 40 miles average run per day achieved by the *Hooghly* on her trial run compared very unfavourably with the 120 miles to 140 miles of the Ohio and Mississippi river steamers. With more powerful engines the steamers could be used as tugs. Separate accommodation for passengers – another most obvious need revealed by the experiment – could be provided in a high wooden poop built on the steamer itself, or in a separate vessel towed beside or behind it. The steamers had to be very slender to pass through the frequent narrow channels.

In January, the *Hooghly* was again steering in a north-westerly direction up the Ganges, this time carrying all the Governor-General's baggage and most of his servants up to Benares, and in March she took the Governor-General's pinnace in tow with him on board back to Calcutta, using only one of her engines. When all the salient design features required for inclusion in future vessels was agreed, Captain Johnston, who had been put in charge of all the government steamers, was sent to London to brief the East India officials

on the requirements for a steam relay service on the Ganges, to supervise the construction of the new steam engines and to draw up plans of tugs and cargo vessels required.

Captain Johnston found a keen listener in Thomas Love Peacock, poet and novelist, who had assumed, by virtue of his post as Senior Assistant Examiner at the East India House, general supervision of all public works. Fortuitously, as in the case of Lord Bentinck, Mr Peacock's imagination had been fired by the challenge of steam and he had spent much time in the experimental steamer on the Thames. Although he supported the enthusiasm shown so far in Calcutta, he was disturbed at the high cost of the experiments to date; there had been considerable depreciation and good money had been thrown after bad by purchasing second-hand steamboats. It was agreed after discussion that the best and latest equipment in Europe should be purchased. Johnston submitted all the relevant statistics and logistics – goods, personnel, treasure – pertaining to transport up and down the Ganges, and these requirements were translated into the number of steamers required and the number of voyages each would need to make. When the resulting costs were compared with those of traditional hiring it was agreed that the much higher costs of creating a steamer service would be more than offset by the revenue the steamers would earn as carriers of light goods.

By a resolution of the Court of Directors in June 1831 liberal support was given for the project. Captain Johnston then left on a tour of Europe to discover what he could from steamers employed on the European rivers, where they were already playing an important part in commercial activity. Conditions on the Rhône he found to be very similar to those on the Ganges, and he was impressed by the 'gondoles' used for towing barges, which lined the Lyons 'quais'. In Paris he found an iron cargo-towing steamer which showed no signs of corrosion after ten years service and another iron boat which drew only 33in. Johnston agreed with Richard Trevithick, a far-sighted engineer who approached the company with plans for an iron barge, that 'it had been ascertained by practice that wrought iron barges on the canals of a quarter of an inch thick, are lighter, cheaper, stronger, draw less water and have more storage room than those made of wood', but would not go along with him on the question of high pressure boilers. Trevithick proposed a high pressure engine of 100hp suitable for strong currents and shoal waters. It was very small and consumed very little fuel, but there had been several cases of exploding high pressure engines and reliable safety devices were still not developed.

By October 1831 the specifications were formulated: four steam tugs and four accommodation boats were to be built with iron hulls measuring 120ft in length with a 20-22ft beam, fitted with iron boilers and low-pressure condensing engines and with a 2ft draught. The court voted to adopt these specifications and invited tenders. Maudslay's submitted

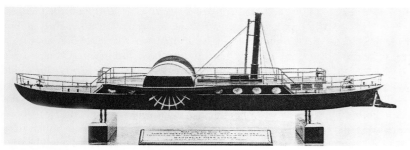

A model of Peacock's 'iron chicks', *Megna* and *Jumna*, built for towing 'flats' up and down the Hooghly.   *(Science Museum)*

an itemised estimate but added that the limits of draught and speed bordered on the impossible. However, at Christmas 1831, Maudslay's were awarded the contract and six months later the first of what came to be called 'Peacock's iron chicks' was hatched. This was the *Lord William Bentinck* tug. These were the only boats built by Maudslay, Sons & Field who, with Boulton & Watt, Rennie, Napier, Penn and Butterly of Derby, led the field in marine engineering.[3]

Four months later, on 13 October 1832, all the Directors, with the chairman and top shipping officials, went to the East India Dock at Blackwall to board the tug with its spoon-shaped hull and tall thin funnel. She had a 22in draught – a great feat of engineering – and she proved her worth at the trials. The *Larkins* East Indiaman weighed anchor in March 1833 bound for Calcutta with the *Lord William Bentinck* and the second steam tug, the *Thames*, contained in innumerable crates in her hold. Her passengers included engineers, boiler-makers and engine drivers going out to assemble the tugs and maintain them.

By April 1834 the *Bentinck* was ready for launching and the *Thames* had been riveted together. Both were on the Ganges by the spring of 1835. They were followed by the *Mwnga* and *Jumna* and all were in operation by 1836. The tugs were 125ft in length overall, with 22ft beam, powered by two 60hp oscillating engines – an invention of Maudslay's, which incurred a great deal of criticism but which had the advantage of being compact and enabling large cylinders to be placed in a limited height, the stresses being taken almost entirely by the engine frame. Penn, another marine engineering firm, took it over and improved it later. The flue boilers were low pressure, working at 7lb per square inch, and coal was consumed at 10lb per hp per hour. The paddle wheels of 16ft diameter were expected to drive the boat at 9mph through still water or 6 to 7mph when loaded. A low mast was rigged for a square sail to supplement the engines when the wind was favourable. There was a light cabin forward of the chimney, a large cabin abaft the boilers and two small cabins and a mess room in between. An awning over the upper deck provided some chance of relaxation in a slightly cooler atmosphere.

The 'flats' or barges, 125ft in length with a 20ft beam, could take 4000 cu ft of cargo weighing 40 tons, and yet, when fully loaded, their draught did not exceed 20in. Above the hold was the accommodation deck, 7ft high, divided into fourteen passenger cabins of various sizes with a cuddy, bathrooms, pantry and store-room, butler's room, guard room and two cabins for the officers. The whole deck was surrounded by venetian blinds and the top deck protected by an awning. Honoria Marshall watched and waited for one of these pairs of tugs and 'flats' to appear round the bend of the Ganges in the summer of 1837, bringing the young Henry Lawrence from the North Western Provinces to Calcutta to marry her.

There were two routes: in the high-water season, from July to October, it was possible to pass from the Hooghly to the Ganges via the Bhagirathi; during the low-water season that river was dry and the steamers had to sail through the channels of the Sunderbans across the Ganges delta, up the Barashee and Goraee rivers and into the Ganges.

The Marine Board arranged the schedule of services, a tug and flat sailing from Calcutta once every three weeks on average. The duration of the passages up to Allahabad and back depended on the season: during the monsoon the upriver journey took only twenty days and the return as little as a week with the current flowing very fast. In the dry season twenty-four and fifteen days were normal. The Government controlled the Ganges navigation until 1846 when private enterprise took over.

Although the prize for enlightened and courageous pioneering work in the field of steam navigation must be awarded to the Bengal presidency, inspired by the Governor-General, the glory was stolen by the enthusiasts on the other side of the peninsula. It was Mountstuart Elphinstone, Governor of Bombay, who first proposed opening up the Red Sea route on a regular basis. It had been used on occasions previously for important despatches - the news of Nelson's victory at the Battle of the Nile was taken to India via Alexandria and Suez and the Red Sea. Sir John Malcolm, who succeeded Elphinstone, concentrated on developing it. He ordered surveys to be carried out in the Laccadive Islands by Commander Moresby of the Indian Navy, to find a suitable harbour for a port of call for steamers sailing from Calcutta and Madras. In 1829 he directed Commander Moresby to transfer to the Arabian coast and the offshore islands to prepare for a trial run between Bombay and Suez. During one of the many prolonged enquiries into the possibility of opening up steam communication between England and India, the court of directors voted for one seagoing vessel for the Bombay Presidency to bring it into line with the Bengal

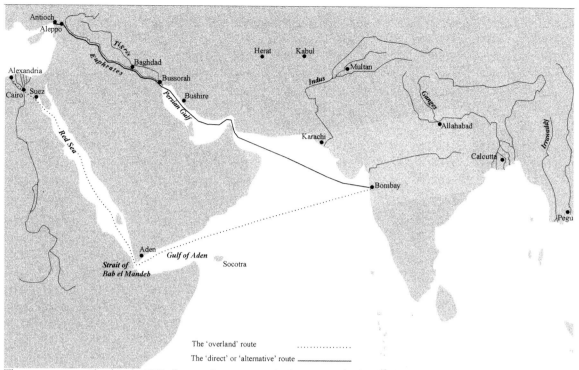

The two routes considered in the 1830s for a regular steamer service between England and India.

Presidency which had three, albeit poor ones. The hull was to be built in Bombay dockyard, the machinery in England and shipped out. Named after one of the Directors, the *Hugh Lindsay* was launched from Bombay dockyard in 1829 – the year the *Rocket* proved her worth at the Rainhill trials. The following March, while the *Hooghly* was towing the Governor-General's pinnace from Benares to Calcutta, the *Hugh Lindsay*, in command of Captain J J Wilson of the Indian Navy, sailed from Bombay bound to Suez with mails for England via the overland route. The *Enterprise* had been intended for this mark of distinction, but on arrival at Bombay from Calcutta her boilers were found to be defective.

Commander Wilson was actually in command of the sloop of war *Coote*, a higher ranking vessel than the noisy and sooty steamer. He did not share his brother officers' contempt of the new steamers and even chose to drop rank to assume the command. As he explained in a pamphlet later: 'I was the staunch assertor that the Red Sea route was *the one* that must become through the means of steam the highroad to India and I was stimulated by a desire to be *the first steam navigator of the Red Sea*'.[4]

The *Hugh Lindsay* was a small steamer of 480 tons, carrying two 80hp engines, drawing 11ft increasing to 13ft when laden. She could carry five days' supply of coal. Additional supplies of 600 tons were taken on ahead to Aden, the first

coaling station, in a collier towed by the *Thetis* brig of the Indian Navy. She reached Aden on 31 March, under steam alone, with only 6 hours of coal left. She stopped at Mocha to deliver despatches, at Jedda for fresh supplies of coal, and arrived at Suez on 22 April. Her total time was thirty-two days sixteen hours including stoppages. On her return passage she called at Kosire, Jedda and Mocha, reaching Bombay on 29 May, nineteen days and fourteen hours actual sailing time, all under steam. Her total distance travelled was 5928 miles at less than 6mph.

This was the first salvo fired by the supporters of the 'overland' – or Red Sea – route, as opposed to the Cape route favoured by the Calcutta merchants, who feared the former route would benefit their rivals. Arguments raged for about fifteen years, occupying thousands of hours of House of Commons time, before a comprehensive service catering for all the presidencies was started by the Peninsular & Oriental Company in 1844.

The Red Sea route was not the only overland route. In 1827 Thomas Peacock had been asked to look into the whole question of the communication by steam between England and India. Giving evidence in March 1832 before a Select Committee on the affairs of the East India Company, he was probably expressing the majority informed view when he came down quite heavily in favour of the 'direct' or 'alterna-

East India Company steam frigates, possibly *Phlegethon* and *Nemesis*, in action at Chusan, China, 1841.　　　　　　　　*(D F Harding)*

tive' route via the Persian Gulf , the Euphrates and the Great Desert to some point on the Mediterranean, preferably Aleppo.[5]

The *Enterprise*, though she had certainly laboured under some disadvantage which could have been avoided later, had shown the Cape route to be expensive, the organising of the coals complicated, and the result certainly not worth all the trouble and expense. The Red Sea route had definite limitations, not the least of which was the inability of even powered vessels to beat against the monsoon, thus restricting the service to eight months of the year. This route was also enormously expensive in coals, which had to be taken from England to Bombay in ballast, and from Bombay to coaling stations en route in sailing brigs.

Peacock was pressed hard on the subject of fuel: were there no other supplies in the area – at Cutch? Burdwan? Had New South Wales coal been tried? The Cutch coal had too much earth mixed in with it, the Burdwan coal was inferior. Australian coal had not been tried as yet. Asked what sort of time the mails could be expected to travel between England and Suez, Peacock replied about six weeks. The two timed passages between Bombay and Suez made by the *Hugh*

Lindsay to date had taken thirty-three days – twenty sailing days and thirteen taking in coals; and twenty-three days – seventeen sailing and five coaling. Asked if he thought the Red Sea would be suitable for steam navigation he replied that it was suitable *only* for steam navigation, as steamers could keep to the middle of the channel and the shores abounded with shoals. On the subject of the much-discussed canal linking the Mediterranean and the Red Sea, he said the principal obstacle was variation in levels of the two seas discovered by Napoleon's engineers.

Turning to the possibility of the navigation of the Euphrates – the traditional route used by European travellers to the Indies before the discovery of the Cape route – Mr Peacock was more optimistic: 'I think the Euphrates route would be very practical, and more advantageous than the Red Sea to this country, because it lies more in the way of all our local interests in the East; I mean, that we should pass through the Persian Gulf instead of the Red Sea'. Replying to the question as to which of the three routes mentioned he would give preference, he replied 'that by the Euphrates if it could be rendered safe from the people'. [6]

No official surveys had ever been done on this route: the

basis of all discussions was only speculation and hearsay. It was believe it would be cheaper than running a service via the Red Sea as it was known there was plenty of fuel to hand on the banks of the Euphrates. Bitumen rose to the surface in springs and, mixed with mud or camel dung, proved a most effective fuel – the American river steamers worked on wood picked up from the banks.

A strong argument in favour of developing this route was the Russian threat. Much activity had been taking place on the Oxus and it was known there were steamers on the Caspian Sea. Mr Peacock felt that if Britain could establish a service in the Persian Gulf she could keep the Russians at bay. The chief dangers to establishing a service via the Euphrates were the migrant Arab tribes and the plague, which visited the area regularly. The view was expressed that if both the Red Sea and the Persian Gulf routes could be developed, one could be used when the other was out of action for one reason or another.

Questioned on the possible time taken for the mails to reach England from Bombay via the Gulf, the Euphrates and Aleppo, Mr Peacock felt it would be less than by the Red Sea as the distance was shorter – the route was much more direct. He expected about five weeks to be average. Francis Chesney, the explorer most conversant with the Euphrates, stated that the river was definitely navigable eight months of the year, possibly the other four months with vessels of shallow draught. He agreed that the greatest obstacle was the predatory Arab tribes.

At a Select Committee of 1834, when thirty-five men of note assembled under the chairmanship of Sir Charles Grant, the East India Company chairman, the Russian threat to India was again fully aired, as well as the advantage or otherwise of the 'overland' and 'direct' routes. Thomas Peacock was now in a position to put down exact sums: it would cost £100,000 per annum for four steamers to serve the overland route compared with only £14,000 per annum for two steamers on the Euphrates.[7]

After hearing all the evidence, the Committee agreed that the establishment of a regular steamer service connecting England and India was necessary. The experiment had shown that it was possible to have steam communication between Bombay and Suez during the north-east monsoon, October to May inclusive, and that better arrangements for coaling could reduce the enormous costs. Steam communication via the Red Sea should begin on a regular footing, whether from Bombay or Calcutta depending on consultations between the government and the Company, who would share the cost of establishing the service. Everyone agreed that such a service could not in the foreseeable future be commercially viable, and that the government and Company should show the way and be willing to subsidise private enterprise. The Company ordered two more steamers for the Bombay presidency, again

to bring it into line with the Bengal presidency.

As the Persian Gulf-Euphrates route had not been sufficiently investigated, but promised to have so many advantages, the government voted £20,000 for experiments to be carried out. The Company rather guiltily added a further £5000, the Chairman excusing the paltriness of the sum by pointing out that there were political reasons for developing this route, so the money to finance it should come from parliament rather than the Company. The expedition was led by Francis Chesney, the indomitable explorer who had already spent several years amongst the wild tribes of Arabia, surveying the Euphrates on a raft, taking soundings through a hole to avoid arousing suspicion. He had then returned to London to report to the government and plead his cause with influential people; his had been the chief pressure that resulted in the convening of the 1834 Select Committee.

Two iron river steamers, aptly called the *Euphrates* and the *Tigris*, were provided by the Government for surveying those rivers, the East India Company salving its conscience by promising to buy them into the marine service for navigation on the Indus on the conclusion of the survey, and reminding everyone that the Company had already expended £60,000 to £70,000 in advancing steam navigation. In 1835, Francis Chesney started on his expedition with a small group of chosen surveyors, the chief of whom was Captain Henry Blosse Lynch of the Indian Navy, already a noted river surveyor and one whose name was to be closely associated with Mesopotamia long after the Red Sea had become the accepted route to India. The survey began at the Bay of Antioch and proceeded for several years, suffering a major setback when the *Tigris* sank. Chesney's command of the expedition ended in January 1837 but the survey was continued by officers of the Indian Navy.

Following the enquiry, steps were taken to provide the Bombay presidency with two steamers as had been decided. Orders were placed with Green, Wigram and Green for one steamer, to be engined by Maudslay, and with Robert Napier of Glasgow who was to build both hull and machinery.[7] Napier was a leading marine engineer who had re-designed the ship's hull to offer less frictional resistance to water; he had also worked with Sam Cunard to start the mail service between England and America. Each of the ships was to cost in the region of £29,000. Green informed Thomas Peacock that the *Atalanta* would be ready for launching on Saturday 14 May 1836 in the East India Dock, but Maudslay's were late in supplying the engines. There was a delay in obtaining parts and a scarcity of good workmen. The Court communicated its 'extreme disappointment' as it had been hoped the ship would reach Bombay under sail before the close of the south-west monsoon. It would now be necessary to work her way out by steam and 'subject the East India Company to considerable additional expense'. On 3 August the court was expressing its 'extreme disappointment' to Napier who had written to report delays, and on 30 August, Napier replied: 'The delay in furnishing the *Berenice* has been caused by a series of unforeseen circumstances over which I have no control, such as weather and men.'

The first of these ships to sail for India was the *Atalanta*, 617 tons and 210hp. She sailed from Falmouth on 29 December 1836 and arrived at the Cape of Good Hope thirty-five days later. She put in at Tenerife, where she underwent repairs, having lost her paddle boxes and jib boom in a gale at Maye and Fernando. After calling at Mauritius and Cochin she arrived at Bombay on 13 April 1837 having passed sixty-six days at sea entirely under steam, and at times by sail. Her sister ship, the *Berenice*, Captain Grant, 756tons and 220hp, carrying a battery of 8in guns, did not leave England until more than a month after the arrival of the *Atalanta* at Bombay. She too sailed from Falmouth, on 10 March, touching at all the same ports except Cochin, and arrived at Bombay on 14 June. She averaged 8mph on the whole passage, which beat *Atalanta*'s performance by five days sailing time and eighteen days on the whole voyage. Her commander declared the *Berenice* to be an excellent sea boat; she answered well under canvas in heavy weather and was in as efficient a state as when she sailed.

The Company's policy with regard to the development of a steam packet service was complicated by two things: its own indecision on the future of the Company's Marine based at Bombay – from 1830 onwards termed the Indian Navy – and the government's failure to produce money, which it had repeatedly declared was necessary for the furtherance of steam communication with India. Development was therefore piecemeal, and consequently fell far short of the ideal. The *Atalanta* and *Berenice* were the first of several steamers built to

The Company's war steamer *Berenice*, built on the Clyde by the famous designer and builder Robert Napier, was one of the two first sea-going steamers ordered by the company. *(BL OIOC)*

form part of the Indian Navy but required to perform service as mail packets, an uncomfortable dual role that persisted for twenty years until rationalisation was achieved by granting a subsidy to a private company – the P&O – to provide a comprehensive service covering all the British settlements in the East.

Protection of Indian interests and the maintenance of British influence in the Persian Gulf was left to the Company. Three iron river steamers, *Assyria*, *Nicrotis* and *Nimrod* – similar to those in use on the Ganges – were sent out in sections to be assembled in the Company's shipyard and employed in the Persian Gulf. They were joined later by the ageing *Euphrates*, after she had finished surveying that river in 1842, and the pick of the Indian Navy was selected to command them. Later they were transferred to the Indus and became the core of the Indus Flotilla.

Yet another Select Committee of enquiry into the question of steam communication between England and India was held in 1837, this time under that veteran of steam, Lord William Bentinck, who had finished his term as Governor-General in 1835 and was devoting his last years to promoting steam power of all kinds. This time all the attention was turned on the Red Sea route – the only one in operation. One of the chief witnesses was Mr Thomas Waghorn who had resigned from the Bengal Marine in 1831 in order to devote himself entirely to the opening up of the Red Sea route. At the request of Lord Ellenborough at the Board of Control he had made an experimental journey from England to Bombay via Boulogne, Paris, Milan, Trieste, Cairo and Suez which revealed the possibilities of speedy communication though he suffered many delays. Once convinced of the superiority of this route, no obstacle was too great to overcome. At the 1834 Select Committee, where he gave evidence, one of the arguments put up against the 'overland' route was the cost of getting the coal by ship to Bombay, then on to Suez, said to amount to £20 a ton. After the enquiry, Mr Waghorn went to Egypt and organised the transport of coal by camel caravan from Alexandria to Suez at a quarter the price.

Second only in importance to obtaining the coal and getting it out to the east was the problem of where the coaling stations were to be. This question occupied the 1837 Committee. Apart from Mr Waghorn, several of his former colleagues in the Indian Navy – men who had been engaged for several years in surveying the coast of Arabia and the offshore islands – gave their views as to the suitability of various places for coaling. All experts, they nevertheless had very diverse views: Mr Waghorn favoured Mocha as 'the best place that can be found in the Red Sea, and the only depot required',[8] Lt Wellstead, who had spent three years surveying the Red Sea, thought Mocha was useless as communication with the shore was impossible for nine months of the year owing to the strong winds; Waghorn considered Camaran to

The Company's steamer *Memnon*, built for service with the Indian Navy, was fitted with the inverted paddle-box boats that were popular for some time. Built in 1841, she ended her short life on a reef when approaching Aden in 1843.

(BL OIOC)

be 'altogether useless' while Wellstead thought it was the best station between Socotra and Suez – he also considered that Aden would be a good place for coals in both monsoons, as there were two harbours. Thomas Peacock dismissed Mocha, as no vessel drawing more than 10ft could get into the inner harbour, while the new steamers added to the service drew 16ft. He felt Aden was good but believed the island of Perim in the Bab el Mandeb strait was the best. Camaran, he felt, was the next best. Another question that gave cause for concern was the limitation of a service to the period of the northeast monsoon, for all agreed that any service must be both regular and reliable or there was no point in running it. Captain Brucks of the Indian Navy, giving evidence prior to sailing to India in the latest addition to the Marine – the *Semiramis* – gave his opinion that in vessels of sufficient power of perhaps 750 to 800 tons, it would be possible to make the passage during the south-west monsoon without unduly straining the vessel.

The whole scheme really hinged on the availability of a coaling station which would also serve as a haven for ships in foul weather and a place where minor repairs could be effected. Exhaustive surveys carried out on the coast of Arabia, the offshore islands and the Red Sea ports had proved inconclusive. However, Commander Haines of the Indian Navy

reported to the Governor of Bombay his very favourable impression, for all year round, of the natural facilities of Aden, though the shortage of labour had proved troublesome when coaling the *Hugh Lindsay* on her trial run in 1830.

A fortuitous occurrence in the summer of 1839 decided the issue. The plundering by Arabs (evidently with the complicity of the Sultan of Aden) of a native ship carrying the British flag, provided just that insult to the Crown that resulted in the acquisition of so many strategic areas on the trade routes in the nineteenth century. Sir Robert Grant, Governor of Bombay, was not slow to seize the opportunity: 'The establishment of a monthly communication by steam with the Red Sea, and the formation of a flotilla of armed steamers, renders it absolutely necessary that we should have a station of our own men on the coast of Arabia, as we have in the Persian Gulf; and the insult to the British flag by the Sultan of Aden, has led me to enquiries which leave no doubt on my mind that we should take possession of the port of Aden'.[9]

This was really the deciding factor in the success of the 'overland' route as opposed to the 'direct' or 'alternative' route, which Chesney never ceased to promote and which was successful in other ways. The acquisition of Aden was the first major step, and the opening of the Suez Canal the culmination of this process.

Packet steamers at Suez in the mid-nineteenth century.
(National Maritime Museum)

Arab tribes to gain their confidence so that he would be assured of a safe passage with the mails. He then turned his attention to the provision of facilities for passengers, getting hotels built at the termini and relay stations at five mile intervals along the 80 miles route between Cairo and Suez.

Honoria Lawrence has left an account of her journey on the overland route when returning to India with Sir Henry in 1848, when he was recalled to the Punjab. After suffering from the unwholesome smoky atmosphere of a French steamer from Malta to Alexandria, they went ashore for the night but had little rest for 'the mosquitoes were voracious, jackals howled and yelled; cocks began to crow about sunset, and continued on and off till daylight'. They travelled on the canal connecting Alexandria with the Nile where they boarded a small crowded steamer as far as Cairo. There they began the 80 mile journey across the desert to Suez by 'van' – 'something like an inside Dublin car, mounted on very high wheels, the sides lifted up to admit light and air' – drawn by two mules and two horses which were changed at staging posts every 5 miles. They started at 2am, the way ahead lighted by blazing torches, stopping at every fourth stage for refreshments. They reached one of these at dawn – 'a table prepared in the wilderness; cold fowl, hash, potatoes, tea and coffee; just out little group of life in the midst of that wild waste'.[10]

Only ten years after *Enterprise*'s disappointing performance the Company had laid the foundations of an efficient internal and external communication by means of steam navigation. As with most other aspects of the Company's development, it had been achieved by the exertions of individuals – Lord Bentinck in Calcutta, Sir John Malcolm and Commander Wilson in Bombay, Thomas Peacock in London, Colonel Chesney and Mr Waghorn in the field – while the Company tightly gripped the purse strings. Nevertheless, the number of steamers had to increase. In their role as part of the Company's navy, there was work for them to do. It is to these naval activities that we now turn.

Although the report of the Select Committee of 1837 urged the extension of the service to the other side of the peninsula, the residents and merchants of Calcutta and Madras were neglected by the Company and the provision of a comprehensive service was left to private enterprise. The Peninsular Line, so successful in the Mediterranean and Portugal, eventually extended its service in the East, taking over the reins from the Calcutta Steam Navigation Committee, which had been striving for some years to obtain a service. A monthly Peninsular & Oriental service began in 1844, parallel with that provided by the Indian Navy, making a bi-monthly service from England to India via the overland route and Suez. The P&O service, inaugurated with its first vessel the *Hindostan*, operated between Suez, Madras and Calcutta, the mail for Bombay being left at Galle in Ceylon. The service was later extended to the Straits settlements and China. For providing this service, which would not have been commercially viable, the P&O received an annual subsidy of £160,000 from government. Ten years later, when Sir Charles Wood was at the Board of Control, he put into operation the policy he had advocated in 1830 when he was at the Exchequer: the Indian Navy steamers were to be henceforth ships of war only and not engage in the packet service, the whole of which was pass to the P&O.

Equally neglected by government and Company was the land part of the overland route. A great deal of time and money was devoted to getting the mails – and any passengers that might be travelling – to and from Suez, but how they got from there to the Mediterranean was not of great concern to government. It is this for which Mr Waghorn is most to be remembered. He first of all managed to get Mehemet Ali to sanction the setting up of agency houses to receive mails at each terminus, and he spent three years living with the migrant

Notes:
1. Banbury, Philip: *Shipbuilders of the Thames and Medway*, 179.
2. Bernstein, Henry T: *Steam Boats on the Ganges*, 31.
3. Maudslays started shipbuilding in 1865 but before then produced only these iron river tugs.
4. Low: *op cit*, Vol 1, 526.
5. BL OIOC. L/MAR/C559, for a full report of Thomas Love Peacock's evidence.
6. *Ibid.*
7. BL OIOC. L/MAR/C561, 1834.
8. Low: *op cit*, Vol 1, 54-56n.
9. Parliamentary Papers 1839 No 268 p18. Minute of the Governor of Bombay, Sir Robert Grant.
10. Diver, Maud: *Honoria Lawrence*, 343-344.

CHAPTER 11

THE *C*OMPANY'S *M*ARINE

The Company's Marine was conceived in the very early years when its agents were maintaining a tenuous foothold at Surat in the teeth of Portuguese armed hostility. It developed in size and strength throughout the seventeenth century, defending the Company's bases in western India and ensuring the Mogul Emperor's continued support by protecting native shipping. When Bombay replaced Surat as the chief Presidency in India, the squadron assumed the name it was to hold for 150 years – the Bombay Marine. During the last three decades of its existence the service was dignified by the title Indian Navy and the appointment of a captain of the Royal Navy as its Superintendent.

Mention of the Bombay Marine is usually incidental and yet its contribution to the Company and to the world was immeasurable. For at least twenty years in the latter part of the seventeenth century the Company's presence in western India was in jeopardy. The Marine continued to perform courageous actions with heroism until its demise, but in the early years it was a simple question of survival.

Throughout the eighteenth century this highly mobile, trouble-shooting force was chiefly concerned with combating the pirate menace. By the end of the century it had won the respect of all the maritime peoples of the Indian seas. From 1800 onwards the Marine's role was largely a supporting one as the Royal Navy took over the defence of the Eastern Seas. Its critics, claiming that it was an expensive luxury, especially when steam power was adopted, called for it to be wound up. Not only did it survive for a further three decades but some of its most far reaching successes were achieved in those years: it pioneered the steam packet service to England via the Red Sea and Suez and played a significant part in British imperial expansion.

For almost the last hundred years of its existence the officers of the Marine were engaged in the systematic surveying of the unknown oceans, rivers and coasts of the East; in this the Marine's work was of lasting benefit to the world at large.

In the early days, when the Portuguese were the chief enemy, the small Surat-based flotilla worked on an *ad hoc* basis, helping to oust the enemy from the River Tapti, the Gulf of Cambay and the Island of Ormuz. Seamen from the season's ships were drafted when necessity arose into what was popularly known as the 'grab service' after the type of ship that formed the nucleus of the flotilla, from the Arabic 'gorab' and the Maratha 'gurab,' meaning galley.

Far from being wound down when the Portuguese menace receded, the squadron was kept at full strength protecting native shipping from the multitude of local pirates. An additional threat developed in the early 1660s with the rise of the Maratha prince Sivajee who organised the revolt against the conquering Moslems. For a quarter of a century the successive governors of Bombay and Surat walked a tightrope between the two, trying to maintain a neutral position. The Maratha's swept down on Surat in 1664 with a vast force, threatening the infant town's very existence. The Mogul governor retreated in terror to the castle and the inhabitants into the countryside. Sir George Oxenden, the president, brought all the company's property into the factory, fortified and manned it with the guns and men from the company's trading ships, and deployed his local flotilla of grabs and gallivats in the river in front of the factory. The small garrison resolutely withstood three days of burning and plundering all around. The Sivajee's repeated demands to surrender, Sir George returned the message that he recorded in his despatch to the court: 'we were here on purpose to defend the house to the death of the last man, and therefore not to delay his coming upon us'.

Although the Island of Bombay was a welcome acquisition in view of the chaotic state of Surat, the Company's survival remained in the balance. Not least of the obstacles to turning it into a flourishing port attracting native trade were the predatory Malabar pirates. Governor Gerald Aungier requested the court to send him the means of defending the traders. Mr Warwick Pett of the famous shipbuilding family was sent out to Bombay in 1670 with stores and equipment for building two ships, using native labour and the teak of the Malabar

Above: India Ship Store musket c1825 by Ashton
for the Duke of Sussex.   (D F Harding)

Right: The inspection marks on the breech of this
musket indicate initial inspection and reinspection
for four voyages.   (D F Harding)

coast. The following year two smaller brigantines were added. As relations with the Dutch deteriorated yet again, Aungier obtained the court's consent for the addition of two frigates and three sloops of war and trained one hundred men from the garrison to act as marines. Fryer, a traveller writing in 1673, noted that 'Under the castle, besides innumerable little vessels, as hoys, ketches and the like, lay three men of war, with their top armour out, waste cloths and pennants at every yard-arm; to wit, the *Revenge*, 22 guns; the *Mayboon*, taken from the Dutch, 220 tons; and the *Hunter* 14 guns'.[1]

The expected Dutch attack did not materialise, but unfortunately the Seedee's fleet – the Mogul Emperor's hired navy – appeared unbidden to shelter in Bombay's superb harbour during the monsoon. His men raided Maratha lands to the south of the harbour, drawing 10,000 Sivajee followers to the mainland shore and producing conditions unlikely to foster trade and growth. In the anarchic conditions of 1677 and 1678 Sivajee took the island of Kenery near Bombay. The Governor sent a small force of the *Revenge* and *Dove* grabs backed up by some armed trading boats to blockade the island and prevent Sivajee's men landing. The *Dove* was forced to strike but the *Revenge*, with a mixed force from the garrison, beat off a Maratha attack, sinking five of their gallivats and frightening off the rest.

The Seedee now occupied Henery, a smaller island not far from Kenery, and the two carried on their war uncomfortably close to Bombay. Typically, the Court's answer to the Governor's request for armed help to drive them out was a firm reproof: 'Although we have formerly wrote you that we will have no war for Henery and Kenery, yet all war is so contrary to our constitution as well as our interest, that we cannot too often inculcate to you our aversion thereunto'.

This attitude was suddenly reversed in the changeover of personalities in Leadenhall Street. In the war with the Emperor that followed the Company's attempt to seize trading areas by force, Bombay came under heavy fire from the Seedee's fleet. The whole colony retreated into the castle and the problem of obtaining supplies was exaggerated by the addition of 2500 Sivajee's – for the Governor was forced to sup with the devil.

Captain Alexander Hamilton described the situation. Following the winter months which were passed 'very ill':

At September we went to sea with our small ships to cruise on the Moghul's subjects, and had pretty good success. I was employed in that service and had the command of a small privateer, with twenty fighting men and sixteen rowers. In three or four months I brought nine prizes into Bombay, laden most with provisions and clothes for the enemy's army, which was increased to forty thousand; but we were not allowed any plunder, but were rather plundered ourselves, for when we brought our prizes in, our chests were severely searched, and if we had saved any of our pay, it was seized for the company's use, as money we had found in the prizes, which made us careless of pursuing the enemy at sea.[2]

Despite the Company's hostility, their trading agreement was renewed. The emperor had come to rely on the superior sea-manship of the English to protect his trading ships from the many pirates which infested the seas, chief of whom was the renegade Maratha admiral, Angria, the first of a long line. In 1718, thirty years after the Company's bid for independence, Alexander Hamilton was head of the squadron, which acquired the name Bombay Marine in 1687 when the chief presidency moved from Surat to Bombay. He was termed Commodore and Commander-in-Chief, and had an estab-lishment of twelve captains and nine lieutenants. Some of the ships in the squadron were constructed at Carwar and Surat, but the *Britannia*, Commodore Hamilton's flagship, was Bombay-built. There were nine grabs or frigates, mounting between 12 and 24 guns and carrying between 80 and 200 men, a fireship, and the bomb vessel *Terrible*. This was prob-ably the machine described by Lt Downing who served in the Marine at this time.[3] The governor ordered it to be built fol-lowing an unsuccessful attack on Kenery, which was by this time one of Angria's chief strongholds:

. . . a floating Castle, or a Machine that should be almost Cannon-proof. This Vessel was pretty flat, flowed with little or no Bulge, and but Six Foot Hold; the Thickness of her Sides were made by the nicest Composition Cannon-proof. She was to go with one Mast, and a Top-sail, which was rigged in a very commodious manner, and mounted 12 Guns, carrying 48 Pounders.

This force was back up by a flotilla of armed, oared boats indispensable in the conditions of the Malabar coast. According to Downing:

We had 10 or 12 galleyvats which are large boats . . . generally mount 6 swivel guns and will carry in the way of landing near 100 men. These galleyvats we make great use of; they sail with a Peak Sail like the Mizzen of any of our Ships of War and row with 30 or 40 oars; very few with less than 20 oars. Their com-pliment is generally 20 fighting Men besides the Rowers: but they are fit for no other service.

The Bombay Marine was kept at full stretch dealing with the pirates of all kinds – the Kemshews, the Sanganians, the Molwans as well as the Angrians. Some of the ships were cruising in the Persian Gulf where the Gombroom factory was threatened in 1721 by 5000 Beloochee horse; others sailed to Madagascar where the Marine was committed to tracking down European pirates following the agreement with the

Dutch and French late in the previous century. A large force was despatched down the coast to Carwar to extract treasure, prisoners and compensation from a villainous rajah who had seized the cargo of a Bengal ship, holed it and imprisoned the crew. Two attempts were made at this time to reduce the forts of Gheriah and Sevendroog, the Angrian pirates' strongholds, but without success.

The threat to native trade can well be imagined from Orme's account of the pirates' drill:

Eight to ten grabs, and forty or fifty gallivats, crowded with men, generally compassed Angria's principal fleet destined to attach ships of war or large merchantmen. The vessel no soon-er came in sight of the port or bay, wherever the fleet was lying, than they slipped their cables and put out to sea; if the wind blew, their construction enabled them to sail almost as fast as the wind, and, if it was calm, the gallivats, rowing, towed the grabs; when within cannon-shot of the chase, they generally assembled round her stern, and the grabs attacked her at a dis-tance with their bow-guns, firing first only at their masts. As soon as the chase was dismasted, they came nearer and battered her on all sides until she struck; and if the defence was obsti-nate, they sent a number of gallivats with two or three hundred men in each, who boarded, sword in hand, from all quarters at the same instant.[4]

In the middle years of the century the Government of Bombay decided to make a determined attempt to get rid of the Angrians. The Marine had at this time a first rate leader in Commodore James, who had beaten off a powerful Angrian attack on a fleet of seventy traders he was convoying from Bombay to the North of Goa. Maratha help was sought for a combined naval and military attack on Sevendroog. A treaty was concluded by which the British agreed to blockade the harbour before Sevendroog to prevent the Angrian fleet bringing aid to the fort while the Marathas stormed the stronghold from the landward side. Commodore James in his flagship *Protector*, 44 guns, led the squadron comprising the *Bombay* grab, the *Swallow*, 16 guns, and the *Tiger* and *Viper* bomb vessels. They were joined by the Maratha fleet or seven grabs and six gallivats carrying 10,000 soldiers. The Maratha army showed little taste for battle but James was determined that attack should not end in stalemate. His boats sent to reconnoitre reported sufficient depth of water to stand in between the island and the mainland. He had the *Protector* warped in to a position where she faced tremendous fire from the heavy guns of the forts on the island and the mainland. However, once in position she was able to direct her broad-sides simultaneously while musketeers in the tops dispersed the gunners in the main fort of Sevendroog. After a four hour bombardment a magazine blew up and the fleeing garrison were taken prisoner by the English ships.

Shortly after this encouraging victory Admiral Watson arrived with the Royal Navy squadron and Lt Col Robert Clive with a detachment of troops. After consultations with the Bombay Government and the Superintendent of the Marine plans were drawn up for an attack on the greatest Angria stronghold of all – Gheriah, built in earlier days by the Portuguese. Commodore James reconnoitred the area and took soundings. His report exploded the myth that had surrounded Gheriah for generations:

> I was exceedingly surprised to find the place so widely different from what I had heard it represented. I assure you, sir, it is not to be called high, nor, in my opinion, strong . . . On the west side of the harbour is a fine flat table-land opposite the fort, and I think within gunshot, but I am sure within distance for bombarding, and from whence a very good diversion might be made while the principal attack is carried on by the ships, and from a hill to the southward of the fort. The hill is very near to and full as high as the fort . . . it is also very plain from our depth of water, that the ships can go near enough for battering and consequently for throwing shells. There are also three sandy bays under the hill, without any surf to render the landing difficult . . . The water is deep enough for the ships to cover the descent, and the hill accessible as to make the getting up of cannon etc quite easy afterwards.[5]

Acting chiefly on this report, a combined military and naval expedition sailed from Bombay on 7 February 1756. Lt Clive led a force of 1400 European and native soldiers. There were six men of war supported by the *Protector*, 44 guns, commodore James, the *Revenge*, *Bombay* and *Guardian*, all 28 guns, the *Swallow*, 16 guns, five bomb vessels on which embarked a company of artillery, and a Maratha force of four grabs and forty gallivats. The ships of the line and the *Protector* attacked the fort while the smaller vessels attacked the Angrian fleet and dockyards. A shell falling on an English ship taken prize earlier by Angria set fire to the whole pirate fleet, while another shell shortly afterward fired the fort. Clive landed with his troops on the landward side of the fort to preclude suspected double-dealing between Angria and the Marathas, and the fort finally hoisted the white flag late the following afternoon.

Another thorn in the flesh of the Bombay government was the continued anarchic state of Surat; in fact the situation deteriorated yearly as the Mogul empire collapsed and a free-for-all replaced former order. Surat was a constant battleground for every kind of faction, creating the worst possible conditions for carrying on the Company's trade. To make matters worse, the Seedee and his fleet had for many years been far too weak to execute the traditional role of safely convoying the pilgrim fleet to Jedda – in fact he was by now as great a pirate as those against whom he was supposed to

defend the ships. Only the English commanded any respect in the Indian seas. A bid to take over the Tunkha – the stipend paid by the Mogul emperor for the service – had been made by the Bombay government as early as 1733, but the English had so many enemies on the coast at this time it seemed impolitic to add the Seedee to the list.

A crisis blew up in 1756 when the Seedee supported a rival claimant to the Nawabship of Surat and seized the castle. The displaced Nawab appealed to the English for help, which was offered in return for concessions, amongst which was the Tunkha. Early in February 1759, Commodore Watson, who had succeeded Commodore James, led the expedition of five ships carrying nearly 2500 troops. A grab of twenty guns and four bomb ketches were warped upriver and directed continuous mortar fire on the walls and castle until the Seedee surrendered.

With the company's capture of Surat the Tunkha was conferred as agreed. This at last enabled the Bombay Marine to control the defence of native trade – a development welcomed by the Moorish merchants whose ships' security was greatly improved. For seventy years – from 1759 to 1829 – the East India Company held the position of Admiral of the Mogul's fleet, and so were permitted to fly his flag at the ships' mainmast.

For those individuals in the Marine appointed as admiral, this was a very remunerative position. Traditionally it was an annual post held in turn by retiring officers. The fees for convoy and various tithes amounted to about £10,000 – a welcome fortune which continued until about 1809 when the sum was greatly curtailed.

About this time the Bombay Marine began to acquire a new look; the professionalism and personal integrity of Commodores James and Watson and the close co-operation with the Royal Navy during the French wars of mid-century tended to modify the swash-buckling image of the Marine in its earlier days. Dignity and status were conferred on the service by the introduction of a uniform in 1761; a blue frock coat, dress coat and waistcoat with gold facings for senior ranks. There were modifications at intervals later on, usually inspired, as with the mercantile service, by naval jealousy, but the uniform remained basically unchanged.

The fleet was improved by ships built in the greatly expanding Bombay dockyard by the famous Parsee shipbuilders brought from Surat in 1735. A visitor to Bombay in 1758 noted that the Marine had eight or ten small ships of war and a number of armed barks, amongst which was the *Bombay* grab, a long-surviving ship whose age was already a legend. By 1775 there were reportedly more than twenty ships, of which the largest was the *Revenge*, 28 guns, including twenty 12pdrs. All the warships had marines on board. Up to 1777 these were soldiers raised from the land forces when the need arose, but in that year the Bombay Marine

Ships of the Royal Navy and cruisers of the Bombay Marine attacking the Angrian pirate stronghold at Gheriah in 1756. A gallivat can be seen in the left foreground with two grabs to the right.
(BL OIOC)

Battalion was formed, consisting of eight companies.

During the twenty of so years of war with France that began in 1793 the resources of the Bombay Marine – about sixteen ships and one hundred officers – saw action all over the eastern Seas from Suez in the west to the eastern islands in the east.

It was the French threat to India via Egypt that most worried Lord Wellesley. A naval force was sent from Bombay to cruise in the Red Sea and in 1799 the Bombay government was ordered to secure the island of Perim destined to become, with Aden, the guardian of the route to India. Several ships of the Marine transported the three hundred troops who formally took possession of Perim for the East India Company. The Marine's ships also transported the army of General Baird, to whom Alexandria capitulated in 1801, from Madras to Suez.

About this time, on the other side of the Indian Ocean Bombay Marine brigs *Swift*, Capt Hayes and *Star*, Lt Scott, were engaged in a gruelling blockade of the island of Ternate, on which there were three strong Dutch forts, monuments to the dominion achieved by the Dutch in those seas two hundred years earlier. At the risk of exceeding his orders, Lt Hayes first advanced with escalading ladders and forty-five seamen with the backing of an advance division of troops, but the concentrated heavy fire forced them to retreat with heavy losses. He followed this up by attacks from the sea on two other forts at very close range, silencing the guns and enabling the troops to take the forts. The despatch from the Company's resident at Amboyna to the Secretary of State referred to 'that gallant officer, Captain Hayes' and noted that 'the difficulties the Hon Company's forces at sea and land had to encounter in this arduous service, and the spirit and intrepidity which they manifested during a siege of nearly two months do them infinite credit and have seldom or ever been exceeded in this part of the world'.

It was the problem of keeping the trade moving in the Bay of Bengal that occupied the attention of the Governor and Superintendent of Marine of Bombay and the Government of India in Calcutta. In 1795 the *Bombay*, Commodore Pickett, and some smaller vessels of the Marine supported the pre-emptive seizure of Ceylon by a combined naval and military force. If the superb harbour of Trincomalee had fallen into French hands circumstances would have been worse. Even so, the situation was so desperate by the time of the renewal of the war in 1803 that captains of country ships could no longer afford to insure them. The appointment of Captain Hayes, now commodore of the Marine, as commodore of all the ships of the Bombay Marine, the Bengal Marine – a temporary uncommissioned service – and the regular and extra commercial ships of the Company, with full naval powers to take the ships and goods of the French and Batavian Republics, was one attempt to protect the trade.

Captain Frost's personal contribution to increasing the safety of the Bay has become legendary. Commanding the new sloop of war *Mornington* he cruised round the Sandheads on the look-out for two French privateers which alone had made the Bay unsafe for shipping – M Surcouff's *La Confiance* and the American-built schooner *L'Eugenie*. Captain Frost disguised the *Mornington* as a country ship by adding dirty patches of canvas to the sails and building a false poop. When the *Mornington* came up with *L'Eugenie* the latter was completely fooled. She came right alongside the *Mornington* and called on her captain to strike. Captain Frost then ordered the gunners to discharge a broadside, crippling the Frenchman aloft so that she was unable to get away. She was taken into service as the *Alert* and given into the command of *Mornington*'s first officer.

However, while the French ships could still repair and refit at their bases of Isle de Bourbon and Isle de France to the east of Madagascar, the source of the threat to the trade of the Bay of Bengal remained. The taking of the island of Rodriguez nearby enabled an attack to be made. The Bombay Marine cruiser *Wasp*, Lt Watkins, was present at the capture of St Pauls, Isle de Bourbon in 1809, the whole island being taken the following year. In November 1810 the *Malabar*, *Benares* and brigs *Thetis*, *Vestal* and *Ariel* sailed from Bombay as part of the force of seventy ships of war and transports carrying 10,000 soldiers which took the Isle de France without much opposition. The island became British under its former Dutch name of Mauritius.

In 1811 ships of the Bombay Marine were again involved in action further east. Commodore Hayes hoisted his broad pennant on board the *Malabar*, Captain Maxfield, and led a squadron of the *Aurora*, *Nautilus* and *Mornington*, all 14 guns, with the 10-gun brigs *Ariel*, *Psyche*, *Thetis* and *Vestal*, to join a naval force which rendezvoused off the south-west coast of Borneo and sailed for Java on 27 July 1811. The Commander-in-Chief of Madras, Lt General Achmuty, sailed in the *Akbar*, formerly the Marine frigate *Cornwallis*. The Marine's ships protected the landing of the troops at Chillingching a few miles from Batavia, then sailed round to the Anjole river where they made a bridge of boats enabling the troops to march on the capital. The town was surrendered without a struggle, but the Marine was kept policing the area for some time and was engaged in a punitive expedition to Palimbang.

Heroic action throughout the French wars and in Burma ten years later did not influence the opinion of some people in high places who had felt for some time that the Bombay Marine had outlived its usefulness and should be disbanded. The officers of the Marine, on their part, were dissatisfied with their conditions of work – so much so that Captain Maxfield addressed a special meeting of the General Court listing their grievances: lack of status compared with the regular captains despite the 1798 regulations; poor pay; the indignities often suffered because of the lack of a code of laws governing the service; and the overcrowded conditions on the ships.

The officers did not have long to wait for partial redress at least. Only seven months later the Court of Directors despatched a letter to the Governor of Bombay ordering a remodelling of the Marine. Officers were in future to enjoy relative rank with the Royal Navy, and the martial law applying to the Company's army was extended to the Bombay Marine. The position of Superintendent, a post previously held by a civilian, would in future be held by a captain in the Royal Navy and the senior officers were to have retirement on the senior list in England with pensions equivalent to colonels. Captain Sir Charles Malcolm was appointed Superintendent according to the new decision and the Duke of Clarence, Lord High Admiral, issued an Order in Council conferring on the officers of the Marine the privilege of taking rank with officers of the Royal Navy and flying the Union Jack. On 1 May 1830 the Governor of Bombay communicated to the Marine the Court of Directors' decision to designate the Service 'the Navy of India'.

However, respectability and stability were not to be achieved without sacrifice. The establishment of the Bombay Marine was severely curtailed by seventeen to make one hundred and twenty. The shore establishment particularly was greatly reduced, and many officers found their sinecures had disappeared.

The tide that threatened to sweep away the Indian Navy was not stemmed by reorganisation. Many people in power

Sir Charles Malcolm, the first officer of the Royal Navy to hold the post of Superintendent of the Indian Navy, fostered the surveys of the Eastern Seas for which many of its officers received worldwide recognition.
(National Maritime Museum)

considered it had outlived its usefulness and agreed with Lord Bentinck that here was an obvious means of cutting back on expenditure. A scathing attack on the India Navy was included in a minute to the Court of Directors from Sir Robert Grant, Governor of Bombay, in 1836.[6] He doubted if the Indian Navy had any useful function to perform. Commenting in turn on each of its duties, he said though the Indian Navy ships were excellent of their type, they were unsuitable for carrying troops, and transports usually had to be hired at great cost. They were also unsuitable for carrying mails, since they were sailing ships and so likely to miss their passage; he felt that the Indian Navy's warmest supporters would never argue that it was capable of coping with the naval force of the pettiest European state. This left only one function – the suppression of piracy in the Red Sea and the Persian Gulf. But when was a pirate last captured, Sir Robert asked? It was notorious that our sloops and brigs were unable to compete with Arab vessels if there was a breeze, and when there was no breeze the Arabs used their sweeps and were sway. There had been an instance a short time previously when a squadron of pirates drew up in battle formation. The

Elphinstone, Captain Sawyer – one of the finest ships in the service commanded by an excellent officer – ran between the two lines of ships and emptied both broadsides at once. The pirates had given up immediately and fled. Despite the confusion the *Elphinstone*'s guns had thrown them into, they had been able to collect themselves and escape, leaving the English ship standing.

Turning to the personnel of the Indian Navy, Sir Robert revealed that it was not only the officers that had complaints. He pointed to 'the want of sufficient stimulus to exertion' as the chief danger and its effect on the officers. They felt inferior, and many were. A 'thorough weeding' was required before any real reform could be attempted. It was, Sir Robert felt, quite unnecessary to keep the shore establishment 'on its present extended scale'.

Sir Robert's solution to the problem was the suppression of the Indian Navy and the creation of a steam flotilla. He pointed to the recent experience in Jamaica where a steamer used for transporting troops had made a contribution equivalent to that of a whole additional regiment. In India, where sail was limited by the monsoon to part of the year, steam would be doubly useful. The question of whether the steamers could sail against the monsoon remained, he agreed, unsolved, but the Mediterranean packets had stood up to far worse weather than the *Hugh Lindsay* had had to face. Sir Robert was sure a steam flotilla could carry out all the duties at present performed by the Indian Navy and give Britain dominion in all the rivers and ports in the Indian seas, constituting a great deterrent to the Russians. He felt that twelve steamers of 250 and 500 tons could undertake all the work at present done by the Indian Navy.

Another member of the Bombay council agreed that there was incredible waste in the Indian Navy. 'I was not before aware', he commented on Sir Robert's minute, 'that such a charge could be advanced against this department of the public service to ensure efficiency considerable outlays of public money must necessarily take place – but it is for the first time I learn that reckless expenditure is to be found abounding in all quarters.'

While the arguments for and against continuing the Indian Navy carried on, the Court went ahead and ordered two steamers 'for occasional despatches and emergent [sic] services'. The *Atalanta* and *Berenice* duly arrived from England in 1837 and the *Atalanta* sailed on 25 August 1837 with the mails for Mocha where the *Hugh Lindsay* was to take them on to Suez. The monthly packet service between Bombay and Suez – with the exception of the monsoon months June to September – was thus inaugurated.

The fourth steamer of the Bombay squadron, the *Semiramis*, 720 tons and 300hp, arrived in Bombay in April 1838. Her commander, Captain Brucks, lost no time in attempting to prove the assertion he had made before the assembled dignitaries at the ceremony following *Semiramis's* trial run between Purfleet and the Nore. He had stated there was an enemy to steam navigation in India that he was ready to meet, and staked his professional reputation on conquering it with the new steamers possessed by the Company. He was referring to that 'bugbear of the Bombay imagination, the south west monsoon'. He sailed in the *Semiramis* on 15 July 1838 and battled for eight days against the mighty seas, which split his fore and aft sails and threatened to extinguish the fires. He was forced to admit defeat and put back to Bombay. For another twelve years, until Commodore Young's passage by another direct route to Aden in twelve days four hours, beaten the following year by Commander Hewett in the *Moozuffer* by twenty-three hours, officers had to 'go down to see how their friend the Equator was getting on' during the south-west monsoon.

But the fate of the Indian Navy remained undecided. Sir Robert Grant's proposal to the court had created a large question mark that hung over all the establishment from Sir Charles Malcolm down. Morale, discipline and standards deteriorated. 'Passed' midshipmen – those who had passed their final examinations – were ordered to serve on packet steamers as lieutenants, but without the rank and pay, which lowered morale still further. Rumours of large numbers of officers being laid off, of reduced pensions, were rife. Eventually many complained to the Court, forcing a decision.

The solution was a typically English compromise: the Indian Navy emerged as neither a steam packet service nor a navy, but a combination of the two. The establishment was fixed at one hundred, the absolute minimum: four captains, eight commanders (this rank being re-introduced), forty lieutenants and forty-eight midshipmen. Retirement was offered to thirty-four senior officers. Lieutenants were to command the steam packets 'unless a commander shall especially apply for the appointment'. An engineer class of officer was created and a steam department formed. Captain Sir Charles Malcolm, who would have looked uncomfortable with an oily rag in his hand, was replaced by Captain Robert Oliver, RN, an excellent steam officer, who set about moulding the service into an efficient hardworking force at the expense of personal popularity. The officers' complaints that they were overworked and undermanned were recognised as having some foundation very soon afterwards, and in November 1841 the establishment was increased to one hundred and thirty-eight, and again in 1847 to two hundred and two.

Space must be found at this point for a brief consideration of an aspect of the service's work that resulted in widespread benefits: the marine surveys. The Bombay Marine and the Indian Navy proved to be a nursery of surveyors, producing over a period of nearly one hundred years a number of highly skilled officers out of all proportion to its establishment. Many of them possessed, in addition, outstanding linguistic

Detail of the buttons of an East India Company officer's maritime service uniform. *(Museum of London, Docklands Collection)*

ability and a wide knowledge of the countries bordering the oceans, rivers and coasts being surveyed. Without their diplomatic missions amongst these peoples, the surveys would not have been possible. Little would have been achieved, either, without the encouragement of people in power: under Mountstuart Elphinstone and Sir John Malcolm at Government House; and under the latter's brother Sir Charles, Commodore Lushington and Sir Henry Leeke as heads of the service, the surveys flourished. Under Lord Bentinck, for reasons of economy, and Captain Oliver, who saw no need for them, the surveys died.

The earlier surveys were chiefly concerned with laying down in the charts the chief danger areas that caused such losses of ships, men and cargoes on the routes to the trading posts. Among the very first surveyors was one of the greatest the Marine produced: John McCluer, who followed up a fairly good chart of the Persian Gulf by an excellent one of the west coast of India – supported by drawings of the coast that Dalrymple liked so much – which put him, by common consent, in the same class as Cook.

The loss of two Indiamen led to surveys on the route to China: the *Antelope*, lost in the Pellew Islands in 1783, and the *Earl Talbot*, believed lost on the dreaded Paracel Shoal in 1800. Lt McCluer was sent to the Pellew Islands to look for a suitable harbour to shelter Indiamen caught in hurricanes in the China Sea. The Marine surveying ships *Comet* and *Intrepid*, sent to look for the *Earl Talbot*'s survivors and to survey the area, were themselves never seen again. It fell to one of the greatest of the Marine's surveyors to tackle this problem. Captain Daniel Ross, who was known as the 'Father of the Indian Surveys' through his advanced methods and high standard of attainment, spent from 1806 to 1820 surveying the coast east and west of Macao, the coast of Cochin China, Hainan, Formosa and the straits of Malacca.

The shoals of the Bay of Bengal were tackled by Captain Maxfield who also verified the existence of an anchorage inside the Armagon shoal north of Madras, providing a haven during the north-east monsoon on an otherwise dangerous coast. Captain Maugham headed a very talented team including Lt H B Lynch, Cdr Ormsby, Lt Ethersy, Capt Haines and Lt Wellstead in a survey of the Persian Gulf in an attempt to get to grips with the pirate menace.

While Captain Ross was Marine Surveyor General, a post was set up in Bengal in 1809 to organise and rationalise the surveys, the focus of attention shifted to the Arabian Sea. The future steamer routes and the urgent need to find suitable ports of call and coaling stations occupied the government at Bombay. Cdr Robert Moresby started a survey of the Laccadive Islands to find a suitable port of call for steamers en route for the Persian Gulf or Suez from Calcutta and Madras. As the *Hugh Lindsay* neared completion he was transferred to the Red Sea to make a quick preliminary survey of this unknown sea beyond the 'Gate of Tears'. Immediately afterwards he and Capt Elwon, in the *Palinurus* and *Benares* surveying vessels respectively, were sent back to the Red Sea to carry out a thorough survey. Each was assisted by what can only be described as an all-star cast, all of whom agreed that the survey would be 'as perfect as labour and skill can make it'. Their work, carried out over the next four years and seven months in gruelling conditions which took a heavy toll of health and life, resulted in charts of exceptional quality backed up by notes on the peoples bordering the Red Sea by Lt Wellstead and others. Capt Haines sailed in the *Palinurus* for the Hadramaut coast of Arabia to establish coaling stations, but was transferred to Socotra to make a quick survey of the island, completing it in three months.

The surveys of the great rivers were as crucial to the furtherance of trade and imperial expansion as were those of the seas and coasts. Lts Wood and Carless surveyed the Indus and its mouths while Lt Christopher surveyed the upper rivers. Although the survey of the Euphrates was originally govern-

ment sponsored, Lts Lynch, Jones and Selby continued surveying the whole area until the Indian Navy was disbanded, Lt Selby proving 'the practicability of rivers the course of which was hitherto almost unknown'. The posts of Surveyor of Mesopotamia and Surveyor of the Punjab Rivers were created to organise these surveys. Following the second Burmese war and the annexation of Pegu, the Irrawaddy was added to the list of great rivers surveyed.

Most of the surveying of the Arabian Sea and surrounding territories aroused the suspicions of the wild Arab tribes; continuing without first ensuring their assent was dangerous. Lt Lynch travelled 900 miles among the Arab Sheikhdoms before Col Chesney carried out his survey of the Euphrates and Tigris, assuring them the results would be mutually beneficial. Capt Haines' knowledge and understanding of the peoples of Arabia qualified him for negotiating the sale of Socotra and Aden, neither of which in fact was effected as both were seized by force, but this was through no fault of his.

The last word on the question of surveys carried out by the Marine and the Indian Navy can be left to Cdr Taylor. Ten years after the Indian Navy had been brought to an end he said:

> I search the Admiralty catalogue of charts in vain to find any really new charts of India for the last ten years . . . They who rashly undertook to succeed 'the pioneers of navigation in the Eastern Seas' have certainly not rendered a good account of their ten years' stewardship, much less have they given to India such an extension of hydrographic knowledge as she was entitled to expect.[7]

A comparison of the fleet just prior to the launching of the *Hugh Lindsay* in 1829 with that of 1841 after the second reorganisation, reveals the great revolution that had taken place in the short space of ten or twelve years. In 1829 the *Hugh Lindsay* was a curiosity, an oddity in the midst of a fine squadron of sixteen sailing ships ranging from a 32-gun frigate to a bomb vessel.

Twelve years later the *Bombay Times*, in an article on the squadron, mentioned the fifteen 'ordinary sailing vessels' of 3419 aggregate tonnage, which 'though not apparently a very formidable fleet, are smart, light, teak-built craft, chiefly employed in protecting the trade along the coast'. The article continues: 'It is to their steamers that the Company now look as the right arm of the strength of their Marine. These consist of 9 splendid vessels . . . of an aggregate burthen of 15,658 tons and a gross value of about £500,000.' That harbinger of a new technical era, the *Hugh Lindsay*, is now dismissed as 'old-fashioned and slow'. The latest additions were still on the stocks or in dock: the *Auckland*, waiting for the first spring tide to float her out, was 900 tons or more; the *Semiramis* – the second of that name – still on the stocks, of 1143 tons and

350hp. The *Cleopatra*, Commander Sanders, 814 tons, 220hp, arrived at Bombay on 19 April 1840.

Built by William and Henry Pitcher, she was the first ship launched from the Northfleet Dockyard, where their father Thomas had built many Indiamen, after the reopening in 1839. Designed by Samuel Ritherden, Surveyor of Shipping, who also designed *Sesostris* and *Queen* for the Indian Service, the *Cleopatra* was an elegant ship. Her commander, Captain Basil Hall, complained of the wheel being placed right at the stern in the old way when American paddle steamers had a high bridge forward enabling the pilot to see clearly ahead. Otherwise she was a fine ship with a superbly fitted saloon, good accommodation, and an array of stern windows. The Bombay-built teak ship *Victoria*, Commander Ormsby, had excelled herself in the packet service, beating every other ship. *Zenobia* had started life as the *Kilkenny*, built at Waterford and purchased into the service by the company in 1839. She was never popular, always being referred to as the 'pig boat' as rumour had it that in her humbler life she had transported pigs.

The English-built ships were never good. The *Cleopatra* was having trouble as early as 1846 when, during a voyage from Bombay to Aden, her paddle boxes had to be secured by chains. When the ship was ordered to Singapore with convicts the following April, her commander told the Superintendent that he considered her to be unfit to make the voyage but the order stood. She sailed in company with six other ships, met one of the worst cyclones on record, and neither she nor any of her complement of one hundred and fifty-one, her marine guard, nor the one hundred and fifty convicts on board were ever seen again. Her sister ship the *Sesostris*, Commander Campbell, reported in April 1848 that she was so loose in frame and decayed in timber that in a seaway the butts of her decks opened and closed and she made so much water he had to ease off the engines. She had to have new decks laid. *Victoria*, the Bombay-built *Semiramis* and *Auckland* were considered the best ships by the officers of the Indian Navy.

What the critics of the Indian Navy in the early 1830s did

The Company's packet *Swallow*, typical of many teak-built cruisers built in the Bombay dockyards, had a sailing life of nearly fifty years in tropical waters.   *(Science Museum)*

the effect of the iron on the compass – had been overcome by Sir George Airey, the Astronomer Royal. The first to arrive – and the first iron war steamer ever to round the Cape – was the *Nemesis*, soon nicknamed *Nevermiss*, which was able to get close inshore to land troops. After the commission, when she was examined in Bombay Dockyard, her bottom was pronounced whole in spite of obvious groundings, and her commander reported that he was well pleased with her on all counts. The fleet was joined by others of her class: *Medusa* and *Ariadne* which unfortunately holed on a submerged rock which still bears her name and sank in spite of repairs at Chusan.

Three other iron steamers built by Lairds formed the nucleus of the Indus Flotilla. These were *Assyria*, *Nicrotis* and *Nimrod* which were sent out in 1838 in sections for assembly at Bussorah by the court of directors when they entertained high hopes of starting a steam packet service in Mesopotamia. They were rushed to the Indus in 1837 when the Russians incited the Persians to besiege Herat – the gate to India – in Afghanistan. The following year they did good service in Lord Auckland's expedition to Kabul. There was a flotilla of nine boats by 1840. Typical of these steamers was the *Indus*, 304 tons, 60hp with a complement of fifty-two, about half being Europeans. Her armament was a 12pdr howitzer and a 3pdr brass gun.

When Moolraj, the Sikh leader, rebelled in 1848, the Company's troops besieged his stronghold at Mooltan. The Indus flotilla under its Superintendent, Commander Powell, transported men, guns and stores 800 miles up the Indus to within a mile and a half of Mooltan. Credit for this was due to Lt Wilmott Christopher of the Indian Navy, who the previous year had sailed up the Indus, the Sutlej and the Chenab with the *Meanee* steam tender towing the iron flat *Ravee*, demonstrating the practicality of navigating the upper rivers.

Commander Powell, reporting on the role of the Indus flotilla during the operations, said the *Comet* and *Conqueror* steamers were still above Mooltan 'stopping all water communications. The *Napier* and *Meteor* are stationed off Raj Ghaut, protecting the bridge and pontoon boats, also those the siege train came up in, and the *Meanee* is towing up commissariat grain boats to the same ghaut. The *Planet* also arrived there yesterday, with two ten inch mortars, six hundred and thirty shells . . .' Later the same steamers were employed carrying wounded officers down to Karachi, while the *Conqueror* stopped all water communication.

The seagoing war steamers of the Indian Navy proved their worth in the second war with Burma as they had in the China war. Capt Oliver's successor as superintendent, Commodore

not foresee was the great part its war steamers would play in securing strategic places on the trade routes of the world. Nor did they realise the great contribution this handful of experienced seamen with their expert knowledge of the Eastern Seas and rivers and their skilled seamanship would make to this important phase of British history.

In China in 1841-43 during what came to be known as the Opium War, in Burma in 1852-53, on the Indus between 1838 and 1848, and in Persia in 1856, the war steamers of the Indian Navy and their officers played a crucial role.

It was in China that the steamers were given their first opportunity to demonstrate all their capabilities to the full. The steam frigates *Sesostris*, her sister ship the *Queen* and others were lashed to the sides of the men of war and towed them into position for attack. They shelled the Chinese batteries to cover the landings, and transported the troops up-river. A new class of flat-bottomed iron steamer, with a drop keel, built at Birkenhead by MacGregor Laird, joined the naval force during the war. The great drawback to ocean-going iron ships –

India Ship Store pistol by Debenham c1775-1788.   *(D F Harding)*

Lushington, appointed Capt H B Lynch, commodore of the squadron of four steam frigates and two sloops: the *Ferooz*, flagship, the *Sesostris*, Commander Campbell, *Moozuffer*, Commander Hewett, *Zenobia*, Commander Bell, all armed with 8in guns throwing hollow shot as well as 32pdrs, and the *Berenice* and *Medusa* steam sloops.

The ships transported a brigade from Madras to the mouth of Rangoon river where they joined up with a squadron of steamers of the Bengal Marine and some ships of the Royal Navy. After a short, sharp attack by the steamers' combined armament and that of HMS *Fox*, which they towed into position, a stretch of coast was cleared for the troops to land. Rangoon fell quickly and the steamers moved upriver to the new town. Commander Campbell displayed a ruthless ingenuity in the use of his ammunition: he had the 68pdr iron shot heated in the furnace before firing from the 8in guns. At the same time he fired shrapnel loaded in only 6lb of powder, which rent the stockades of the defending forces. Later he headed a brigade of seamen in an assault on the battery, as he had done at Mooltan. A letter in the *Times* of 1 June from an officer stated '. . . we shelled away from two days and two nights, Capt Campbell firing 68-pounder red-hot shot, the first, I think, every fired afloat on board ship. The effect was tremendous. The whole place was set on fire and two thirds of it burnt down . . . the Indian Navy seems to stand high in the good opinion of all.'

The fruits of Captain Oliver's insistence on good gunnery training, which he had arranged to be studied at HMS *Excellent* at Portsmouth, were well in evidence at Rangoon. The *Bombay Times*, reporting on 8 May, disarmingly ate its own words: '. . . though we have always heard the merits of the gunnery instruction spoken of in the highest terms, we have at times expressed our opinion that more than enough of time and attention was devoted to the subject, the result shows . . . the time has been well spent'.

Bassein was the next target. A small squadron of the *Moozuffer*, *Sesostris* and the Bengal Marine's *Tennasserim* carried the eight hundred troops 160 miles round the coast and 60 miles up the river '. . . the poor fellows being all crowded into every corner we could stuff them. We anchored that night and next day all steamed up this noble river, following the little *Pluto* as out guide, having no pilots and but a poor map dated 1754'. On reaching Bassein they found the Burmese throwing up 'sloping-sided mud forts in European style' to resist the shot which the timber stockades of Rangoon had disastrously failed to withstand. Again Commander Campbell led an attack by seamen of the *Sesostris* and *Moozuffer* on one of the defences while the main body of troops took the main fort. The steamers' value as troop carriers was fully shown in the latter part of 1852 ferrying troops across the Bay of Bengal from Calcutta to Rangoon to reinforce the army, each steamer making three or four round trips. It was chiefly the steamers of the Bengal Marine – *Nemesis*, *Phlegethon*, *Mahanuddy*, *Proserpine* and *Enterprise* – that bore the brunt of the expedition upriver to Prome; and the first of Peacock's iron chicks, the *Lord William Bentinck*, and two other boats from the Ganges flotilla, carried out the protracted attack on Pegu, which was annexed, bringing the whole coastline from the borders of Siam into British hands.

The high standard of seamanship and skill in gunnery were shown in the war with Persia in 1857, caused by a suspected instance of Russian intrigue resulting in a Persian attack on the sensitive Herat. The new steamers formed part of the fleet despatched from Bombay: the *Assaye* 177ft in length 'overall' and 39ft 6in in breadth, of 1800 tons and 650hp, was launched in March. Her sister ship *Punjaub*, 7ft longer and 700hp, followed in April, Commander Young taking the command. With them were the *Semiramis*, *Adjaha*, *Victoria* and *Ferooz* steam frigates, the steam sloops *Berenice* and *Hugh Lindsay*, and the sailing sloops *Clive*, *Euphrates* and *Falkland*, a fine, recently-launched corvette.

Following the taking of Bushire, the Commander-in-Chief, General Outram, planned to attack the fort at Mohamra at the junction of the Karoon and Shatt-ul-Arab. Commander Young in his flagship *Ferooz* was appointed commodore. The fort was of solid earth, 20ft thick and 18ft high with powerful batteries commanding the main channel. Everyone considered the task impossible; a French commander forecast the loss of at least three steamers. Commander Rennie, known for his ingenuity, suggested building a raft for the mortars, with screwed hay bales to protect the gunners. This was done and the raft towed under cover of darkness to a position opposite the fort. At the same time the channel was buoyed by Lt Sweeny, who had become a specialist on this are through his survey work, in preparation for the attack at dawn. The steamers taking part defended their bulwarks with screwed bales of hay, as only those of the *Semiramis* were musket-proof. At daybreak *Ferooz* and *Assaye* steamed up to a point 300 yards from the fort, then closed to 60 yards, protected by the mortar shells that exploded every three minutes for five hours. The operation demanded great skill in seamanship, keeping the steamers, particularly the *Assaye* with her great length, in position in the narrow fast-flowing channel. The steamers kept up a constant fire with their broadsides, despite the heavy bombardment from the fort, until a series of explosions within the fort brought the Persian defence to an end. The *Berenice* now moved up through the steamers, carrying the Highlanders and towing two transports – a very risky operation as the decks were crammed with men and the officers packed on the bridge. Parties of seamen stormed the fort, followed by the troops, who took possession.

The axe which had hovered uncertainly for more than thirty years finally fell in the aftermath of the Indian Mutiny. When the new Secretary of State, assuming authority in 1858 over all the Company's former property and administration, looked around for likely ways of effecting economies, his eye alighted – as had so many before – on the Indian Navy. He felt that in future the Royal Navy would be better suited to perform most of the services previously performed by the Indian Navy in the Eastern Seas, and that the few remaining functions could be undertaken by a temporary uncommissioned unit like the Bengal Marine. As it was generally thought, not least by its officers, that a service with the honourable history of the Indian Navy could not be relegated to the position of such an organisation, disbandment was agreed on and effected in April 1763. The officers were offered posts in the newly formed Bombay Marine or awarded pensions. The ships were all disposed of, some destined for a glamorous future, others for a useful one; all the sailing ships were sold. Of the steamers, *Ferooz* was to be kept on hand to serve as the Governor-General's yacht when required. *Semiramis*, *Berenice* and *Zenobia* were fitted out as transports. *Auckland* was to serve as a floating battery to defend Bombay or Karachi. *Assaye* and *Punjaub* were bought up by Jock Willis who had an eye for a good ship: he resold *Assaye* at a large profit but kept *Punjaub*, renamed *Tweed*, and built sister ships *Blackadder* and *Hallowe'en* to her design. Tweed earned him a fortune and inspired the beautiful bow lines of *Cutty Sark*.

It has been possible only to suggest the main aspects of the Company's Marine and its contribution to the Company's involvement in India. The service was never fully accepted by anyone. For the Directors in Leadenhall Street it represented a heavy drain on expenditure. The Royal Navy, whose operations the marine frequently supported, never took it seriously and either deliberately withheld recognition or simply forgot to mention it. The Indian Government in Calcutta viewed with suspicion a force which history had dictated should be in the control of a minor presidency. In view of these attitudes, the officers of the Indian Navy were highly indignant when a person of some authority referred to it as a 'pet service'. In many ways, however, this was a fair judgement. It was a service with its own distinctive history, and consequently a strong *esprit de corps*. It was a small service numerically, answerable only to the Governor and Council in Bombay, not to come remote department in Calcutta or London – all these characteristics made for a great deal of flexibility and a minimum of petty restrictions. Within this framework individual officers could develop their own strengths without bureaucratic inhibitions: Commanders Campbell and Rennie organised the seamen into brigades for land warfare; some of the leading surveying officers grew into figures of world renown, nurtured by the peculiar conditions of the Marine.

When the 'Company Jack', the Indian Navy's flag, was struck on board *Adjaha* at midday on 30 April 1863, it marked the end of a unique chapter in the extraordinary history of the East India Company.

Notes:

1. Dr Fryer was physician to the company's ships between 1672 and 1680.
2. Hamilton, Alexander: *A New Account of the East Indies*, Vol 1, 128.
3. Downing: op cit, 39.
4. Orme, R: *History of the Military Transactions of the British Nation in Hindostan for the year 1745*, Vol 1, 409ff.
5. Report by Commodore James to Admiral Watson, 22 December 1755, quoted in Low: op cit, Vol 1, 133.
6. BL OIOC L/MAR/C580 (A) Minute of Sir Robert Grant, Presidency of Bombay, to East India Company, on role of Indian Navy.
7. *Memorandum on the Marine Surveys of India* by Cdr A Dundas Taylor, 10 March 1871, submitted to the Indian Government.

APPENDICES

APPENDIX 1: Chart showing the payment of share capital by the owners of the ship *Bowscawen*

Owner	Share	1747				1748				1749				1750				1751			
		1	2	3	4	1	2	3	4	1	2	3	4	1	2	3	4	1	2	3	4
J Wauhemart	1/16	125					125	250				280									
H Crabb (Boulton)	1/16	125					125	250					280								
S Nicholson	1/16	125					125		250		280										
A Harrison	1/16	125					125		250		280										
J Tonson	1/16					125	125	250			280										
C Child	1/32						62½	125			140										
W Baker	1/16						250	250				280									
C Harris	1/32						125	125			140										
J Harrison	1/32						125	125			100	40									
J Small	1/16						250			350					180						
L Pead	1/16						250	250					280								
J Fisher	1/32						125		125			140									
N Fletcher	1/32							125	125					140							
W Braund	1/16							275						250	255						
A & J Crowley	1/16									100	680										
J Shipston	1/16														780						
S Braund	1/16 + 1/32																		1170		
C Pole	1/16									400	100	280									

APPENDIX 2:
Positions held by William Larkins and his sons Thomas and John Pascal between 1776 and 1805

Ship	Tons	Voyage		Position	Sailed	Returned	Destination
Lioness	693	4	William	Husband	14.3.1766	23.7.1777	Coast and Bay
			Thomas	Captain			
			John P	3rd Mate			
Nassau	723	3	John P	2nd Mate	7.3.1788	14.9.1780	Coast and Bay
Nassau	723	4	John P	1st Mate	8.2.1782	21.8.1785	Bombay and Bengal
Warren Hastings	755	1	William	Husband	6.2.1782	21.9.1784	Coast and China
			Thomas	Captain			
Warren Hastings	755	2	Mrs Larkins	Husband	8.4.1785	20.5.1786	China
			Thomas	Captain			
Warren Hastings	763	3	Thomas	Husband	13.4.1787	23.9.1788	Bombay
			John P	Captain			
Warren Hastings	786	4	Thomas	Husband	6.5.1790	9.10.1791	Bengal
			John P	Captain			
Warren Hastings	783	5	Thomas	Husband	7.7.1793	30.8.1794	Bengal
Warren Hastings	716	6	John P	Husband	24.5.1795	13.2.1797	China
Warren Hastings	1000	1	John P	Husband	24.2.1809	1.8.1810	Bengal and China
			Thomas	Captain			
Royal Admiral	914	5	Thomas	Husband	17.4.1790	26.6.1791	China
Royal Admiral	914	6	Thomas	Husband	30.5.1792	24.8.1793	New South Wales and China
Royal Admiral	914	7	John P	Husband	14.8.1794	19.3.1796	Bengal
Walmer Castle	1200	1	John P	Husband	11.8.1796	20.3.1798	China
Walmer Castle	1200	2	John P	Husband	2.4.1799	17.4.1801	Bombay and China
Walmer Castle	1200	3	John P	Husband	12.2.1802	27.4.1803	Bombay and China
Walmer Castle	1200	4	John P	Husband	13.2.1804	12.9.1805	St Helena, Benkulen and China
Warren Hastings	1200	1	John P	Husband	6.4.1803	13.8.1804	China
			Thomas	Captain			
Warren Hastings	1200	2	John P	Husband	17.2.1805	–	St Helena, Benkulen and China
			Thomas	Captain			

APPENDIX 3: Instrument appointing Samuel Braund as husband to the ship *Durrington*

We Whose names are hereunto Subscribed, Partowners of ye Good Ship or Vessell called ye *Durrington* whereof Capt Rich[ar]d Crabb is Commander now bound on a Voyage to ye East Indies and back, do hereby Authorize Impower and Appoint Mr S Braund To be ye Sole Husband and Manager of all affairs relating to ye Said Ship during any Voyage or Voyages that shall be made by her till it shall be otherwise ordered by ye Majority of ye said partowners and we do hereby Severally promise and Agree to Ratify and Confirm all and what ye said Samuel Braund shall lawfully do or Cause to be done in or about ye premises by virtue of these presents witness our hands together with our Several parts the Sixth day of November in ye year of our Lord One thousand Seven hundred and forty six.

On condition that ye said Samuel Braund enter into bond to render an Acc[omp]t to ye Majority of ye said Owners and pay such sums of money as are in his hands to ye said Owners on their Disapprobation of ye Conduct of ye said Samuel Braund in ye penalty of two thousand pounds, which Acc[omp]ts are to be laid before ye Owners in two Months after ye Acc[omp]ts of Freight and Demorage is settled with ye East India Company.

Signatures of part-owners.

Samuel Braund's Bond

Know all men by these present that I Samuel Braund of London Merchant am held and firmly bound unto John Blachford Esquire one of the Aldermen of the City of London and William Allix two of the owners of the Ship Durrington in the service of the East India Company on the behalf of themselves and the rest of the Owners of the Said Ship in the penal Sum of two thousand pounds of Lawful money of Great Britain to be paid unto the said John Blachford and William Allix or their certain Attorneys Executors Administrators or Assigns To which payment well and truly to be made I bind myself my heirs Executors and Administrators or Assigns and Every of them firmly by these presents Sealed with my Seal this Seventh day of March in the Twentieth Year of the Reign of our Sovereign Lord George the Second by the Grace of God of Great Britain France and Ireland King defender of the Faith etc in the year of our Lord One thousand Seven hundred and forty-six.

APPENDIX 4:
A summary of the accounts relating to the building of the *Boscawen* and her first voyage

Launched 1748
Sailed for Bombay March 1749
Arrived Bombay August 1749
Returned London June 1751

Income		Expenditure	
From owners 18/2/47 – 6/6/51	£12,480 0 0	Building, Fitting, provisioning and voyage expenses	£19,927 8 11½
Sundry receipts relating to Voyage	£59 17 0	27.8.51 Owners 1st Divi £210 per ¹⁄₁₆	£ 3,360 0 0
East India Co 10/2/49 impress	£1247 10 0	15.4.52 Owners 2nd Divi £100 per ¹⁄₁₆	£ 1,600 0 0
East India Co 10/7/50 – 7/2/52	£15,373 13 4 £29,161 0 4	15.4.52 Balance due to owners	£ 4,273 11 4½ £29,161 0 4

APPENDIX 5:
A summary of the accounts relating to the private trade of Captain John Stevens of the *Godolphin*

Goods sold in September 1749 and March 1750 at the company's sales

Income		Expenditure		
28 Tubs Hyson Tea	£ 600	Custom	£ 1710	
10 Chests Hyson Tea	550	Duty	360	
12 Chests Benjamin	940	Indulgence	140	
15 Chests Cassia Lignea	330	Warehousing	150	
2 Chests Camphire	45	Almshouses at Poplar	30	
159 Tubs Camphire	3700	Freight	NIL	
1 Cask Tamerinds	10	Goods to clear	90	
5 Lots Oranges (71.166)	950			
20 Casks Arrack	550		2480	
6336 Rattans	20	Balance due		
1 Chest White Pepper	45	(to Captain Stevens)	4760	7240
	7740			
Less 6½% discount for cash payments	500 7240	NB All figures have been rounded off		

APPENDIX 6:
Monthly wages of men employed in ships in the Company's service for the years 1746 and 1813

1746	£	s						
Commander	10		Butcher	2		Carpenter's servant		15
Chief mate	5		Baker			Surgeon's servant		15
Second mate	4		Poulterer			Foremastmen	2	5
Third mate	3	10	Coxswain	2	5			
Fourth mate	2	10	Boatswain's mates	2	10			
Fifth mate	2	5	Gunner's mates	2	10	Wages for 1813 were the same in all cases		
Sixth mate			Carpenter's first mate	3	5	except the following:		
Midshipmen (4)	2	5	Carpenter's second mate	2	10	Surgeon	£ 5	
Surgeon	3	5	Caulker's mate	2	15	Surgeon's mate	£ 3	10
Surgeon's mate	2	5	Cooper's mate	2	10	*Poulterer	£ 2	5
Purser	2		Captain's cook	3	5	Butcher	£ 2	5
Boatswain	3	10	Ship's cook	2	10	*Baker	£ 2	5
Gunner	3	10	Captain's steward	2		*These posts did not exist on board ship		
Carpenter	4	10	Ship's steward	2	10	in 1746		
Caulker	3	15	Quartermasters (4)	2	10			
Cooper	3		Captain's servants	1	5	The list for 1746 is taken from Samuel		
Sailmaker	2	10	Chief officer's servant	1		Braund's paper in Essex County Record		
Armourer	2	10	2nd mate's servant		18	Office (D/Dru B9). Those for 1813		
			Boatswain's servant		15	appear in Hardy, Charles: *A Register of*		
			Gunner's servant		15	*Ships employed in the service of the East*		
						India company, 1820.		

APPENDIX 7: Extract from the victualling bill and stores for the ship *Durrington*, 1746, 100 men, and list of prices for 1746

Item	Amount	Item	Price	
Ale, strong beer, cyder, rum	5 tons			
Beer (strong)	6 tons		£6	per ton
Beer (small)	40 tons		£2 2 0	per ton
Brandy and English spirit	250 gallons		3 6	per gallon
Wine in casks and bottles	6 tons		10 0	per cwt
Bread	30,000 weight		10 0	per cwt
Beef, pork, suet, tongues	25 tons	(beef, pork)	£1 2 0	per cwt
Fish	7000		17 0	per cwt
Red and white herring, salmon	5 barrels			
Peas	180 bushels		3 0	per bushel
Oats, barley, bran	300 bushels	(barley)	2 0	per bushel
Flour	70 cwt		11 6	per cwt
Cheese	50 cwt	(average)	£1 6 0	per cwt
Butter	30 firkins		£1 6 0	per firkin
Fruit (raisins and currants)	15 cwt		£1 14 0	per cwt
Mustard seeds	10 bushels		16 0	per bushel
Oil sweet and lamp	300 gallons	(sweet)	4 0	per gallon
Oranges and lemons	6 chests			
Salt White and Bay	40 bushels		4 0	per bushel
Sugar and Spice	15 cwt			
Vinegar	6 hogshead		10	per gallon
Sauces, all sorts	5 cases			
Limejuice	100 gallons		3 0	per gallon
Water (minimum)	40 tons			

Papers of Samuel Braund, Essex County Office (D/Dru B20)

APPENDIX 8: A typical contract specification for an East Indiaman

Articles of Agreement made the Twenty second day of December in the Twenty first year of the Reign of our Sovereign Lord George the Second By the Grace of God King of Great Britain ye Anno Dom 1747 Between John Perry and Company of Blackwall in the County of Middlesex Shipwrights of the one part and Samuel Braund Esq. of London in the County of aforesaid . . . of the other part Witnesseth that the said John Perry for himself and Company by these presents does covenant and agree to and with the said Samuel Braund that they the said John Perry and Co. shall and will at their Dockyard at Blackwall aforesaid at his and their own proper Cost and charge for him the said Samuel Braund Esq. or his Assigns Build and Erect in good and workman Like manner the Hull or Body of a new Ship Conformable to all the articles hereinafter mention'd Viz't

		feet	Inch
1.	Length by the Keel one hundred and five feet	105	
2.	Breadth from out to out of a three Inch Plank either above or below the Wale	33	4
3.	Depth in the Hold from plank to plank fourteen feet two Inches	14	2
4.	Height between Decks next the side five feet ten Inches	5	10
5.	Height in the Waist: five feet	5	
6.	Height in the forecastle Steeridge and great Cabbin next the side five feet ten Inches	5	10
7.	Rake afore to be three fifths of the Breadth ten feet of which to go into the Rake if thought proper the Keel		

		feet	Inch
8.	Stern post to rake three Inches in a foot		
9.	Lengths of the floor timbers to be twenty two feet four Inches and to carry the Lengths and Breadths with Dead flatts forwards as the Chesstree and as far aft as the Timb: light	22	4
10.	Dead Rising to be no more than Eight Inches		8
11.	Height in the Roundhouse afore five feet ten Inches	5	10
12.	Height abaft Six Foot Two Inches	6	2
13.	Length of the Roundhouse Eighteen foot	18	
	The Ruther head to come up into the Great Cabbin w[i]th a hole for a Tiller		

SCANTLINGS

14. Keel of fourteen Inches square with scarfs of four feet long and six bolts and a false keel of four Inches thick English oak plank

15. Keelson fourteen Inches square and to let down one inch into the Timbers a stemson abaft the Apron to work a three Inch Plank on the Keelson fore and aft in the wake of the pillers Stern post the Butt end downwards

16. Stem twelve and a half by fourteen Inches with an Apron to run down the Rising wood twenty two Inches broad and nine Inches thick the Stem and hawse pieces to be of good height

17. The Stern post at ye head to be fifteen Inches and a half square and two false ports to ye same the after one to be Eighteen ins abaft the Broad below: sufficient Dead wood on the Keel for the security of the [?] Timbers and two Knees on the same one arm twelve foot long the other arm to [?] the lower Transom and the Bolts [?] . . . Deadwood to be Clinch'd before the . . .

18. Wing transom fourteen Inches by Eighteen Inches

19. The same to be in Length

20. Knees sides twelve Inches

21. One arm to be ten foot and a half long the other arm to be six foot and a half at least

22. To add a false post if Required of sixteen Inches at the Lower end and five Inches at the upper end all the other [?] transoms to be whole Transoms and fashion Ones [?] in proportion all to be substantially kneed the fashion pieces to be sides the same at the upper futtocks.

23. Floor timbers to be twelve by thirteen Inches and to be in and out at the floor heads nine and a half

24. Lower futtocks Eleven and a half by nine and a half and to run to the Limber rooms but on the bearing to be sided twelve Inches

25. Middle futtocks Eleven by nine Inches

26. Upper futtocks ten and a half by Eight and half and to run two foot nine Inches above the Lower Deck

27. Top timbers to Tumble home at least three foot

28. All the Timbers and Plank to have six foot and a half scarf where the work will allow of it and none were less than six foot all the Timbers to butt four Inches good wood at least

29. To have broad Timber at the end of every Beam and in the wake of the Channills to take the Chain and Standard Bolts

30. Top timbers ten and a half Inches broad at the foot and eight at the head and to be in and out at the head five Inches wrought

31. All the timbers to be ten and Eleven Inches in the wake of the Channils for the main and fore Channil Bolts

32. A piece of Deadwood Elm fore and aft on the Keel of five Inches thick and nineteen Inches broad to save the Rabbets

33. Lower Deck Beams to be fourteen Inches by twelve and a half to be double-kneed at each end with one Lodging and one hanging knee to five to six Beams the other Beams to be kneed as Customary to have the same number of Beams in

this Ship as Capt Petre's Ship has in to lay but four foot six Inches or five feet asunder the Deck to hang twenty six Inches

34. The upper Deck Beams twelve Inches by ten Inches to be double-kneed at each end and to be spaced to come under the ports, lay right over the Lower Beams the knee to be sided six Inches with sufficient Ledges and Carlings to the said Deck the Beam afore and the Beam abaft the mainmast to be twelve Inches by ten Inches and half for the partners of the Mast and to have two hanging Knees of each side in the Gunroom in the Wake of the Transom

35. Quarter Deck and forecastle Beams Eight Inches by Six and to lay but two foot four Inches asunder and all to be single kneed at each End and well pillard, all the Beams of the great Cabbin to be well kneed if Required

36. All the Beams of the Lower and Upper Decks to be well pillard and all the Beams to be well pillard in the Hold the pillars to be Eight Inches Square

37. The half Deck to go to the Mainmast

38. The Timbers on the Quarter Deck to be high enough for an Awning

39. Main-wales to be four Strakes ten Inches by six Inches and to have three Strakes of four Inc[h] Plank below the Wale

40. All Butts to be Bolted

42. One Strake above the Wale of fourteen Inches broad of English Oak plank and four Inches thick

43. All the Rest of the Bottom of the Channill wales to be three Inch English Plank wrought except under the water which may be East Country plank if the said Samuel Braund Esq. approve of it

44. Channil Wales three Strakes full four Inches thick and Eleven broad one Strake above of two and a half Inches thick English plank

45. Waist Rail ten by four Inches and the same within board and to Run as to give good scarf to the forecastle and quarter Deck Clamps

46. All the rest of the upper works to be two Inches plank

47. The ends of all the scarfs and winding Butts to be Bolted with three quarter Inch Bolts

48 & 49. Main and fore Channils to be lift nine Inches higher and Cutt off in the wake of the ports to be full five Inches thick and proportionable in Length and Breadth

PLANK WITHIN BOARD

50. Foot waling at the floor head three Strakes two of four Inch and one of five Inches and a half

51. Next the Limbers one Strake of four Inch English plank and three Strakes of middle Bands of four Inch English plank

52. Lower Deck Clamps two Strakes of English Plank of fourteen Inches board to hook and Butt one of six Inches the other of five and one Strake of four Inches under the Clamps

53. All the Rest in the Hold to be three Inch English plank neither slappy nor sappy and well fayed

54. Lower Deck Spurkitting two Strakes of four Inches

55. Upper Deck Clamps four Inches thick and fourteen Inches broad to hook and Butt and to shutt in between the Spurkitting and the Clamps w[i]th three Inch English plank

56. Upper Deck Spurkitting four Inches two Strakes

57. Forecastle Clamps to be four Inches Quarter Deck Clamps three Inches and all the Rest the Quick work to be two Inches Oak or Deal as the said Samuel Braund Esq. shall Direct and the Quarter Deck Spurkitting to be three Inch English Plank and to work a plank round the Timb[e]r heads upon the forecastle

58. A String under the Beams in the great Cabbin of six Inches thick if Required the said Beams to be tayld and Bolted into the same or single kneed as the said Samuel Braund Esq shall direct

59. The Beams in the Round house to be the same

PLANK ON THE DECKS

60. Lower Deck Waterways to be full four Inches Chim'd down one Inch and a four Inch Strake next the Hatchways of each side of good lengths and all the Rest of the Deck to be good three Inch English plank or spruce Deal as the said Samuel Braund Esquire shall direct

61. Upper Deck water ways to be four Inches. Rabbitted down three quarters of an Inch for the Spurkitting to fay into in and four Strakes nex[sic] the same of two and a half Inch and one Strake next the Cumings of three Inch plank and all the plank in the forecastle to be two Inch and a half except which [is?] in the fall which is to be three Inch English oak Plank and to run out and give good scarfs in [the?] waist all the Rest of the Deck to be two and a half Dantzig long Deals

62. Quarter Deck Roundhouse and forecastle to be two Inch Deal Except the Waterways which is to be full (three) Inch plank Chim'd down an Inch

63. Sufficient and Convenient partners to all the Masts Capstands and Pumps

64. The main partners to be seven Inches thick

65. The fore partners to be six Inches thick and to run down the Stem

66. The Missen partners to be four Inches thick and to run quite Aft

67. Upon the upper Deck the partners of the foremast Missen mast and main Capstan to be four Inches thick and Jeer Capstan four Inches thick and to Run from Hatch to Hatch and the partners of the foremast to run down to the Stem and as far aft as the fore Hatch way

68. To have two Crutches and seven Breasthooks in proper places of sixteen foot long and nine bolts in Each the Breasthooks under the Bowspreet to be twenty two foot long if to be got

69. Limber holes to be Cutt in Every timber fore and Aft All the Timber and plank to be well fayed fastened and Shifted

SIZES OF IRON AND ALL TO BE GOOD SPANISH IRON

70. Bolts in the Keel Keelson Deadwood Breasthooks Crutches and Wing Transom Knees to be one Inch and quarter to be bored with one Inch and half quarter Augar with nine Bolts in Each knee

71. Bolts in Lower Deck Knees and Standards to be one Inch and one Eighth six in each knee and to forelock the End Bolts

72. Six Bolts in Each upper Deck hanging knee as several of the new Ships have full Inch

73. Chain plates as many and Substantial as usual w[i]th fourteen preventer plates and twelve backstay plates and Bolts

74. Six pair substantial Rudder Irons a Bolt and strap for the Tiller two false posts and Steps for the Braces to be bolted through the posts

75. A good Rudder with Eye Bolts and Ring bolts on the back of it with Swivel Rings for Boat rope Guest[?]

76. The Ring and Eye Bolts of the posts to be full Inch the ten stoppers on the deck one Inch & three Eighths and to have Bolts to hook the Jeer and Toptakle Blocks to and to have four Ring plates and to fix two Iron pawls to the Jeer Capstan and one Iron pawl to the main Capstan and Ring Bolts for the Bowspreet Shrouds to the Chain Bolts to be one Inch and five Eighths substantial Iron hoops on the head of the Rother Capstans and Catheads as many as the said Samuel Braund Esq shall Direct to have twelve bars to the Jeer Capstand and twelve in the main Capstan to have one Iron hoop on the Drumhead of Each Capstan

77. Build a Stair Case with handsome turn'd Bannisters to go from the Quarter Deck into the Steeridge

78. To have two sets of Iron Pins and chains for the Capstans and Eye Bolts to hook the Toptakle Halliards and shank painters to and as many Bolts in the thick stuff as may be thought Convenient

STANDARDS

79. Standards between Decks seven pair sided twelve Inches to run up to the Deck, upon the upper Deck seven pair sided nine ins and at the Bulkhead of the Roundhouse one pair of standards sided nine Inches

80. A Roundhouse sixteen foot long completely finished with Copper Funnels to each Gallery to be lined and made Convenient and all the sashes belonging to the Roundhouse and great Cabbin to be good Crown Glass

81. To build two Bread Rooms and Batten them to fix a powder Room and Bulkhead Lined, with a Light Room

82. To make a Lazaretto and a powder Room Scuttle and a Capscuttle with a Gunroom Bulkhead & a capscuttle & [?] to the Bread rooms to make a passage to the powder room & inclose the scuttle

83. A great Cabbin with a Leaden or Copper Funnel to each Gallery the said Gallery to be Completely finished with handsome sashes and good Crown Glass where usual

84. The Treenails that are drove inward to be wedges and Rim'd

85. To Compleatly Build, Eighteen standing Cabbins with Lockers and shelves four Cabbins to be lined and scuttle cut in them & lined and a pantry to be built and Compleatly finished with shelves in the Steeridge or where else the said

Samuel Braund Esq shall Direct

86. The build a substantial well in the Hold with good two and a half Inch plank Rabitted

87. Fix two hand and two Chain pumps to come upon the upper Deck with Cisterns and everything thereto belonging Except the pumps and Iron work

88. To sheathe the Bottom with good three quarter Inch board to sire (?) and Tarr the parselling and to nail it on, to Cant the Wales as usual and to pay the Bottom with white Stuff and find spunyard and Nails

89. To find a good suit of masts and yards of the Growth of Gottenburg the main mast to be full twenty four Inches Diameter free from sap the foremast the same bigness as the mainmast and the other in proportion to Build a Substantial head with two pair of cheeks and to fix Bumkins to lead the Stem Hawes and Cutwater

90. To have two Good Capstans twenty three Inches at least with Drumheads of sufficient bigness for twelve Bars with a suit of ashen bar pins and chains to each Capstan with bitts and Rings for the Cables w[i]th Rings Kavels and Cleats

91. Main Bitts to be seventeen Inches square the Cross pieces to be sixteen Inches by Eighteen Inches the Gallows Bitts to be ten Inches and a half square to have as many ports Gratings Ladders Hatches and Scuttles as the said Samuel Braund Esq shall Direct and also as many leaden pipes Hawes and Scuppers as he shall think proper

92. To fix a sweep and Tiller and strapp in the Rudder head to fix linings for the Anchors and Skidds over the sides down to the main wale and to fix wash boards and to fill up under and between the Cheeks

93. Find what plank or Elm may be necessary for Cleats and Rings for the masts and fix them

94. Fix a Belfry and Gallows

95. All the Timber and plank to be of the Growth of England Except the Bottom plank underwater as aforesaid

96. All Red sappy shaken or Defective Timber or plank if at any time put in to be taken out again and Good put in its Room at the Builders Charge

97. All Knees Breasthooks Crutches and all the whole frame to be well Grown and free from sap

98. The floor Timbers to be placed no more than fifteen and a half Inches asunder

99. To make a handsome Bell Ladder at the fore part of the awning to go from the Quarter Deck to the top of the Roundhouse

100. To find as much three Inch Deal as may be sufficient for Russtrees and fix them

101. To fix an Iron Rowl of the Ensign staff

102. Pay the Stem and Stern post Keel and Transom with Rosin and Cutt Loopholes in ye Bulkheads

103. Treenails to be wedged fore and Aft in all the thick stuff

104. To paint the Ship within board and without and also the steerage forecastle Quick work waist all the Cabbins together with the Gunwales Capstans awnings and whatever else the said Samuel Braund Esq Directs that is belonging to the Hull of the said Ship

105. All Glaziers Joyners Plumbers Painters and Smiths work to be done at the Builders charge as Capt Petrees Ship

106. That the East India Company Surveyors shall have the Liberty from time to time to survey and inspect ye work

107. That the said Samuel Braund Esq. shall have Liberty of Choosing and appointing a proper person or persons to over-look and inspect the particulars of the whole work and if any dispute arises to be Determined by two persons indifferently Choses and these two if necessary to Choose a third person

108. To lay in the Dry Dock for the cleats to be taken off without any charge from the Builder

109. To fix a Steering wheel on the Quarter Deck with proper Blocks to the same the owners finding the wheel

110. The cell of the ports not to be cutt into the thick Brake of the spurkitting

111. The Gun Deck Transom to be Bolted with two good Bolts through the Stern post

112. To make a Sail Room Gun Room Table with a proper Bulkhead for the Gun Room

113. To make an handsome awning on the Quarter Deck of whole Deal Rabitted to come as far forward as the Missen Mast with Quarter Deck Table and two Binicles Glazed

114. To marke the ship fore and aft with Lead

115. To Lead the upper Gallerys as shall be Directed and also the Brace and stirrups

116. To fix dark shutters to the Roundhouse and great Cabbin windows with substantial Dead lights to the great Cabbin & also ye Bulkhead of the Steerage Roundhouse & forecastle and all the Bulkheads to be fill'd up with 4 Inch plank and also thick doors to the Gallery

117. To pay the said John Perry & Co Eight pounds ten Shillings pr Ton Sheathed for as many tons as the said Ship shall meas-ure according to the aforesaid Dimensions and not to be oblig'd to pay for any such increase

118. All the payments to be endorsed on these presents from and after which Time the Hull of the said Ship or so much there-of as shall be then built to be the proper Goods of the said Samuel Braund Esq and not liable to any Debts or incum-brances whatsoever of the said John Perry & Co

119. That all such Damage or Loss as shall or may happen to the said hull or Body of the said ship by Fire or any other casu-alty before the said ship shall be Launch'd and safe in the River of Thames shall be sustain'd by the said John Perry & Company their Execut[o]rs or Administrators

120. The said Ship to be Launch'd on or before the first spring in July . . . next ensuing this date

121. The said John Perry & Co do further oblige themselves to work no North country wood plank or Timber but what the said Samuel Braund Esq his surveyors shall approve of under the penalty of Fifty pounds over and above the charge of ye taking any such out that may be put in and so put good Timber or plank in the Room

122. To case the pump in the head to find five anchor stocks
123. The measurement of the Breadth of the Ship shall only from a three Inch Plank either under or over the wales

PAYMENTS

The payments to be at five several payments before and at Launching the said Ship and a Bill of Sale executed

1st One Thousand pounds at the enclosing these presents 1000
2nd One Thousand pounds when the frame is fully
      Erected and ready to go to Planking 1000
3   One Thousand pounds when the Gundeck Beams
      are all in and fastened 1000
4th Eight hundred pounds when the upper Deck Beams
      are all in and fastened 800
5   The Remainder when the ship is Launched and compleated according to these Agreements and a Bill of Sale executed

For the true performance of all and every the foregoing Articles the said parties do by these forms [?] Bind themselves, their Heirs Executors and Administrators firmly to each other in the penal sum of Two thousand pounds of Good and Lawful Money of Great Britain in Witness whereof the said Parties to these present Articles have interchangeably sett their Hands and Seals the Day and year first above written
John Perry for self and Company

Sam Braund
Received the Within 22nd December 1747 of Samuel Braund Esq. one thousand Pounds being for the first Payment of the Within Contract
£1000-0-0   Signed John Perry

Received the 23rd March 1748 of Samuel Braund Esq. one thousand Pounds being for the Second Payment of the Within Contract
£1000-0-0   Signed John Perry

Received the 25th of May 1748 of Samuel Braund Esq. one thousand Pounds being for the third Payment of the Within Contract
£1000-0-0   Signed John Perry

Received the 13th of July 1748 of Samuel Braund Esq. Eight hundred Pounds being for the fourth Payment of the Within Contract
£800-0-0   Signed John Perry

APPENDIX 9: Ships in the Service of the East India Company 1600-1834

This list has been compiled from the following sources: Bal Krishna's book (see **Bibliography**) for the period 1601-72; Add. MSS 38872, Ship book, East India Company Records, Vol. II, (British Museum) for the period 1673-1790; Hardy's Register of Ships, (see **Bibliography**) for the period 1791-1832.

To facilitate reference while keeping the list within manageable proportions, the ships have been arranged alphabetically by name and grouped in the four periods into which the Company's trading life naturally falls.

1600-57 witnessed the early successes followed by decline culminating in near cessation of trade by the final years.

1658-1703 was a period of growth following the introduction of a new charter and advantageous conditions. Desire to share in the profits led to a spate of licensed ships – private, permission, and finally ships of rival Companies.

1704-73 is the period of regulations and consolidation of trade carried on in ships of roughly similar size and capacity taken up by the new United Company.

1773-1834 sees a return to diversification in response to considerable changes in the pattern of trade established in the previous period.

Tonnage is extremely unreliable throughout the period apart from a short time following the Act of 1773. Such diverse figures are given by various authorities in the early period that it is difficult to determine if they refer to one ship or several. Similarly it is difficult to ascertain when one ship was taken out of service and replaced by another of the same name. Ships were frequently almost completely rebuilt and so could perform several voyages, often with several years' interruption.

Where ships have the same name and the records show there is ownership in common, they have been marked (1), (2), etc. Where no connection can be found the similarity of name has been assumed to be coincidental.

The dates given for the first and final voyages refer to the season in which a ship sailed, not to the individual voyage: eg the *Warren Hastings* actually sailed on 24 February 1809, in the season beginning in 1808.

Key to abbreviations:
(ES) Extra ship
N   New company
P   Permission
Pr   Private
M   Merchant

A:	Name of ship
B:	Tonnage
C:	Number of voyages
D:	Period of Service

PERIOD I – 1601-57

A	B	C	D
Abigail	150	1	1623
Advice	160	1	1614
Advice	350	5	1637-58
Aleppo M	400	3	1642-50
Anne	700	1	1616
Anne	300	3	1649-58
Anne Royal	750	2	1618-21
Antelope	350	1	1646
Ascension	260	3	1601-7
Assada M	250	1	1650
Attendance	100?	1	1614
Bee	150	1	1616
Blessing	260	3	1644-51
Blessing	700	6	1622-42
Bonito	400	2	1648-50
Bull	400	2	1616-18
Caesar	400	1	1640
Centaur	100	1	1619
Charles	1000	2	1615-19
Charles	700	2	1629-31
Christopher	300	1	1626
Clove	527	3	1610-17
Coaster	260	1	1635
Comfort	200	1	1633
Concord	213	1	1613
Consent	150	1	1606
Crispian	400	4	1635-44
Darling	150	1	1610
Defence	400	1	1614-17
Diamond	300	1	1619
Discovery	500	9	1617-60
Dolphin	500	2	1621-25
Dolphin	300	4	1631-48
Dove	300	3	1628-53
Dragon	600	6	1601-18
Dragon's Claw	100?	1	1618
Eagle	280	1	1620
Eagle	400	4	1624-49
Eagle	600	8	1637-73
East India M	330	7	1650-72
Elizabeth	978	1	1619
Endeavour	400	1	1643
Endyman	300	3	1646-56
Exchange	700	2	1626-31
Expedition	240	7	1608-34
Falcon	560	2	1625-45
Farewell	140	1	1647
Flour	200	1	1617
Fortune	200	1	1621
Gift	130	1	1601
Globe	527	3	1610-17
Godspeed	50	1	1620
Golden Fleece	550	2	1648-50
Greyhound (ex-Swan)	400	2	1646-48
Hart	500	5	1620-36
Hart	220	1	1643
Hector	300	5	1601-13
Hind	300	1	1643
Hope	533	2	1615-19
Hopewell	240	5	1627-41
Hosiander	213	2	1611-15
Hound	250	1	1615
Intelligence	100	1	1631
James	600	2	1611-15
James Royal	1000	3	1616-30
Jewel	250	3	1631-38
John	500	1	1644
Jonas	700	5	1621-40
Katherine	200	2	1654-58
Lanneret	200	1	1614
Lanneret	160	1	1645
Lesser James	500	1	1621
Lion	386	4	1614-25
Lionness	350	1	1650
Lion's Claw	100?	1	1618
Little James	260	1	1627
London	800	7	1620-41
Love	450	3	1650-58
Mary (Mary Royal)	800	7	1627-47
Merchant's Hope	533	2	1613-19
Moon	600	1	1617
Morris	400	1	1626
New Year's Gift	867	2	1613-16
Palsgrave	1083	4	1619-33
Pearl	200	2	1610-31
Peppercorn	342	3	1610-17
Reformation	400	5	1622-41
Refuge	150?	1	1627
Relief	50?	1	1610
Richard	20	1	1621
Roebuck	300	3	1620-52
Rose pinnace	140	3	1615-21
Royal Exchange	700	1	1619
Ruby	700	1	1619
Ruth	400	1	1649
Samarian	453	1	1614
Samson	600?	1	1617
Samuel pinnace	180	1	1610
Samuel	300	1	1629
Scout	100?	2	1624-27
Seaflower	180	1	1643
Seahorse	150	1	1630
Smirna M	450	3	1652-59
Solomon	400	2	1611-13
Speedwell	200	3	1614-31
Spy	100?	1	1624
Star	250	4	1619-30
Sun	700	1	1617
Supply	100?	1	1619
Supply	250	1	1650
Susan	240	2	1601-04
Swallow	100	2	1625-31
Swan	400	1	1615
Swan (later Greyhound)	400	4	1632-46
Thomas	340	2	1610-14
Thomasine	133	1	1614
Tiger	240	1	1604
Tiger's Whelp	100?	1	1604
Three Brothers	260	1	1655
Trades Increase	1293	1	1610
Trail	500	1	1621
Ulysses	350	2	1642-46
Unicorn	700	2	1615-17
Union	400	1	1607
Unitie	300	1	1619
Welcome	240	3	1651-58
Whale	700	1	1621
White Bear	900	1	1619
William	700	9	1626-50
William	450	1	1656

PERIOD II – 1658-1703

A	B	C	D
Abingdon	400	4	1703-11
Advance	220	1	1670
Adventure	220	1	1684
Advice pinnace	150	1	1673
Advice Frigate	130	1	1700
African	240	3	1660-64
Albermarle N	350	1	1699-1704
American M	240	2	1692-94
American	225	4	1660-64
Amity	120	2	1693-96
Amoy M	310	2	1681-83
Andulasia Pr		1	1686
Ann	300	3	1670-74
Anna	350	4	1697-1707
Anne	120	1	1687
Anne	450	8	1669-83
Antelope	400	3	1668-72
Antelope	470	2	1659-98
Arabia M N	300	2	1701-04
Armenian M	220	3	1692-98
Asia	450	1	1683
Aurengzeb	450	4	1701-13
Bantam Pink	120	1	1667

Name			
Barbadoes M	240	1	1659
Barnardiston	400	5	1671-83
Beare Pr		1	1686
Beaufort	775	2	1683-85
Beaufort Frigate	100	1	1685
Bedford	800	3	1697-1700
Bengal M	390	1	1700
Bengala M	550	5	1676-86
Bengal Sloop	150	1	1683
Benjamin	460	3	1689-98
Berkley Castle (1)	500	7	1669-81
Berkley Castle (2)	630	2	1686-91
Blackmoor	240	3	1658-67
Blessing Pr		1	1686
Bombay	370	5	1668-76
Borneo N	600	1	1700
Bowden	150	1	1686
Bowen Frigate	150	1	1660
Buckhurst	300	1	1698
Caesar	500	7	1672-86
Caesar	380	1	1703
Canterbury N	350	2	1699-1701
Carolina	290	1	1682-86
Castle Frigate	240	3	1659-68
Chambers Frigate	350	3	1695-1701
Chandois	660	2	1684-88
Charles	140	1	1666
Charles	370	2	1682-84
Charles the Second	775	4	1683-95
China M	170	3	1681-1700
Coast Frigate	300	6	1658-83
Colchester	400	2	1699-1701
Concord	300	1	1659
Constant M	430	6	1658-67
Constant M	300	2	1664-69
Convertine	240	1	1661
Coronation	400	2	1660-63
Crowne	250	2	1668-70
Crown P		2	1681-88
Curtana	140	1	1685
Dashwood	320	1	1700
Defence	650	6	1681-92
Degrave	520	1	1698
Degrave	300	1	1700
Delight	100	1	1682
Diamond	80	1	1685
Diana	170	1	1688
Discovery N	500	1	1700
Donegal	240	2	1703-07
Dorcas	75	1	1665
Dorill	300	2	1695-99
Dorothy	225	4	1687-97
Dover	180	1	1703
Dragon	400	1	1658
Dragon	180	2	1681-84
Duke of Gloucester	400	1	1697
Dunkirk	150	1	1661
Dutchess	430	4	1700-09
Eagle	500	5	1673-83
Eagle P	240	1	1697
East India M	370	4	1674-83
East India M	450	2	1696-98
Eaton	340	2	1699-1703
Edward and Dudley	300	2	1701-06
Elizabeth	280	1	1691
Emerald	103	1	1685
Endeavour P		1	1688
European M	380	2	1670-73
Expectation	400	4	1671-77
Experiment	260	2	1669-71
Falcon	360	7	1670-83
Fame	420	2	1697-99
Featherstone	180	1	1703
Fleet Frigate	280	4	1694-1707
Flying Eagle	120	1	1670
Formosa	200	1	1675
Frederick	350	4	1699-1712
George	500	5	1676-84
George & Martha	300?	1	1661
Gilbert	250	1	1658
Gloucester Frigate	350	1	1702
Golden Fleece	500	5	1673-82
Good Hope	200	1	1661
Gosfreight P	300	1	1699
Gracedew	300	1	1698
Greyhound	280	2	1664-70
Halifax N	350	3	1701-08
Hampshire	400	3	1698-1704
Hannibal	350	2	1669-71
Happy Entrance	240	2	1663-69
Hare	500	1	1682
Hawk	400	1	1692
Henry P	350	1	1693
Henry & William	250	1	1682
Herbert	750	3	1682-89
Herne Pr	200	1	1699
Herne	150	1	1701
Herne Frigate N	200	1	1701
Herne	350	3	1703-11
Howland	400	4	1699-1710
Humphrey & Elizabeth			
	320	2	1668-70
James P	300	2	1687-90
Johanna	500	5	1671-81
John & Alexander		1	1673
John & Express	200	1	1695
John & Margaret	425	2	1668-70
John & Martha	300	2	1668-70
John & Mary	150	3	1683-1701
Jonah	500	1	1673
Jonas Frigate	80	1	1686
Josiah	570	7	1680-1703
Julian N	260	1	1698
Katherine N	495	2	1700-02
Kempthorn	640	3	1682-88
Kent	140	2	1681-84
King Fernandez Pr		1	1658
King William	800	3	1690-1699
Lancaster	500	5	1673-81
Laurell	250	1	1682
Leghorn Frigate N	170	1	1701
Liampo N	160	2	1699-1705
Little James	80	1	1678
Little Josiah	200	1	1691
London	380	1	1658
London	400	9	1658-74
London	515	1	1685
London Frigate	350	2	1693-98
Loyal Adventure	220	1	1684
Loyal Bliss	350	4	1701-12
Loyal Captain	150	1	1685
Loyal Cooke	330	3	1700-08
Loyal Eagle	250	1	1681
Loyal M	450	6	1660-87
Loyal M P	450	1	1689
Loyal M	400	2	1699-1703
Loyal Subject	500	6	1667-78
Macclesfield N	250	2	1698-1701
Macclesfield Frigate N			
	310	1	1701
Madras	250	2	1696-99
Madras M	250	2	1661-67
Madraspatan	250	1	1658
Marigold	200	3	1658-63
Martha	700	4	1693-1703
Mary	330	3	1671-75
Mary	150	1	1684
Mary Pr	150	1	1687
Mary	420	1	1693
Mary Pr	420	1	1697
Mary	350	1	1697
Mary N	468	1	1702
Mary	300	1	1702
Maryland	300	1	1682
Massingbird	470	5	1670-83
Mayflower	250	1	1658
Maynard	200?	1	1695
Mediterranean	240	2	1669-71
Merchant Adventurer	430	1	1658
Merchants Delight	350	1	1658
Mexico M	200	1	1682
Mocha Frigate	150	1	1694
Modena	775	2	1685-91
Montague	410	4	1698-1710
Morning Star	200	2	1663-68

Nassau	520	2	1693-97	Sarah Galley N	275	2	1696-1700		
Nathaniel	550	7	1675-85	Satisfaction	400	1	1670		
Nathaniel	250	5	1700-14	Sceptre	360	2	1695-98		
Nathaniel Frigate	100	1	1685	Scipio Afric[anus]	390	5	1675-83		
Neptune N	275	3	1698-1703	Scipio	350	2	1703-07		
New London	540	4	1674-82	Seaford	240	3	1700-02		
Norris	520	2	1699-1701	Sedgwick	100	1	1696		
Northumberland	250	4	1698-1706	Seymour Pr	200	1	1694		
Oaklander	150	1	1681	Shrewsbury	360	2	1684-87		
Orange (Tree)	350	2	1686-90	Shrewsbury Pr	180	1	1697		
Panther N	350	3	1699-1704	Sidney	500	4	1696-1702		
Pearl	80	1	1685	Smyrna M	190	2	1682		
Persia M	360	6	1658-87	Society	240	1	1658		
Phoenix	380	4	1670-77	Society	550	4	1675-83		
Phoenix	400	3	1700-09	Sommers N	480	4	1699-1711		
President	540	5	1672-81	Starling Adv[venture]	200	1	1661		
Princess of Denmark	670	2	1687-92	Streatham	350	4	1700-1711		
Prysaman	150	1	1683	Success	500	7	1674-93		
Prudent Mary	350	2	1682-84	Surat Frigate	150	2	1658-60		
Queen	320	1	1702	Surat M	350	4	1671-81		
Rainbow	380	7	1667-87	Susannah N	350	1	1700		
Rapier		1	1702	Susan M	330	1	1683		
Rebecca	170	4	1663-85	Tankerville N	430	4	1699-1708		
Rebou N	150	1	1701	Tavistock	750	4	1696-1707		
Regard	230	1	1702	Taywan	140	1	1675		
Resolution	650	4	1681-91	Thomas	400	2	1693-97		
Restoration	400	1	1660	Thomas & William Pr		1	1658		
Return	370	4	1665-71	Thorndon	500	1	1697		
Richard & Martha	450	4	1660-67	Tonqueen	130		1681-94		
Rising Eagle N	600	1	1700	Tronbail N	250	2	1697-99		
Rising Sun N	140	1	1700	Truroe	270	1	1659		
Robert & Nathaniel	230	1	1701	Tuscan Galley N	220	1	1699		
Rochester	775	3	1683-88	Unicorn	330	4	1667-77		
Rochester Frigate	100	1	1685	Union N	140	1	1701		
Rook Frigate	250	1	1699	Unity	300	4	1670-76		
Rose	150	1	1661	Upton Galley N	180	1	1701		
Rose	100	1	1685	Vine	150	1	1658		
Royal Charles	500	2	1660-63	Virgin Pr		1	1658		
Royal James	650	2	1683-85	Welcome Pr		1	1686		
Royal James & Mary	670	2	1687-92	Welfare	250	2	1681-84		
Royal James & Henry	400	1	1660	Wentworth	350	4	1699-1707		
Royal Katherine	380	1	1662-67	Westmorland	340	2	1703-07		
Royal Oak	400	1	1663	William & Herbert	240	1	1682		
Ruby	80	1	1685	William & John Pr		1	1681		
Ruby	450	1	1698	William & Mary	170	1	1690		
Russell Frigate	350	2	1694-97	William & Richmond					
St George	230	1	1664		220	1	1697		
Samaritan	250	1	1658	Williamson	600	5	1677-86		
Sampson	340	4	1668-74	Worcester	220	1	1685		
Sampson	600	6	1677-95	Zant Frigate	180	2	1669-71		
Samuel	200	1	1691						
Samuel & Anna	300	1	1702						
Samuel & Henry	350	1	1673						
Sapphire	320	1	1685						
Sarah	340	1	1694						

PERIOD III 1704-1773

A

	B	C	D
Addison	470	2	1717-20
Admiral Pocock	499	3	1761-69
Admiral Vernon	493	4	1740-51
Admiral Watson	499	4	1757-66
Aislabie	380	4	1720-30
Ajax	499	1	1758
Albermarle	330	1	1704
Alfred	758	4	1772-81
Anglesea	490	1	1737
Ankerwyke	679	4	1764-74
Anson	499	3	1746-53
Anson	499	4	1763-71
Arabella	140	1	1713
Asia	657	4	1763-73
Augusta	495	4	1738-48
Averilla	300	2	1710-13
Beaufort	490	4	1734-43
Beckenham	350	1	1763
Bedford	490	3	1731-39
Bengal Gallery	160	1	1721
Benjamin	350	4	1741-49
Berrington	440	3	1722-29
Blenheim	280	3	1704-11
Bombay Castle	160	1	1721
Bombay Castle	498	4	1745-57
Bombay Frigate	300	1	1706
Borneo	180	2	1713-18
Boscawen	499	4	1748-60
Bouverie	420	4	1709-21
Bridgewater	360	4	1719-29
Bridgewater	804	4	1769-79
Britannia (1)	490	4	1732-41
Britannia (2)	498	4	1745-57
Britannia	499	4	1761-70
British King	499	4	1762-72
British M	200	1	1715
Bute	657	4	1762-72
Cadogan	450	4	1718-28
Caernarvon	376	4	1717-25
Caernarvon	499	3	1755-63
Caesar	430	4	1721-30
Caesar	495	4	1739-50
Calcutta (1)	499	4	1758-66
Calcutta (2)	761	4	1770-81
Cardigan	400	4	1712-22
Cardonnell	300	3	1714-19
Carlton Frigate	275	2	1705-08
Cassandria	380	1	1719
Catherine	200	1	1704
Catherine	450	3	1709-15
Chandois	440	1	1719
Chesterfield	498	4	1747-58

Name				Name				Name			
Clinton	499	3	1752-58	Edgecote	498	4	1747-58	Hawke (2)	723	4	1769-81
Clive	499	4	1761-70	Egmont (1)	499	4	1752-62	Heathcote (1)	400	4	1708-17
Colchester	495	4	1739-51	Egmont (2)	700	4	1766-76	Heathcote (2)	480	4	1720-30
Colebrooke	499	3	1770-78	Elizabeth	498	4	1743-56	Heathcote (3)	490	4	1732-42
Craggs	370	4	1718-29	Elizabeth	499	1	1762	Heathcote (4)	498	1	1746
Compton	440	4	1722-35	Enfield	450	4	1721-31	Hector (1)	499	4	1750-64
Cruttenden	499	4	1762-70	Essex	300	4	1716-25	Hector (2)	688	4	1766-75
Dartmouth	440	4	1710-20	Essex (1)	498	4	1744-53	Herbert Galley	210	1	1707
Dawsonne	480	4	1718-29	Essex (2)	499	3	1758-67	Hertford (1)	290	2	1717-19
Deckar	490	2	1732-36	Europa	676	4	1766-76	Hertford (2)	440	4	1722-33
Defence	480	3	1735-41	Europa	300	2	1704-09	Hester	250	3	1710-15
Delaware	450	4	1747-58	Exeter	498	4	1742-54	Heston	350	1	1704
Denham	499	2	1753-58	Eyles	480	4	1721-31	Horsenden	499	3	1764-70
Deptford	499	4	1762-70	Falmouth	499	5	1752-64	Houghton (1)	450	4	1724-34
Derby (1)	450	4	1710-19	Fordwich	480	4	1718-28	Houghton (2)	495	3	1738-45
Derby (2)	480	4	1722-34	Fort St George	160	1	1721	Houghton (1)	499	4	1751-61
Despatch	110	1	1707	Fort St George	498	3	1740-47	Houghton (2)	707	4	1766-76
Devonshire (1)	480	4	1721-23	Fort William	499	1	1763	Huntingdon	499	2	1769-72
Devonshire (2)	495	1	1736	Fox (1)	499	4	1756-68	Ilchester	498	4	1745-56
Devonshire	495	4	1763-71	Fox (2)	758	4	1771-83	Indian Frigate	130	1	1705
Doddington	499	3	1748-54	Francis	390	4	1720-30	James & Mary	300	4	1720-30
Dolphin	370	2	1744-47	George	480	4	1727-36	Jane Frigate	240	1	1704
Dover	180	1	1704	Glatton (1)	499	4	1762-70	Kent	350	4	1703-14
Dragon	310	4	1745-52	Godfrey	220	2	1718-21	Kent (1)	498	4	1740-53
Drake	390	5	1720-33	Godfrey	716	4	1770-79	Kent(2)	499	4	1763-72
Drake	499	3	1751-57	Godolphin	280	1	1708	King George	450	5	1715-25
Duke	490	2	1739-42	Godolphin (1)	480	4	1734-43	King George	270	1	1719
Duke of Albany	499	4	1763-71	Godolphin (2)	498	4	1747-58	King George	200	1	1729
Duke of Cambridge	400	4	1712-22	Good Fellow	140	1	1720	King William	400	4	1709-18
Duke of Cumberland	470	4	1726-37	Grafton	350	2	1733-36	King William	490	4	1733-43
Duke of Cumberland	499	1	1749	Granby	786	4	1767-78	Lapwing	260	4	1743-49
Duke of Cumberland	499	4	1765-76	Grantham (1)	470	4	1711-20	Latham (1)	499	4	1756-66
Duke of Dorset (1)	460	4	1733-43	Grantham (2)	480	4	1724-35	Latham (2)	699	5	1769-80
Duke of Dorset (2)	498	4	1747-58	Grantham (3)	490	2	1738-41	Lethieullier	470	4	1721-32
Duke of Gloucester	499	3	1763-69	Grantham	499	4	1746-56	Lioness	693	4	1765-75
Duke of Grafton	804	4	1768-79	Greater London Pr	620	1	1705	Lincoln	498	2	1744-47
Duke of Kingston	499	2	1765-68	Greenwich	450	4	1719-30	Litchfield	420	2	1707-10
Duke of Kingston	723	4	1772-82	Greenwich	676	4	1766-75	Little London Pr		1	1704
Duke of Lorraine	490	4	1731-41	Grenville	499	4	1764-74	London (1)	500	1	1710
Duke of Newcaste	380	1	1748	Griffin	499	4	1748-58	London (2)	480	4	1719-29
Duke of Portland	723	4	1769-79	Grosvenor (1)	499	3	1761-67	London (3)	490	4	1734-44
Duke of Richmond	499	4	1759-70	Grosvenor (2)	729	4	1770-79	London (1)	499	4	1749-59
Duke of York	400	4	1716-29	Guardian	300	1	1751	London (2)	499	2	1763-66
Durrington	495	4	1739-51	Haestinfield	490	3	1735-42	London (3)	723	3	1770-78
Dutton	676	4	1764-73	Halifax	490	2	1735-39	London (4)	728	4	1779-88
Eagle Galley	200	1	1713	Hampshire	499	4	1765-74	London Packet	120	1	1761
Earl of Asburnham	499	4	1761-71	Hannover	460	4	1712-21	Lord Anson (1)	499	4	1749-59
Earl of Chatham	499	1	1766	Harcourt (1)	499	4	1752-61	Lord Anson (2)	499	1	1763
Earl of Elgin	499	4	1760-69	Harcourt (2)	499	4	1764-72	Lord Camden	707	4	1765-75
Earl of Holderness	490	3	1754-60	Hardwicke (1)	495	5	1739-53	Lord Clive	499	1	1762
Earl of Lincoln	499	4	1763-71	Hardwicke (2)	499	3	1754-64	Lord Holland (1)	499	3	1763-68
Earl of Middlesex	499	3	1762-68	Harrington	490	4	1732-41	Lord Holland (1)	804	4	1770-79
Earl Temple	499	1	1759	Harrison	460	4	1727-36	Lord Mansfield	499	4	1759-60
Eastcourt	498	4	1746-57	Havannah	499	4	1762-71	Lord Mansfield	499	4	1772
Edgebaston	495	4	1739-52	Hawke (1)	499	4	1756-65	Lord North	761	4	1770-80

Ship	Tons	No.	Dates
Loyal Hester	350	1	1704
Lyell	460	5	1721-36
Lynn (1)	450	4	1724-35
Lynn (2)	495	4	1738-49
Macclesfield	450	4	1720-1730
Marlborough (1)	480	4	1711-20
Marlborough	490	2	1731-34
Marlborough (2)	480	4	1724-41
Marlborough (3)	498	3	1745-52
Mary (1)	450	4	1711-19
Mary (2)	490	4	1722-32
Mead	310	1	1709
Marquis of Rockingham	400	3	1768-75
Mercury Packet	210	4	1770-77
Middlesex	430	4	1720-33
Monmouth	480	4	1720-31
Montagu	380	4	1719-29
Montagu	490	4	1733-42
Montfort	498	4	1742-52
Morice	400	4	1716-28
Morse	864	3	1769-77
Nassau	480	4	1731-40
Nassau	723	4	1771-80
Neptune	300	1	1740
Neptune	499	4	1759-68
Newcastle	490	2	1732-36
Nightingale	480	1	1721
New George	400	1	1708
Norfolk (1)	499	4	1745-56
Norfolk (2)	499	1	1759-68
Norfolk (3)	723	4	1771-81
Normanton	490	3	1732-38
Northampton	498	2	1740-43
Northington	676	4	1766-76
Northumberland	657	4	1763-73
Nottingham	490	3	1736-43
Nottingham	701	4	1765-74
Ockham	420	3	1727-33
Oley Frigate	180	1	1705
Onslow	480	4	1734-44
Onslow	499	4	1750-59
Orford	300	2	1743-47
Osterley (1)	499	4	1757-68
Osterley (2)	758	3	1771-77
Oxford	498	4	1746-58
Pacific	668	4	1764-73
Pelham	480	1	1735
Pelham	498	4	1744-54
Pigot	499	4	1762-70
Pitt	600	3	1757-62
Plassey	499	4	1760-68
Pocock	499	2	1758-62
Ponsborne	499	4	1764-72
Portfield	400	4	1745-55
Portland Packet		1	1770
Porto Bello	300	3	1740-46
Prime	864	5	1769-82
Prince Augustus	495	4	1722-32
Prince Edward	498	5	1745-59
Prince Frederick	420	4	1715-27
Prince George	499	4	1750-60
Prince Henry	499	4	1750-60
Prince Henry Packet	167	1	1760
Prince of Orange	480	4	1731-40
Prince of Orange	495	1	1744
Prince of Wales	200	1	1729
Prince of Wales	495	4	1737-46
Prince of Wales	499	4	1751-61
Prince of Wales	716	5	1763-75
Prince William	460	4	1726-35
Prince William	495	3	1738-46
Princess Amelia	340	4	1715-24
Princess Amelia	495	3	1739-45
Princess Anne	350	4	1716-26
Princess Augusta	499	4	1753-63
Princess Caroline	195	1	1728
Princess Louisa	490	4	1733-42
Princess Mary	480	3	1737-44
Princess Royal	470	2	1733-37
Princess Royal	864	4	1769-78
Princess of Wales	480	4	1726-35
Princess of Wales	495	3	1740-45
Protector	580	1	1751
Queen	300	2	1714-17
Queen (1)	804	4	1767-80
Queen Caroline	490	4	1734-44
Recovery	330	2	1707-11
Resolution	495	1	1737
Resolution	804	4	1769-78
Rhoda	498	4	1747-57
Richmond	350	4	1706-13
Rochester	350	4	1706-13
Rochford	723	4	1770-79
Royal Captain	499	4	1764-72
Royal Charlotte (1)	499	3	1764-68
Royal Charlotte (2)	758	5	1771-85
Royal Duke	498	4	1747-59
Royal George	490	4	1737-47
Royal George	758	5	1758-79
Royal Guardian	490	4	1732-42
Royal Henry	804	4	1771-81
St George	420	1	1706
St George	450	4	1709-19
St George	498	4	1742-53
Salisbury	485	4	1741-52
Salisbury	657	4	1764-74
Sandwich	498	5	1745-59
Sarum	400	4	1715-25
Scarborough (1)	480	2	1735-45
Scarborough (2)	495	4	1740-50
Sea Horse	676	4	1767-76
Severn	498	3	1741-48
Shaftesbury (1)	495	4	1735-45
Shaftesbury (2)	499	3	1749-57
Sherbourne	250	1	1709
Shrewsbury	676	4	1767-77
Solebay	350	1	1763
Somerset	495	4	1738-47
Speaker	499	4	1762-71
Speke	726	4	1764-73
Stafford	498	4	1743-52
Stafford	804	3	1769-77
Stanhope	420	4	1714-25
Stormont	499	4	1755-76
Streatham	430	4	1720-30
Streatham	498	4	1746-57
Stringer Galley	220	4	1706-15
Success	180	2	1710-12
Success	250	2	1711-16
Success	499	1	1763
Suffolk	499	4	1749-58
Sunderland	360	4	1718-27
Susannah	300	4	1709-18
Sussex	490	1	1736
Swallow	180	2	1747-49
Swallowfield	250	1	1722
Swift	100	4	1741-46
Talbot	657	4	1762-74
Tavistock	498	4	1745-56
Thames	676	4	1764-73
Thistleworth	250	4	1710-18
Tilbury	499	3	1757-67
Todington	220	4	1704-10
Townsend	400	4	1716-25
Triton	499	4	1750-59
Triton	637	4	1766-75
True Britain (1)	400	4	1746-57
True Britain (2)	499	4	1760-69
Tygris	270	1	1740
Valentine (1)	499	4	1758-69
Valentine (2)	499	2	1772-76
Vansittart	480	1	1718
Vansittart	499	4	1763-72
Verelst	499	2	1767-69
Wager (1)	490	2	1734-37
Wager (2)	498	4	1740-50
Walpole (1)	490	4	1721-35
Walpole (2)	495	4	1738-48
Walpole	499	3	1752-58
Warwick	495	3	1738-45
Warwick	499	4	1750-59
Warren	499	4	1748-60
Wilmington	490	4	1733-41
Winchelsea (1)	498	2	1742-46

Winchelsea (2)	499	2	1752-57
Winchester	490	3	1736-42
Windham	470	4	1724-35
Windsor	200	1	1710
Worcester (1)	499	4	1756-66
Worcester (2)	723	4	1769-81
York	498	4	1740-49
York	499	4	1753-63
York		4	1767-76

PERIOD IV – 1774-1832

A	B	C	D
Abberton	451	4	1818-27
Abercrombie Robinson	1331	4	1825-31
Admiral Alpin	558	2	1801-2
Admiral Barrington	527	1	1786
Admiral Gardner	813	6	1796-1808
Airley Castle	813	8	1787-1806
Albion	961	8	1787-1808
Albion (ES)	462	2	1820-24
Alexander	600	7	1803-15
Alfred	1198	8	1790-1809
Alfred (ES)	716	1	1826
Almorah	416	1	1818
Alnwick Castle	1200	7	1801-1814
Ann	508	8	1800-15
Ann & Emilia	600	1	1781
Ann & Amelia	587	3	1825-31
Antelope Packet		1	1781
Apollo	690	5	1811-1818
Arniston	1200	8	1794-1811
Asia (1)	816	6	1780-95
Asia (2)	820	5	1798-1807
Asia (3)	958	10	1811-31
Asia (ES)	410	1	1819
Asia (ES)	536	3	1825-28
Astell	820	10	1809-29
Atlas	763	4	1778-86
Atlas	1200	9	1812-28
Baring	820	6	1801-12
Barksworth	505	1	1815
Barossa (ES)	698	4	1818-31
Barwell	796	6	1782-94
Batavia	555	3	1809-15
Bellmont	758	5	1779-92
Belvedere	987	6	1786-1800
Bencoolen (ES)	416	1	1831
Bengal (1)	818	5	1799-1807
Bengal (2)	950	2	1811-13
Bengal M (ES)	501	2	1829-32
Berrington	816	6	1783-1797
Berwickshire	1322	6	1821-31
Bessborough	870	4	1772-85
Blandford	606	1	1780
Boddam	1021	6	1787-1800
Bolton (ES)	540	1	1831
Bombay	1242	11	1809-32
Bombay Castle	1200	6	1792-1804
Boyne (ES)	402	2	1823-25
Brampton (ES)	432	1	1819
Bridgewater (3)	799	6	1785-1797
Bridgewater (4)	1200	9	1812-28
Brilliant	703	1	1781
Britannia	770	12	1779-1804
Britannia	1200	2	1806-1808
Brothers (ES)		1	1819
Broxbornebury	720	4	1811-31
Brunswick	1200	6	1792-1803
Buckingham	1369	10	1817-32
Busbridge	771	7	1781-95
Cabalva	1200	4	1811-18
Caesar (ES)	620	1	1831
Calcutta	819	5	1797-1807
Caledonia	612	2	1797-1800
Cambridge	756	2	1810-15
Camden (ES)	399	1	1819
Canning	1326	8	1818-31
Canton	1198	8	1790-1809
Carmarthen	550	8	1802-16
Carnatic (1)	1169	7	1785-1800
Carnatic (2)	820	6	1808-18
Castle Eden	818	6	1799-1810
Castle Huntley	1200	10	1813-32
Catherine (ES)	535	3	1818-32
Ceres (1)	723	4	1773-81
Ceres (2)	1180	11	1787-1814
Ceylon	818	4	1802-09
Chapman (1)	538	2	1780-85
Chapman (2)	558	1	1811
Charles Grant	1246	11	1810-31
Charles Mills	564	2	1810-12
Charlton	818	6	1798-1808
Childe Harold (ES)	463	2	1824-26
Cirencester	1200	8	1794-1811
City of London	820	6	1799-1811
Claudine (ES)	452	1	1823
Clyde (ES)	479	1	1819
Coldstream	693	3	1811-15
Comet	530	3	1800-1804
Contractor	777	7	1779-97
Cornwall	789	2	1815-18
Cornwall (ES)	872	1	1825
Coromandel (ES)	645	1	1819
Countess of Harcourt (ES)	517	1	1824
Coutts	1200	8	1796-1813
Cuffnells	1200	8	1795-1814
Cullands Grove	576	1	1801
Cumberland	1200	7	1802-15
Cambrian (ES)	720	1	1825
David Scott	1200	5	1801-09
David Scott	736	3	1810-14
Deptford	784	6	1780-94
Devaynes	600	6	1801-12
Devonshire	820	5	1804-12
Diana	600	4	1804-11
Dorsetshire	1260	9	1799-1821
Dover Castle	820	6	1797-1810
Dover	700	1	1786
Dublin	786	6	1784-97
Duchess of Atholl	1330	6	1821-30
Duke of Argyll (ES)	600	1	1832
Duke of Atholl	755	1	1781
Duke of Auvergne (ES)	441	1	1832
Duke of Buccleuch	1182	6	1788-1800
Duke of Buccheuch (ES)	619	1	1830
Duke of Montrose	755	8	1784-1806
Duke of Northumberland (ES)	608	1	1830
Duke of Sussex	1300	4	1826-32
Duke of York	1327	9	1817-32
Dunira	1325	8	1817-31
Dutton	761	5	1781-93
Eagle	220	1	1776
Earl of Abergavenny	1182	7	1789-1804
Earl Balcarras	1417	9	1815-31
Earl of Camden	1200	4	1802-09
Earl of Chesterfield	758	4	1780
Earl Cornwallis	755	7	1783-98
Earl of Dartmouth	758	1	1779
Earl Fitzwilliam	803	5	1786-96
Earl of Hertford	758	1	1780
Earl Howe	876	8	1794-1811
Earl of Mansfield	758	5	1777-88
Earl of Mornington	241	1	1799
Earl of Oxford	758	6	1778-94
Earl of Sandwich	804	4	1771-82
Earl Spencer	645	6	1796-1809
Earl St Vincent	818	7	1799-1811
Earl Talbot	767	6	1778-91
Earl Talbot	1200	2	1796-99
Earl of Wycomb	643	6	1786-96
Edinburgh	1326	4	1825-31
Elizabeth	600	1	1800
Elizabeth	363	1	1814
Elizabeth	544	1	1832
Elphinstone	1200	7	1802-15
England (ES)	420	1	1825
Essex (1)	793	6	1780-95
Essex (2)	1400	7	1802-17
Euphrates	590	5	1802-11
Europa	755	6	1781-95

Name	Tons	No.	Years
Europe	820	6	1802-16
Exeter	1200	8	1792-1809
Experiment	549	4	1802-06
Fairford	755	1	1781
Fairlie	698	3	1811-14
Fame	492	3	1801-05
Fame (ES)	432		1818-22
Farquharson	1326	7	1820-32
Florentia (ES)	452	3	1820-25
Fort William	798	6	1785-1800
Fort William	1137	1	1815
Fortitude	758	1	1780
Foulis	755	3	1783-89
Fox Packet	240	2	1780-83
Francis	789	6	1781-94
Ganges (1)	784	6	1778-93
Ganges (2)	1200	4	1796-1804
Ganges (ES)	627	1	1830
Gatton	758	4	1771-79
General Barker	758	1	1778
General Coote	787	6	1781-94
General Elliot	800	6	1782-93
General Goddard	755	6	1781-95
General Harris	1200	9	1812-29
General Hewitt	894	5	1815-23
General Kyd	1200	9	1814-30
General Palmer (ES)	531	1	1832
General Stuart	1329	6	1800-1812
George IV	1329	4	1825-31
Georgiana	285	7	1798-1808
Georgiana (ES)	496	1	1831
Glatton (2)	758	4	1777-86
Glatton (3)	1200	9	1792-1813
Glory	502	3	1802-06
Good Hope	885	2	1795-97
Guildford (ES)	533	2	1824-26
Halsewell	758	3	1778-85
Harleston	528	1	1810
Harriet	549	6	1802-11
Hartwell	937	1	1786
Hastings	676	1	1780
Hawke (3)	779	6	1786-1800
Hebe	413	1	1809
Henry Addington	1200	9	1795-1813
Henry Dundas	802	5	1786-1800
Henry Porcher (ES)	465	3	1817-29
Herculean	609	2	1799-1801
Hercules (ES)	483	1	1827
Herefordshire	1200	10	1814-32
Hillsborough (1)	723	3	1774-79
Hillsborough (2)	764	6	1783-96
Hinchinbrooke	528	1	1780
Hinde Packet	200	1	1777
Hindostan	1248	6	1789-1802
Hooghly (ES)	480	2	1818-30
Hope	1200	9	1796-1814
Houghton	778	7	1782-98
Huddart	600	8	1802-16
Hugh Inglis	1200	6	1799-1822
Hyperion (ES)	402	1	1819
Hythe	1333	6	1820-30
Indus	590	6	1803-13
Inglis	1200	11	1812-32
Isabella (ES)	579	1	1825
James Pattison (ES)	513	1	1827
Java (ES)	1175	1	1824
James Sibbald	667	4	1810-19
Jane Duchess of Gordon			
	820	2	1804-07
Juliana	540	2	1809-11
Juliana	498	1	1823
Kellie Castle	1332	7	1818-32
Kent	755	7	1781-99
Kent	1332	3	1820-23
King George	776	6	1784-96
King George IV (ES)	470	1	1819
Kingston	504	2	1818-20
Lady Burgess	820	4	1799-1805
Lady Carrington	564	4	1811-19
Lady Castelreagh	821	7	1802-15
Lady East (ES)	650	1	1829
Lady Campbell	684	2	1815-19
Lady Jane Dundas	820	5	1799-1807
Lady Kennaway (ES)	573	3	1825-29
Lady Lushington	594	4	1808-17
Lady Melville	1200	10	1813-32
Lady Raffles (ES)	647	3	1819-25
Lansdown	574	1	1785
Larkins	670	5	1809-18
Larkins (ES)	647	4	1826-32
Lascelles	758	8	1779-95
Lacko	758	3	1780-86
Layton	498	3	1821-31
London (2)	836	7	1779-97
London	1322	8	1818-32
Lord Amherst (ES)	506	2	1825-31
Lord Camden	775		1783-95
Lord Castlereagh	812	7	1802-18
Lord Duncan	830	7	1797-1811
Lord Eldon	538	6	1801-14
Lord Forbes	513	2	1810-12
Lord Hawkesbury	803	8	1787-1806
Lord Hungerford (ES)	736	1	1826
Lord Keith	599	8	1803-17
Lord Lowther	1332	4	1825-30
Lord Lynedoch	589	1	1815
Lord Macartney	755	6	1782-95
Lord Melville	818	6	1802-14
Lord Melville (ES)	425	1	1826
Lord Mulgrave	692	1	1780
Lord Nelson	818	5	1799-1807
Lord North	758	1	1785
Lord Thurlow	805	6	1789-1800
Lord Walsingham	559	6	1786-99
Lord William Bentinck (ES)			
	564	1	1827
Lowther Castle	1427	12	1810-32
Macqueen	1300	6	1821-31
Major	755	1	1781
Malabar	884	2	1795-97
Malcolm (ES)	600	3	1825-29
Mangles	560	1	1815
Manship	812	7	1785-1800
Marchioness of Ely	952	9	1811-27
Marchioness of Exeter	820	7	1801-15
Marquis Camden	1200	10	1812-31
Marquis of Ely	1267	8	1801-18
Marquis of Hastings (ES)			
	450	4	1818-29
Marquis of Huntley	1200	11	1811-32
Marquis of Lansdown	647	5	1786-98
Marquis of Wellesley	818	6	1799-1810
Marquis of Wellington	961	9	1812-28
Mars	696	1	1785
Martha	406	1	1795
Matilda	774	1	1818
Melville Castle	806	7	1786-99
Metcalfe	819	6	1804-14
Midas	414	1	1809
Middlesex	755	5	1783-93
Minerva	798	7	1786-1801
Minerva	534	2	1810-12
Minerva	976	10	1814-32
Moffat	717	3	1810-19
Moffat (ES)	821	3	1823-31
Moira (ES)	650	7	1819-32
Monarch	600	5	1800-10
Montagu	755	3	1781-84
Morley (ES)	492	1	1828
Morse	864	1	1781
Mountstuart	758	2	1777-79
Neptune (2)	758	4	1779-87
Neptune (3)	1200	8	1796-1813
Neptune (ES)	644	1	1826
Northampton	545	8	1800-17
Northumberland	755	6	1780-94
Northumberland	600	6	1800-1816
Nottingham (1)	1152	6	1786-1800
Nottingham (2)	1152	2	1806-08
Ocean (1)	1189	4	1788-96
Ocean (2)	1200	5	1800-10
Orient (ES)	596	4	1822-33
Orwell	1335	8	1817-30
Osterley (3)	753	7	1780-97
Parmelia (ES)	443	1	1826

Name	Tonnage	Voyages	Years
Perseverence	1200	7	1801-17
Phoenix (1)	800	6	1785-99
Phoenix (2)	818	6	1804-17
Phoenix (ES)	493	1	1819
Pigot (2)	758	5	1779-92
Pitt	775	4	1785-95
Ponsborne (2)	758	6	1779-93
Potton	396	2	1814-22
Preston	671	6	1798-1809
Prince Regent	953	10	1811-32
Prince of Wales (4)		1	1802
Prince William Henry	803	5	1787-1800
Princess Amelia (1)	808	4	1786-96
Princess Amelia (2)	1275	10	1808-25
Princess Charlotte (1)	610	4	1795-1803
Princess Charlotte (ES) (2)	400	1	1818
Princess Charlotte of Wales	978	9	1811-28
Princess Mary	462	4	1795-1802
Princess Royal	805	3	1786-92
Protector (ES)	511	1	1829
Providence	631	1	1815
Providence (ES)	678	1	1819
Queen (2)	801	5	1785-99
Ranger	537	1	1785
Ranger Packet	135	1	1785
Ravensworth	512	1	1785
Raymond	793	6	1782-96
Regent	916	3	1815-21
Repulse	1334	6	1820-30
Retreat	505	5	1804-12
Richmond (ES)	466	1	1819
Rockingham	798	7	1785-1799
Rockingham (ES)	427	1	1822
Rodney	772	6	1781-94
Rose (1)	810	6	1786-98
Rose (2)	955	11	1810-32
Roxburgh Castle (ES)	599		1824-29
Royal Admiral	914	8	1777-95
Royal Bishop	720	2	1781-85
Royal Charlotte (1)	1252	2	1789-92
Royal Charlotte (2)	1252	8	1795-1813
Royal George	758	2	1777-80
Royal George	1333	7	1802-17
Royal George (ES)	486	1	1822
Royal Henry	804	4	1771-81
St Helena Packet	130	2	1814-21
Sarah Christina	557	4	1800-08
Scaleby Castle	1242	14	1806-32
Severn (ES)	586	1	1832
Sir David Scott	1342	6	1821-30
Sir Edward Hughes	957	9	1787-1803
Sir Godfrey Webster	541	1	1811
Sir Stephen Lushington	608	7	1795-1809
Sir William Bensley	547	6	1801-11
Sir William Pultney	565	6	1804-14
Skelton Castle	584	4	1799-1805
Southampton	758	3	1777-85
Sovereign	617	7	1800-15
Stakesby (ES)	450	1	1829
Streatham	850	7	1804-18
Stormont	723		1772-85
Sulivan	755	6	1782-96
Surat Castle	1139	5	1806-15
Susan (ES)	569	2	1827-29
Surrey	819	6	1804-15
Surrey	461	1	1828
Swallow Packet	345	9	1784-1799
Syren	250	1	1774
Tartar	496	1	1780
Taunton Castle	1198	9	1790-1810
Telegraph	165	1	1801
Tellicherry	465	4	1795-1801
Thames (1)	1200	8	1795-1813
Thames (2)	1330	7	1819-32
Thetis	804	6	1786-98
Thomas Coutts	1334	8	1819-31
Thomas Grenville	886	13	1809-32
Tigris	525	6	1802-13
Timandra (ES)	367	1	1819
Tottenham	517	6	1801-12
Travers	577	5	1799-1807
Triton	800	4	1787-94
True Briton (1)	758	4	1773-82
True Briton (2)	1198	8	1790-1808
Tyne	480	1	1809
Union	550	8	1802-16
Union	600	5	1804-12
United Kingdom	820	4	1801-08
Valentine	790	6	1780-93
Vansittart (2)	828	4	1779-88
Vansittart (3)	1200	10	1814-32
Walmer Castle	1200	9	1795-1814
Walpole	758	7	1778-97
Walpole	820	5	1797-1806
Walthamston	820	6	1799-1810
Warley	1200	9	1788-1814
Warren Hastings (1)	716	6	1781-94
Warren Hastings (2)	1200	2	1802-04
Warren Hastings (3)	1064	11	1808-32
Warren Hastings	1276	3	1814-22
Waterloo	1335	9	1816-32
Wexford	1200	7	1802-15
William Farlie	1348	6	1821-31
William Pitt	798	6	1785-98
William Pitt	819	7	1804-19
William Pitt	572	3	1803-13
Winchelsea	1331	10	1805-25
Windham	823	6	1800-15
Windsor	1332	7	1818-31
Winterton	771	4	1781-91
Woodcot	802	4	1786-96
Woodford	1180	8	1790-1809
Woodford (ES)	594	1	1819
Worcester (3)	798	8	1785-1806
York (3)	475	1	1818
Zenobia (ES)	588	1	1828

APPENDIX 10: Chronological outline of the development of the East India Company

1600 Elizabeth I grants charter to Governor and Company of Merchants of London trading to the East Indies.

1601 First separate stock voyage: James Lancaster, General.

1602 Formation of the VOC, the Dutch East India Company.

1604 Second voyage: Henry Middleton, General.

1605 Death of Akbar; accession of Jahangir.

1607 Third voyage: Captain Keeling, General. Captain Hawkin's mission to Mogul Emperor to seek trading concessions.

1610 Sixth voyage: Sir Henry Middleton, General, captured and imprisoned at Mocha.

1611 EIC establishes factory at Masulipatam on Coromandel coast.

1613 First joint stock voyages: Nicholas Downton, General. Defeats Portuguese at Swally Hole and establishes factory at Surat.

1615 Sir Thomas Roe's embassy to Mogul Emperor at Agra: secures farman to trade.

1618-20 War between EIC and VOC. Dutch capture Jakarta, renamed Batavia: becomes capital of VOC empire.

1622 English drive Portuguese from Ormuz.

1623 Dutch massacre EIC merchants at Amboyna.

1627 Death of Jahangir; accession of Shah

Jahan.

1629 Surat became EIC HQ in India and chief presidency in the east.

1630 Famine in Gujarat affects textile trade.

1635 Treaty with Portuguese eases tension on west coast of India.

1639 EIC acquires Madras.

1641 Madras fortified: Fort St George.

1651 Madras becomes a presidency. EIC establishes a factory at Hooghly in Bengal.

1652 First Anglo-Dutch war: Dutch colonise Cape of Good Hope as port of call.

1655 *Ann Frigate* (Robert Knox) sails for Fort St George and Bengal. Returns July 1657.

1657 Death of Shah Jahan: accession of Aurengzeb. Cromwell confers new charter on EIC, establishing a permanent joint stock company.

1657 *Ann Frigate* (Robert Knox) sails for Malabar coast: Knox captive in Ceylon for twenty years.

1664 Formation of Compagnie des Indes Orientales. Charles II confirms Cromwell's terms in new charter.

1665-7 Second Anglo-Dutch war.

1667 Dutch capture Macassar from Portuguese.

1668 Charles II hands over Bombay to EIC.

1670 *Experiment* (Edward Barlow) sails March for Bombay and Surat. Returns July 1671.

1671 *Experiment* (Edward Barlow) sails September bounds to Bantam and Formosa. Captured by Dutch ship returning through Sunda Strait.

1672 Third Anglo-Dutch war.

1673 St Helena acquired by EIC as port of call for home-bound ships.

1674 French secure Pondicherry.

1681 *Tonqueen Merchant* (Robert Knox) sails September bound to Bantam and Tonking.

1683 Dutch take Bantam.

1683 *Delight* (Edward Barlow) sails January bound to Achin and Formosa.

1684 *Tonqueen Merchant* (Robert Knox) sails May bound to Tristan de Cunha, Madagascar and Bali. His piratical crew seizes ship. *Kent* (Edward Barlow) sails

December bound to Bombay and Surat. Returns July 1687.

1685 EIC declares war on the Mogul Emperor: factory at Hooghly abandoned. EIC develops pepper plantation at Benkulen in west Sumatra.

1687 Bombay replaces Surat as chief presidency on Malabar coast.

1687 *Rainbow* (Edward Barlow) sails December bound to Batavia and Tongking. Returns January 1689.

1688 Accession of William III who confers charter on new rival company. 'Old' and 'New' companies trade competitively for twenty years.

1690 'Old' EIC re-establishes factory on the Hooghly at (future) Calcutta.

1690 *Tonqueen Merchant* (Robert Knox) sails January bound to Madagascar.

1696 Factory on Hooghly fortified: Fort William, nucleus of future Calcutta.

1696 *Sceptre* (Edward Barlow) sails May bound to Malabar coast and Mocha. Returns July 1698.

1699 Trade opened with China.

1699 *Wentworth* (Edward Barlow) sails November bound to Batavia and Macao. Returns August 1701.

1700 Fort William becomes a presidency.

1701 *Fleet Frigate* (Edward Barlow) sails March bound to Batavia and Canton. Returns November 1703.

1707 'Old' and 'New' companies merged in United Company of Merchants of England trading to the East Indies. Death of Aurengzeb and beginning of break-up of Mogul Empire.

1747 Struggle for supremacy in India between Britain and France really begins. Madras (Fort St George) taken by French but in 1748 returned by treaty.

1747 *Edgecote* (Captain Pearse) sails December bound to Fort St David and Canton.

1749 *Boscawen* and *Warren* sail March bound to Bombay, and further ports. *Grantham* sails December bound to Fort St David and Canton.

1756 Calcutta taken by Nawab of Bengal: Black Hole incident. Pirate stronghold of Gheriah taken by Admiral Watson and Col Clive.

1757 Battle of Plassey makes EIC virtual

ruler of Bengal. Clive appointed Governor.

1759 Dutch expedition to Bengal: annihilated by English. Surat attacked by Bombay Marine. EIC acquires 'Tunkha'.

1765 Battle of Baksar assures British supremacy in Bengal. Clive's second governorship.

1769 *Plassey* (William Hickey) sails January bound to Madras and Canton. Returns April 1770.

1772 Warren Hastings appointed Governor-General.

1773 Regulating Act marks beginning of British government's control of Indian affairs. Governor-General supreme over all three presidencies.

1777 *Sea Horse* (William Hickey) sails November bound to Bengal.

1779 *Nassau* (William Hickey) sails May bound to England.

1780-84 Anglo-Dutch war. Dutch colonies suffer.

1783 *Earl of Sandwich* (Captain Wordsworth); private trade investment recorded.

1784 Pitt's India Act increases parliamentary control over Indian Affairs through newly created Board of Control.

1793 War with France begins.

1795 British seize Ceylon. First British occupation of the Cape of Good Hope. VOC formally dissolved. William V orders many Dutch possessions to be handed over to Britain to prevent their falling into French hands.

1798-1805 Lord Wellesley Governor-General: greatly expands British territories in India. Delhi taken: Mogul emperor under EIC protection.

1808 *Castle Eden* (William Hickey) sails February from Bengal bound to England; arrives July.

1810 British capture Isle de Bourbon and Isle de France from French.

1811 British take Java.

1824 Treaty of London determines future British and Dutch spheres of influence in the east.

1824-6 First Anglo-Burmese war: Britain acquires Assam, Tennasserim and Aracan.

1826 Paddle Steamer *Enterprise* completes

an experimental passage from England to Calcutta via the Cape of Good Hope.

1830 Bombay Marine renamed Indian Navy.

1830 Paddle steamer *Hugh Lindsay* completes experimental passage from Bombay to Suez.

1833 Division of Presidency of Bengal into Bengal and the North West Provinces by Act of Parliament. Capital at Calcutta.

1834 EIC withdraws from all commercial activities: restricted to administration of its Indian territories.

1839 Governor of Bombay orders seizure of Aden.

1839-42 First Afghan war.

1840 Indian Navy supports actions against Chinese in 'Opium War'.

1843 Annexation of Scinde.

1845-48 First and second Anglo-Sikh wars. Punjab annexed.

1852-3 Second Anglo-Burmese war: Pegu annexed.

1856 Anglo-Persian war.

1857 Indian Mutiny.

1858 Government of India Act ends all EIC powers. Viceroy of India replaces Governor-General.

1861 East India House demolished.

1863 Indian Navy disbanded.

1874 Final EIC charter expires.

APPENDIX 11: L/MAR/C656 F7

Authenticated certifiacte submitted by Thomas Munden on applying for the post of second mate of the *Bombay Castle* in 1794.

Thomas Munden Second mate of the *Bombay Castle*

	Yrs	Months
27 years of Age used the Sea 12 years 4 Voyages to India		
To the West Indies in the *Sally Transport* as seaman	-	9
In the Royal Navy as Midshipman	1	-
To America and up the Straights as Chief Mate in the *Three Brothers*	1	2
1st voyage to India in 1779 in the *Belmont* to Coast and China as Midshipman	3	1
2nd voyage to India 1782 in the *Pigot* to Coast and Bay as seaman	2	-
3rd voyage to India in 1786 in the *Earl of Wycombe* to China as Midshipman & Coxswain	1	4
4th voyage to India in 1792 in the *Bombay Castle* to Bombay & China as Fourth Mate for which Station he was approved 17th October 1792	1	11
	11	3

Approved 17th December 1794
   By Stephen Williams
   Walter Ewer   Esqs.
   T.T.Metcalfe

BIBLIOGRAPHY

Manuscript and unpublished sources:

BL OIOC: Marine Records listed in Danvers, F.C.: *List of Marine Records* (1896) with an introduction.

Essex Record Office, Chelmsford: The papers of William and Samuel Braund, particularly Samuel Braund's shipping papers: D/Dru, B9-B26.

Berkshire Record Office, Reading. Papers of Richard Benyon, D/E BY B6 and D/ESy(M)f8.

Cumberland, Westmoreland and Carlisle Record Office, the Castle, Carlisle. Personal and trading accounts of John Wordsworth of Penrith, commander of the *Earl of Sandwich* for the year 1783-4.

BL. Papers of Henry Johnson, Add MSS 22, 184-6.

BL Ship Book, East India Company Records, 2vs Add MSS 38872/3.

BL OIOC Court books of the Court of Directors.

BL OIOC Tract 133, Barlow.

Guildhall Library. Memorandum Book Ms 31376.

Willson, M: The East India Company Warehouses and quays in the Port and City of London 1680-1800. King Alfred's College, Winchester: unpublished dissertation.

Secondary sources:

Abell, Sir Westcott: *The Shipwright's Trade* (1948, reprinted 1981)

Albion, R C: *Forests and Seapower* (1926)

Auber, Peter: *An Analysis of the Constitution of the East India Company* (1826)

Banbury, Philip: *Shipbuilders of the Thames and Medway* (1971)

Barnard, J E: *Building Britain's Wooden Walls: the Barnard Dynasty, 1697-1801* (1997)

Bernstein, Henry T: *Steamboats on the Ganges* (1960)

Brown, R Stewart: *Liverpool Ships in the Eighteenth Century* (1932)

Bulley, A: *Free Mariner* (1992)

Chatterton, E K: *The Old East Indiamen* (1933, reprinted 1973)

Chaudhuri, K N: *The English East India Company, 1600-1640* (1965)

Childers, Colonel Spencer: *William Richardson, a Mariner of England* (1908, reprinted 1970)

Cotton, Sir Evan (Charles Fawcett ed): *The East Indiamen* (1949)

Country Life Book of Nautical Terms under Sail (1978)

Course, Captain A G: *A Seventeenth Century Mariner* (1965)

Danvers, F C: *List of Marine Records at the India Office Library, with an introduction* (1896)

Davis, Ralph: *The Rise of the English Shipping Industry in the Seventeenth and Eighteenth Centuries* (1965)

Dews, Nathan: *A History of Deptford* (1884, reprinted 1971)

Diver, Maud: *Honoria Lawrence* (1936)

Downing, Clement: *A Compendious History of the Indian Wars* (1737)

Eastwick, R W (H Compton ed): *A Master Mariner* (1891)

Evans, C: 'Power on Silt: Towards an Archaeology of the East India Company', *Antiquity* vol 64 no 244 September 1990

Falconer's *Marine Dictionary* (1778, reprinted 1970)

Fenwick, W and Redknap, M (eds): 'Ships, Cargoes and the East India Trade', Nautical Archaeological special issue printed from the *International Journal of Nautical Archaeology*, vol 19 no 1 (1990)

Fletcher, R A: *In the Days of the Tall Ships* (1928)

Forbes, James: *Oriental Memoirs: A Narrative of Seventeen Years Residence in India* (1834)

Foster, Sir William (ed): *Letters Received by the East India Company from their Servants in the East, 1602-1617*, 6 vols (1896-1902)

Foster, Sir William: *England's Quest of Eastern Trade* (1933)

Foster, Sir William: *John Company* (1926)

Fry, Howard T: *Alexander Dalrymple, 1737-1808, and the Expansion of British Trade* (1970)

Furber, H: *Henry Dundas, First Viscount Melville, 1742-1811* (1931)

Gill, Conrad: *Merchants and Mariners in the Eighteenth Century* (1961)

Green, H and Wigram, R: *The Chronicles of Blackwall Yard* (1881)

Hamilton, Alexander: *A New Account of the East Indies* (1725) with introduction and notes by Sir William Foster (1930)

Hannay, D: *Friends and Enemies* (1912)

Hannay, D: *Ships and Men* (1910)

Hannay, D: *The Sea Trader* (1912)

Hardy, H C: *A Register of Ships employed in the Service of the East India Company* (1820)

Hedges, W: *Diary* (1887)

Hickey, William (edited by Alfred Spencer): *Memoirs* (1913)

Horne, D B, and Ransome, M: *English Historical Documents* (1957)

Hunter, Sir W W: *A History of British India*, 2 vols (1899)

Ingram, B (ed): *Three Sea Journals of Stuart Times* (1936)

Ingram, E (ed): *Two Views of British India: Private Correspondence of Mr Dundas and Lord Wellesley 1798-1801* (1969)

Keay, J: *The Honourable Company* (1991)

Knox, R: *An Historical Relation of Ceylon* (1911)

Krishna, B: *Commercial Relations between India and England 1601-1757* (1924)

Lawson, P: *The East India Company, Studies in Modern History* (1993)

Lubbock, B (ed): *Barlow's Journal* (1934)

MacGregor, D R: *Merchant Sailing Ships 1775-1815* (1985)

Masefield, J: *Sea Life in Nelson's Time* (1905)

Morse, H B: *Chronicles of the East India Company trading to China 1635-1834* (1926)

National Maritime Museum: *The Birth of Navigational Science*, Monograph no 10 (1974)

Nightingale, P: *Trade and Empire in Western India 1784-1806* (1970)

Parkinson, C Northcote: *Trade in the Eastern Seas, 1793-1813* (1937)

Parkinson, C Northcote: *War in the Eastern Seas, 1793-1815* (1954)

Parliamentary Papers, House of Commons, 1801-1900, IV

Philips, C H (ed): *The Correspondence of David Scott, Director and Chairman of the East India Company relating to Indian Affairs 1787-1805*, Camden Third Series, vol LXXV, Royal Historical Society.

Philips, C H: *The East India Company, 1784-1834* (1940)

Rand, F P: *Wordsworth's Mariner Brother* (Mass 1966)

Roberts, E: *The East India Voyager or the Outward Bound* (1845)

Roddis, L H: *James Lind, Founder of Nautical Medicine* (1951)

Sainsbury, E B (ed): *Calendar of the Court Minutes of the East India Company, 1635-1679*, 11 vols (1907-1938)

Sainsbury, W N (eds): *Calendar of State Papers, East Indies 1513-1634* 5 vols (1862-1892)

Sherwood, Mrs (F J Harvey-Darton ed): *The Life and Times of Mrs Sherwood, 1775-1851* (1910)

Sutherland, L S: *A London Merchant* (1933, reprinted 1962)

Sutherland, L S: *The East India Company in Eighteenth Century Politics* (1952)

Temple, Sir R: *Papers of Thomas Bowrey*, Hakluyt Society Series 2, vol LVIII (1925)

Thomas, J H: 'Portsmouth and the East India Company in the Eighteenth Century', *The Portsmouth Papers* no 62 (1993)

Vincennes Service Historique: *Les Flottes des Compagnies des Indes 1600-1857*. Proceedings of conference (1994)

INDEX

References in *italics* refer to illustrations.